THE
LAST
THOUSAND

THE
LAST
THOUSAND

ONE SCHOOL'S PROMISE
IN A NATION AT WAR

JEFFREY E. STERN

St. Martin's Press
New York

THE LAST THOUSAND. Copyright © 2016 by Jeffrey E. Stern. All rights reserved. Printed in the United States of America. For information address St. Martin's Press, 175 Fifth Avenue, New York, N.Y. 10010.

www.stmartins.com

The Library of Congress Cataloging-in-Publication Data is available upon request.

ISBN 978-1-250-04993-3 (hardcover)
ISBN 978-1-4668-5099-6 (e-book)

Our books may be purchased in bulk for promotional, educational, or business use. Please contact your local bookseller or the Macmillan Corporate and Premium Sales Department at (800) 221-7945, extension 5442, or by e-mail at MacmillanSpecialMarkets@macmillan.com.

First Edition: January 2016

10 9 8 7 6 5 4 3 2 1

To Jenna and Margot

CONTENTS

THE
LAST
THOUSAND

1

ELEVEN MONTHS LEFT

A policeman is holding the Teacher at a checkpoint.

There's an event at the military base down the road, an important one with generals and ministers and members of parliament, so police set up a perimeter with checkpoints and big concrete blocks. Only the big people with the big cars get by, the big black up-armored bulletproof Land Cruisers riding low on their suspension. Smoked-glass windows are rolled down and arms emerge with credentials, and then these vehicles are waved on. The Teacher is made to stay.

He pleads his case but gets nowhere. He is not persuasive in this particular kind of situation; he's a little man, physically unimpressive, the influence he's won among his tribe has to do with the fact that this is a country where a lot of business gets done in rooms without furniture. Men sit on the floor and talk, their size becomes secondary, and the idea that tends to win is the one that's delivered with the most poetry. In darkened rooms after power has gone out for the night, around the blinking lights of cell phone screens and single bulbs connected to generators, the Teacher is something of a master, a man with a golden tongue, soft-spoken and long-winded, whose circuitous explanations slowly unfold until he woos people to his side and makes admirers out of skeptics.

★ ★ ★

The policeman at the checkpoint knows none of this. All the police-man knows is that there is a small man with a small taxi and a bad suit asking to get by. It does not seem possible that the person stand-ing in front of him is a leader of men. It does not seem possible that he is a person with influential friends, or that he and the two youths with him—malnourished-looking kids, really—have been invited to the very event for which this policeman is providing security. That General Allen himself, the man with his finger on the trigger, the owner of military power in this country, has requested their presence.

The Teacher can see this, and he knows that these checkpoints are places that produce violence. He's familiar with the flinty way men's pride becomes combustible when one tries to exert authority the other doesn't recognize. He decides to stop arguing. He will sim-ply walk the remaining mile to the base.

Or rather, he will run. This is not the kind of thing one should be late to, after all, and the Teacher knows the whole ritual that will play out when he arrives on base: the checks of identification, retinal scans, fingerprinting. After being booked he will be late, and then General Allen will be upset with him, so he and the two undersized teenagers pick up the pace. Soon they are sprinting, and he's aware of the symbolism here, the locals running toward the foreign forces.

They dodge obstacles on the dimpled streets, trying and failing to avoid the puddles in old bomb craters, potholes born from shoddy construction and carved out by Kabul's excited drivers. And from mortars. It is February 2013, over a decade since America began its campaign here with a series of air strikes, followed by special forces and then a convoy of aid groups. Many roads have been fixed since then, to cover up the scars of war; many haven't. Some were fixed and have cracked again from bombs on belts strapped to men, or built into the trunks of cars. February, so there's melted snow and cold, raw rain. Mud and dirt splash up on the Teacher's clothes, waist high on the youths, and when they finally get to the gate they look like the filthy street urchins who orbit the base like an asteroid belt, hawk-ing crappy trinkets to soldiers from *Amrika* and *Englistan*.

Only they're not treated like street urchins. Now that they are in the embrace of the American military, no longer beholden to their own countrymen, it's as if they've stepped across a threshold to an alternate universe. A man by the gate recognizes the three immediately and whisks them inside without even asking for identification, marches them past sandbags and giant cargo containers into the gymnasium where the event will be held.

Now *they* are the ones breezing through, past all the important government types who drove by them fifteen minutes before. Among the Americans, the Teacher is treated like an important person.

An important person because, like others who found ways to thrive when the foreign armies came, the Teacher provided those armies with a service. His service is less tangible than delivering dried fruit or pirated DVDs or translating conversations with village elders, but maybe more important. It's psychological, and subtle, but critical. Especially for a soldier like the one running the war machine here, General John Allen, who lies awake at night thinking of the men and women lost—541, under his watch—and comes pretty damn close to tears, his voice cracking, when asked about them during television interviews.

For a man like General Allen, the service the Teacher provides is validation.

He's the one they can point to and say, "Here is a thing those good kids died for. Here's why it wasn't all a waste." The good local is what the Teacher is, a man who buys the whole democracy thing, who happens to be a minority, who happens to be concerned with the rights of women. Just one man, maybe, but one is proof of concept. It's not impossible. That there are people like the Teacher means there is at least one good reason why so much has been sacrificed.

Because the Teacher has built something amazing: an oasis in the middle of the desert off the west end of the capital. If you make the drive, over bad roads, past a little bit of misery, past men wrapped in so many blankets they seem to be receding from the world, past women whose faces are wrinkled and leathery and dark, and youths giddy and oblivious, you will arrive at a school where a few thousand boys and girls, mostly poor, mostly happy, all members of the same oppressed minority group, are *learning*. Not just learning to read and write and add, but to question, criticize, make provocative art.

To sing, poke fun at one another, to protest. Learning to love Islam but actively—not by being administered the religion but by interrogating it. The Teacher named the school Marefat because it means "knowledge" but also all its derivatives: "wisdom," "education," "intellect," "awareness."

And if you make this journey to the outskirts of Kabul, if you witness this diamond in the rough, if a kid comes up to you and shakes your hand and respects you but isn't afraid of you, it all has the effect of making you feel like you yourself are some great explorer; like just by witnessing the thing you are somehow deserving of credit, if only for having abided the long miserable trip to get there.

And it's a feeling the Teacher will let you have, because it is part of a covenant he has made with the foreign armies. He will allow this thing he has built to be theirs, too. He will allow it to be proof that the people who have died and been dismembered, that the empty shirtsleeves and empty pant legs and empty chairs at dinner tables back in Amrika and Englistan have not been for nothing.

In return, the foreigners protect him and his four thousand students.

That is the other part of this covenant. When soldiers came to his land a decade ago and said "Disarm," the Teacher, and his community, said, "Okay." They accepted the deal they thought was on offer: that if you give up your weapons and stop fighting, and if you build yourself up, build institutions for yourself, you will have equal rights. You will have access to positions in the new government if you want them; we will help you build roads and factories and hospitals. We will destroy the Taliban. We will eliminate your enemy for good.

So his people are unarmed, in a country where everyone is armed. His people, nearly all of them, gave up their weapons, which means they depend on America for one thing most of all: protection.

And today, when you get right down to it, they are being asked to celebrate the end of that protection. The Teacher and his students are there to watch the general who ran Operation Enduring Freedom hand command over to the man who will end it.

The general's aide deposits them in the very front row.

★ ★ ★

Today, an hour north of the gymnasium where Aziz and his students sit, the Taliban dismantles a man with an axe. The reason is that this man spied for the Americans. Everyone knows "spied" is synonym for "agreed with." So Aziz is also a spy.

By that logic, he is of course much more than a spy. He's a sympathizer, an appeaser, and an apostate. He's been called these and other things: Communist (although he took up arms against the communists). Christian (although he is a scholar of Islam's holy book). Pimp (although he encouraged girls to protest laws that would legalize their rape). And perhaps most ominously: American.

The Americans are wasting no time: at almost the same moment a man is dying from axe wounds in the north for siding with the Americans, the Americans are getting their military equipment out of the country to the south and east. A local news outlet in Pakistan spotted twenty-five cargo containers marked USFOR-A on their way out of Afghanistan, heading to a port in Karachi, where they'll be put on a cargo ship and taken far away. The things the foreign armies use to fight are leaving; this is the beginning of the withdrawal, the rug being slowly tugged from beneath Aziz's feet by fifty defense ministers from NATO member countries. All around Afghanistan, the lights are going out. Bases are being handed over to the locals, bases are closing, vehicles are being cleaned and inspected and packed up, soldiers are standing next to shipping containers waiting for C-130s to come take it all away.

Aziz tries to push these things from his mind. He takes in the room: big and dull and a kind of purgatorial gray that someone tried to liven up with aquamarine siding. It looks like giant, cheap headboards ringing the room. A sliver of garish morning sunlight arcs down across the crowd like a blade, and it finally makes sense why the generals from America wear their caps indoors, with the brims pulled so low you can't see their eyes. The first infantry division band is playing, poorly: a regal melody made muddy and distorted by a flat tuba and a wobbly clarinet and a room built without acoustics in mind. General Allen enters, a war paint shadow over his eyes. The band switches to a gleeful rendition of Afghanistan's national anthem,

and the four NATO generals, each in camouflage uniform, no two
of which would blend into the same forest, face the audience. They
salute, then sit down, then stand back up for the American national
anthem.

President Karzai, as of late in one of his fugue states, having
blasted the British on a trip to Britain with a rhetorical wad of phlegm
for their failure to secure a southern province, is not in attendance;
Aziz makes note of his absence. He makes note of who *is* in attendance: next to him sit Kabul's police commander and the chairman
of the country's armed forces. These men, upon whom he and his
four thousand students will soon be dependent for security, are right
now chatting and tittering like adolescents. Aziz thinks they're not
even listening. They take off their simultaneous translation headphones, and he *knows* they're not listening. Aziz is amazed. They are
nakedly uninterested in what's going on in front of them. They are the
people charged with keeping the country intact after these foreign
generals up on the podium are gone; these are the men who are supposed to carry on the fight and keep the country together.

Aziz thinks they are not at all ready. He is beginning to think
that at the first possible instant, they will resort to the only sense of
belonging they feel at marrow level. To the people who look like
them and come from the same places they do and speak the same languages with the same accents. These are men who have a shaky understanding of history, who will break off based on allegiance to the
sects of their fathers and mothers, drawn to their separate corners until each side is big enough for it to turn into war. He has seen that
before.

It's a shame, Aziz thinks. If only the men at the top weren't
so . . . "empty" is the word he keeps coming back to. They are
empty and it's not even that they and President Karzai and his cabinet are bad people. They are simply lightweights. Incapable of or dis-
inclined to deep thought. Juvenile, that's what these men sitting next
to him are. They are juvenile and it is what will destroy the country
when the Americans leave.

Aziz now forces himself to stop thinking about this, because to
entertain the thought further leads him to its logical conclusion: in-

stability, collapse, factional war. And the ones who will suffer most will be Aziz and his people, for these three reasons: His people, the Hazaras, look different, in a country where most people look mostly the same; their flat faces and narrow eyes have been their curse for centuries. And where everyone else is Sunni, they are Shia. So they are different, and everyone can see it. And finally, when America came in and asked everyone to disarm, they did. The Hazaras are seen as collaborators. They look different, they are different, and they took our side. So as the ceremony proceeds it is frightening to watch the foreign generals talking about Afghan security forces like they are very close to being ready, while Aziz can see very clearly that they are not. The foreigners talk about "continuing mission momentum" and in the same breath of taking men, women, and equipment out of the theater. They speak of Afghanistan's security forces being just about all trained up, as if it were enough that everyone would really like them to be.

It's not a new idea. All these generals, sitting with their brims pulled low, began their careers when Vietnam was ending, when training up the locals made as much political sense as it did military. If you can train locals to continue the fight, you get to leave without admitting defeat.

A German general takes the podium and speaks from a wistful place, with romance even, about the Afghan forces and the "progress that you can almost touch," and how the "transition has gained momentum to the point that it is irreversible."

These are parents who love their sons too much and are blind to their flaws. "We commend the work of the Afghan national security forces for the way they have risen to the challenge," the German says. Aziz is presented with an ominous image: foreign generals talking about how it will all be okay because the Afghan forces are so professional, while the leaders of the Afghan forces are sitting next to him, not even pretending to listen.

General Allen is a man who prefers to think of war like a grand physics experiment. To imagine it on a big planar field where things like "force vectors" and "threat streams" go about their contest until one triumphs over the other. Thus, the general's job is to arrange the pieces so that the appropriate threat streams are overcome by the correct force vectors and all the bad things are neutralized and the good things prevail. He's a man drawn to the science of warfare. He gave up Princeton to study fighting instead; it was what fascinated him. A week before this ceremony he explained to the *Wall Street Journal* how he planned to solve the logistical brainteaser of removing thirteen years' worth of military hardware from a landlocked country with no catcher's mitt next door, no Kuwait like you had with Iraq, where you could park your planes and tanks for a while. Here the closest ocean was on the other side of Pakistan, where the people were screaming about sovereignty and tended toward the mind-set that dodging drone strikes was plenty of exposure to the American military, thank you very much. Who would be damned if they let us use their backyard to store our weapons Until Further Notice. So Allen took to the chessboard. The military built up an air path, a land path, and a coordinated communication system to keep the whole thing humming. They sent test shipments through to find blockages and bottlenecks, so they could make sure it was all "flowing and to achieve full velocity on all three in order for us to have removed the preponderance of equipment out of theater for all fifty nations by the end of '14."

Problem solved.

That's the disciplined way the general prefers to think, but he's not always the best at maintaining that mind-set. When an interviewer gets Allen off logistics and onto the stories of people, the general needs a minute to compose himself. He's not very good at keeping casualties out of mind. On this mission, Allen has even more emotional exposure, because he made the mistake of growing close to the country. He met Aziz Royesh and the students and started making trips out to the school in the slums. By the end of his tour Allen was so moved by what he'd seen in this country that he donated enough money for twenty-five scholarships to Marefat out of his own pocket. He lobbied the president of the United States not to abandon these people, to keep more troops here for the long haul. Perhaps because he's aware of something the other generals do not acknowledge:

that it is actually going to be very hard to get Afghan forces ready in time. When Allen took command of the NATO mission here there were roughly four hundred thousand Afghans under arms, many of whom were not only poorly trained but illiterate.

Those men will soon be in control of the police and army. Which means that in order for the country to be secure these men who couldn't read now must believe in something called the "rule of law" with more force than they believe in their own ethnicity so that they'll fight for the former, never the latter. Because here's an added challenge the United States never faced in Vietnam: the South Vietnamese might not have been very motivated to fight for us, but they at least weren't motivated to fight against each other. Here, there is a long history of ethnic differences exploited by political leaders, warlords, and foreign countries, including ours.

Though Allen would go hoarse trying to keep the U.S. army in this country, he had little chance of succeeding. He had respect but no leverage in Washington, and the war here was becoming less popular by the day. As he ran directly against political headwinds he was kneecapped by a string of "green on blue" insider attacks, Afghan troops killing their Western mentors. "Even the good guys don't want us there," Americans thought, and Allen was placed in the awful position of wanting the world to keep protecting Aziz and the students and others like them, but having the duty to make the world stop.

When General Allen takes the dais to give his remarks, he speaks first in his earnest but clipped way. He is formal and stolid. He is thanking people, so many people to thank, which is an odd thing, it seems, for a mission that's still very much undecided. But just now his tone is changing. He is becoming looser, he looks up from his notes to address the room, he's actually becoming expressive, his hand moving to the side of the dais and his torso relaxing, sinking, as he explains how he feels about the people in this country, how "in a very real sense, we have become brothers." This is also odd. It's the language of aid workers in their constant state of minor hysteria, not of hardened Marine generals. It is striking and inspiring and disconcerting that a general is doing this, like when a stern father shows warmth, and you are elevated, but also concerned that something must be very wrong.

"The people of Afghanistan have become my family. Part of me." Now Aziz is paying close attention. "And normally on an occasion like this my family would be with me, my wife and my daughters would attend a ceremony such as this, but they're not able to be here, so I asked two young students from a high school nearby with whom we have a strong relationship, Somaya and Mustafa Ibrahim"—now Aziz thinks he must be mishearing—"to join me today, because they are very much my family, they will always be very much my family." The general's voice cracks a little, and he gestures to where Aziz and the two youths are sitting, and they stand up in this room full of all the most powerful people in the country, some of the more powerful people in the world. Aziz and two students from his school in the slums are being shown off by the commander of the most powerful military in the world, who is now transparently emotional—"and in their bright faces, we see the future of this great country. Today they are my precious family and they have served to form the memories that I will take from Afghanistan."

Aziz can't believe what he is hearing. He expected to show up and have a handshake with the general and leave; instead, his students have been called the very future of the country. The commanding general has called them his own family.

Tomorrow, newspapers around the world will report this. They will carry the story of General Allen's emotional farewell, in which he mentioned a school and two of its students. They will not report the name of the Teacher, the name of the school, or the name of the youths. Reporters believe this omission protects them. Aziz thinks that's a mistake. Reporters think an American mentioning your name makes you a spy, and everyone knows what happens to spies. But Aziz wishes the journalists would do it anyway. *Print my name!* he thinks, as if he could will them to do so. *Print the children's names!* He understands something the reporters don't: tying him so closely to the American military doesn't make him a spy. He already is a spy.

At this point, the general's pronouncement means legitimacy. Anyone who might take offense with the school—the students who are always protesting some religious figure or demonstrating against some law, the extracurricular activities in which boys and girls sit in the same classroom, the school's new radio station, broadcasting provocative ideas and women's voices—these people will know that there are powerful American military men who care about the school. For Aziz, being named is not being outed, it's armor.

Press be damned, Aziz will go back and tell all his friends in rooms without furniture about this remarkable moment, when the kids stood up and the room clapped for them and the General seemed close to tears. Aziz will tell his faculty and his students and the students' families that the General thinks they are all his family, and everyone will for a time be just so incredibly hopeful, furnished for the moment with the notion that the Americans might not leave after all, because you don't leave family.

"This spring, our forces will move into a support role, while Afghan security forces take the lead. Tonight, I can announce that over the next year, another 34,000 American troops will come home from Afghanistan. This drawdown will continue and by the end of next year, our war in Afghanistan will be over."

So said the president of the United States during his state of the union address in February 2013, forty-eight hours after the general's speech in Kabul. Back in Washington, the tectonic plates had shifted and made way for the withdrawal. A slack-faced nominee for secretary of defense, a man who always looked like he needed a shower and an aspirin, and who was known to favor the "zero option"— leaving no troops at all behind—was wobbling his way toward Senate confirmation.

Thirty-four thousand troops leaving in a year—the biggest, fastest withdrawal of troops yet. The United States needed one hundred thousand troops here to fight and subdue the Taliban, and by this time next year, they'll have a third of that. Maybe less, if their new defense secretary has his way. Aziz knows that's not a fighting force. That is not enough to hold the Taliban back. Not enough to protect Aziz and his people from whatever new insurgency emerges. The foreigners are saying they're serious that the Afghan commanders, who Aziz can see are not ready, are going to be in charge of securing the whole country by next year. By next year, there will only be enough American troops left here for mop-up and Aziz has seen enough to know that if the United States is done, whoever's left will follow them out. Maybe, by the end of it, a few thousand troops will stay behind for good measure; maybe they won't. What Aziz is hearing is that the troops are leaving faster than ever and that by this time next year, the U.S. mission to protect this place will be as good as done. The clock is ticking.

Aziz tries to be sanguine about this at first. He doesn't allow himself to be down. This is part of his resilience, a key ingredient: he just ignores those things that would upset him. "When God gives you a locked door," he says, "be grateful it's not a wall!" There's always a way, and bad things are not that bad because they're not that real. The United States won't leave.

There were things even at the ceremony that he saw but didn't allow himself to register. How General Allen, after calling everyone's attention to Aziz and the students, had continued a speech that sounded less like a man celebrating a career milestone than one memorializing a catastrophe that has already happened.

"I will miss you all," Allen said, "and I will miss those who are with me here today and I will miss this mission beyond words. I don't want to say good-bye today. Instead I'd like to reflect and to thank and to pay tribute to you," he said. Aziz chose not to see a foreboding in this, to not be concerned by how, for example, the hugs General Allen is administering are a little excessive, the general is *really* emotional. These hugs are uneven, the kind that require large men to adjust ballast, like two seniors slow-dancing. It's been that way all day. His hug with Dumford, the general taking over, was a bit unsteady, a slight sway to the side before they recalibrated. And after his speech, when the ceremony is over and the flags have been passed from the old general to the new, General Allen finds Aziz, and offers him one of these big hugs, just swallows Aziz in his camouflage as if he might hide the little man forever.

After his good-bye Aziz will present himself to the new general, who will receive him kindly but coolly and will say in his disinterested Quincy accent, "So you are members of Allen's family . . ." a comment in unsure space between compliment and condescension. Aziz will not take offense. He knows what this is. The new general is not as invested as the old, and Aziz knows why. It's for the same reason a doctor knows not to be too invested in a patient with late-stage cancer. Both men stand there for a moment after this handover ceremony. Both men know that one, by doing his job, may bring about the demise of the other.

Aziz has eleven months to prepare.

2

THE FIRST THOUSAND

The story of the Hazaras—the people about whom this book is written—might as well start in the twelfth century with a bright-eyed boy born to a concubine mother. Temujin was his name, "Iron Worker" it meant. He grew up in a world of intrigue, with family members constantly jockeying for position. Often violently: Temujin killed for the first time at the age of ten. He was only a teenager when he began a rapid, relentless campaign to consolidate tribes and eliminate those who opposed him. He took the practices of the time and revised them in ways that made him a better commander than any one before, and for a long time after. He adjusted plundering to serve a new purpose: no longer simple enrichment, but also security; not just stealing from your enemies, but also decimating them so that they could never rise up. As he defeated once-dominant peoples, he killed their leaders and absorbed their commoners to swell his own ranks, but split tribes up and dispatched them to different lands so that they couldn't join together against him. It wasn't just "divide and conquer" that Temujin practiced. It was "conquer, then divide even more." His surprise raids at breakneck speeds against larger armies would inspire another consolidating force centuries later, which would call the tactic "lightening war"—*blitzkrieg*—and themselves *Nationalsozialistische*. National Socialists. Or, for short, Nazis.

It would take one final underdog fight before Temujin assumed the name the world would know him by. Facing a larger, stronger army, he sent an order down the ranks that no man was to share a campfire, each was to light his own. That night, from a distance, his army looked several times larger than it actually was. The enemy was thrown into disarray. When the fighting began, Temujin's men won decisively. It was after this last war that a grand congress was convened to bestow upon Temujin the title by which he would be known for centuries to come: Ruler of the Universe. Genghis Khan.

The critical piece, as far as Hazaras are concerned, turns on a technicality.

It has to do with the particular manner in which Genghis Khan designed his army. He divided his military into multiples of ten: ten, one hundred, one thousand. It was a unit of one thousand men, that, according to certain histories, the Mongols left behind after conquering a valley along the Silk Road, in what is today Afghanistan.

"One thousand," in the most commonly spoken language of Afghanistan, is *hazar*. Hazaras, therefore, are the people descended from the one thousand.

The history is neat. (For a list of sources from which this history has been drawn, please see the Author's Note.) The Mongols came, they conquered, they left a thousand men behind, and they begot a people called Hazaras: the children of concubines and the rampaging Mongol army, the children of the one thousand.

But it's a history that makes Hazaras latecomers to Afghanistan. It affixes to them a legacy of invasion, in a country that has a long and complicated relationship with invaders. In their very facial features— "bad features," as one character in this book tells his daughter—they carry a story of violence and rape.

And because of their association with a marauding conqueror, there has always been the lingering notion that the Hazaras' long and ongoing tenure as Afghanistan's underclass was not something anyone should apologize for. To treat Hazaras as servant and slave stock, to prohibit them from the university system—this was not repression. This was justice.

But while Genghis Khan is woven through the history of the Hazaras, it turns out this origin story isn't quite so simple. There are mysteries here, mysteries that have yet to be solved but which the Hazaras, as they've lifted themselves up over the years since the U.S.–led invasion, are beginning to question.

For one, a key piece of supporting evidence is that the Hazaras *look* like Genghis Khan's Mongol army. Visually, the story adds up. Mongols came; a people who looked like them emerged.

But there were people with similar features in present-day Afghanistan long before Genghis Khan's army ever showed up in the thirteenth century. Long before Genghis Khan was even *born*. Traders traveled the Silk Road between China and Europe, as did the ancient Kushans, and Buddhist pilgrims. Even in Bamiyan, a linchpin of the Mongol invasion, there were a pair of giant Buddhas carved into the sandstone, bearing stereotypical Asian features. They predated Genghis Khan's arrival by more than six centuries.

There's also a very basic logical flaw in the Genghis Khan theory. Hazaras are Muslim and Persian-speaking. The Mongol army was neither. If the Mongols came, destroyed what was there, and then repopulated the land, what sense would it make for them to adopt the language of a population they just decimated? Or convert to the religion of people they'd just killed?

This is all evidence many Hazaras cite to reject the "one thousand" theory. The likeliest origin story is a messier one: Hazaras descended from an amalgam of peoples—Mongols, but also Silk Road traders, Buddhist pilgrims, and Kushans. Nevertheless, the simplest story emerged as the dominant one: Hazaras are the ones who came later, the ones who are not really from this place, who aren't *really* Muslim. Complicating matters is the fact that while many Hazaras reject this origin myth, not all do. Some embrace it: there are Hazaras, most of them living next door in Pakistan, who wrap themselves in Genghis Khan's legacy to show they aren't ashamed. Better to have descended from a fearsome conqueror than to just be an underclass.

Maybe, if the Marefat school survives after we leave, and if Hazara men and women keep getting into universities, getting jobs in civil society, and levering themselves into power, they will produce enough of their own scholarship to determine their own provenance once and for all. Until they do, anyone inclined to reject Hazaras as "other," "foreigner," "newcomer," or "infidel," need not look further than Genghis Khan for justification.

Another mystery lies at the center of the Hazara history. Like most Afghans, they are Muslim. But while most Afghans belong to the Sunni sect, most Hazaras are Shia. The split between the two sects dates back to the seventh century, when a dispute arose concerning who should succeed the Prophet Mohammed as caliph, leader of the Islamic community.

Across the world, as in Afghanistan, Sunnis make up the overwhelming majority of Muslims. Exactly how it came to pass that Hazaras are Shia has never been satisfactorily resolved, but it has tremendous bearing on their lives. Being Shia in a country where just about everyone else is Sunni is its own crucible, since the two sects have a long history of conflict, and Afghanistan shares a border with the biggest and most powerful Shia country in the world: Iran. Hazaras are tied to Iran, whether they like it or not, because it's a country with 76 million of their religious kin.

The Hazaras' relationship with Iran is fraught, as is the relationship between Iran and Afghanistan. On the one hand, Iran has accepted millions of refugees fleeing conflict in Afghanistan. On the other, it periodically forces tens of thousands of them at a time to return. Iran has invested heavily in Afghanistan, everything from hospitals to madrassas and other monuments to Shiism. Naturally, monuments to one sect are not always welcomed in a country where most people belong to another. Hazaras are assigned responsibility for all of Iran's activities in Afghanistan—the productive ones, the destructive ones, the ambiguous ones.

The irony is that in Iran, no one has been treated worse than the Hazaras. During Afghanistan's most violent periods, Iran struggled to absorb the millions of refugees coming across the border, and when economic pressure mounted, resentment toward refugees did, too. But most refugees weren't identifiable because most Afghans don't look all that much different from most Iranians. So when Iranians got fed up with refugees, the only people they could tell were refugees were the ones who looked like Genghis Khan. "I was never allowed to think I was Afghan in Afghanistan," a Hazara once told me. "The only time I was ever considered Afghan was when I was in Iran."

Hazaras have often been targets. All the way back to the first Mughal emperor, Babur, who traveled Afghanistan at the beginning of the sixteenth century and considered Shiism to be absurd, heretical, and evil. Never have Hazaras suffered more, however, than they did at the end of the nineteenth century, during the reign of Amir Abdur Rahman Khan. "The Iron Amir," as he came to be known, decided that quieting restive minorities was a measure necessary for modernization.

The amir's campaign against the Hazaras went more or less according to a series of steps familiar throughout history, when one group of people seeks to put down another. First, the inclination to see an entire race of people as unappealing. This was not an uncommon feeling about Hazaras at the time, nor even one reserved to Afghans: an Englishwoman visiting the country and serving as the amir's palace doctor wrote about Hazaras as a strange and underevolved species. "Such a crowd of girls," she wrote, about a trip to a Hazara village, "and every one of them hideous." She specified: "Broad, squat little persons, with faces like full-moons and heads like rugged bullets, all bumps and nodules, covered with straight, coarse, lank-black hair, which only half concealed the curious outline of the skull." As praise, she offered this:

> Hazaras are naturally hard-working and industrious, and being also strong and active, they make excellent servants and even beasts of burden, and in the towns, at any rate, are cheaper to feed than donkeys.

Of course it wasn't just that Hazaras were often viewed as primitive. If it had been solely that, perhaps no one would have cared enough to launch a campaign against them. They were a fairly small population of mostly subsistence farmers, living in the highlands.

It was that they were also seen as vassals of cynical outside forces, of other countries seeking to control Afghanistan by coopting its hapless underclass. If the Hazaras weren't deliberately undermining the country, they were simply too foolish to realize someone else was undermining it through them. The Iron Amir was inclined to see Hazaras as puppets; he believed in the most reductive story of their origin, that they were installed in Afghanistan as a rear guard for the Mongol army. From the very beginning, their loyalties were to be questioned. He believed they were traitorous by constitution, "always ready," he wrote in his memoirs, "to join the first foreign aggressor who attacked Afghanistan."

He took it upon himself to bring them into line. He levied exorbitant taxes, which many Hazaras refused to pay. He accused Hazaras of attacking travelers and denying the amir's own cavalcade safe passage through the highlands. He saw himself (or at least he wrote that he saw himself) as making repeated peace offerings to the troublesome Hazaras, only to have them thrown back in his face. The amir saw his own intentions as solely noble: to unify the land and create a strong new country, protected by its strength and coherence against neighbors and invaders, so was justified when he decided to strike at those standing in his way with overwhelming force.

He ordered a series of brutal attacks against the main concentration of Hazaras in the highlands. His soldiers led Hazaras on long marches to Kabul, during which many died, and those who survived were enslaved. The Iron Amir ushered in a period of genocide against the Hazaras, or at the very least, institutionalized repression. When news of a victory over a Hazara faction reached the capital, the amir was overjoyed, and moved to generosity: "All the property and wealth of that ill-favored group is licit for you," he told the military leaders. "Nothing but the prisoners of that wicked tribe should come to the government. Bring them back with you and divide the spoils up equally." They did as instructed. "Hazara slaves were so plentiful in Kabul at that time," the British doctor wrote, "that there were not masters to be found for them all."

Hazaras who survived and managed to escape enslavement found much of their land destroyed or confiscated; hundreds of thousands were driven into poverty and out of Afghanistan. For those who had doubts, it was now abundantly clear that this was not a country for them. In Kandahar, the dismembered heads of Hazaras were displayed in the bazaar, and taken down only so they could be fashioned into a tower of skulls, erected as a warning.

In the years since, Hazaras have continued to flee, mostly to Iran and Pakistan, especially in times of intense violence or persecution. But even in their places of refuge they've been targeted, particularly after the Iranian revolution. In 1979, when Iran was seized with Shia-flavored revolutionary zeal, a wave of Shia influence spread throughout the Muslim world and a countering wave of anti-Shiite influence rose to meet it. In Pakistan, fear of Shiism found its outlet in violence against the sect's most easily identifiable followers, the ones who looked different from everyone else: the Hazaras.

In the 1980s, Hazaras in Pakistan clashed with Pakistani police, and Hazara communities were placed under dayslong shoot-on-sight curfews. Hazaras were killed, police were injured; the military was called in. By the 1990s, new groups had emerged in Pakistan animated solely by a desire to kill Hazaras and seal off Pakistan from Iranian influence, real and imagined.

After the U.S.–led invasion of Afghanistan in 2001, Hazaras embraced the United States and the international community, so a new offense was added to the list of complaints against them—helping us. In Pakistan, anti-Shia groups merged with anti-American ones. Hazaras became victims of "target killings," shootings, and massive bombings in Hazara communities. Even in Pakistan, their country of refuge, Hazaras are still being killed by the dozens, sometimes the hundreds.

They have not always been passive victims, of course. They formed their own military factions to fight against the Soviets, and then to fight against other Afghan factions—Aziz was a leader in one of these factions—and they have their own warlords. Still, they have suffered more bloodshed and oppression than they've imposed, and they're the only tribe for whom oppression has been institutionalized: from the state-backed massacres and enslavement during the time of the Iron Amir, well into the twentieth century, when Hazaras were barred from attending government schools and universities, banned from military and civil services jobs, and prevented from owning property in downtown Kabul.

It all began to change when we arrived. Hazaras seized upon the opportunity to recover, and to do it in their own country. With a new constitution overseen by the Americans, an ostensible democracy was born, minority rights were on the books, and discrimination was illegal, at least on paper. Hazaras expanded into positions they'd never held before. They started to succeed in business and filled important roles in government, moving upward so quickly that they have a new criticism to contend with: "People see them as being uppity," one American foreign service officer said. "Remember that word? They'd been regarded as the underclass for so long that a lot of Pashtuns and Tajiks assumed they really were. And people don't trust their underclass. They think that the underclass is going to subvert society."

Hazaras have existed for the better part of a millennium with a kind of triple curse. In a country that is almost entirely one kind of Muslim, they are another. In a country traumatized by a procession of invaders, they're associated with one of the most violent ones. And for anyone inclined to regard Hazaras as an offending party for any of these reasons, it's always been easy to identify them, because in a country where most people look more or less the same, Hazaras look different.

But their greatest offense may be the most recent. They're not just adherents of a different faith, not just physically distinct in their own country, and not just associated with a nine-hundred-year-old invasion. Now, they're associated with us.

It was less of a problem in the early years of the occupation, when the Taliban had fled and the foreigners kept arriving: troops, aid organizations, embassy workers. Everywhere you looked, buildings were being built, roads were being cleared and paved. There seemed to be interest from every corner of the world in a safe and democratic Afghanistan.

It was hard to imagine a day when the Western world would tire of its "good war" in Afghanistan. Just as it was hard to imagine that the Taliban could ever come back. Or that both things—the return of the Taliban, and the fading of international interest—would begin right around the same time, placing Hazaras squarely in harm's way. Disarmed and guilty of collaborating with a foreign army, just as the foreign army leaves, and the rest of the world mostly looks away.

The school at the center of this book emerged during one of the most tragic chapters of Afghanistan's history. It is a place of knowledge and enlightenment that began at the very depths of violence and oppression. At the moment the idea for this school was realized, in a refugee camp next door in Pakistan, Afghanistan was a hopeless place. It had been through a Soviet invasion that split the country and left millions of people dead, many of them civilians. It had been through a brutal civil war, in which cities were destroyed, no one ever held control for long, and there was rarely meaningful authority. There was a hopeful moment when a group of young religious students seemed destined to secure the whole country and finally restore order. But by 1996, that group—calling themselves "Knowledge Seekers" or *Taliban*—had taken Kabul, demonstrated that they had very little capacity to govern, and shown themselves to be perhaps the most oppressive regime operating anywhere in the world.

Random violence began again, the country was moving toward drought, and there was no longer anything to look forward to; it felt like the country had already tried every kind of government and none of them worked. Maybe Afghanistan was a doomed place. Especially for Hazaras, for whom the Taliban reserved special ire, as they were, once again, the wrong kind of Muslim. It was a country in its darkest hour, with no upcoming election that might change things, no movement forming on the horizon that might bring about a more just government, and no conceivable way Hazaras might change their fate themselves.

It was in Pakistan, in the city of Rawalpindi, that a young Hazara man in exile—a holy warrior who had fought against the Soviets, and then against other holy warriors in the civil war, but who had now taken his family into hiding—decided that his people were becoming so fatalistic they'd reached a change-or-die moment. He had just survived a massacre, barely, in which the whole world seemed to fall down on the Hazaras, and they didn't even try to help one another. Their collective attitude was that the only way for people from this place to have any kind of life was to abandon it and find a way to Germany or Australia or the United States. There was nothing here for them now and nothing good was coming.

This young man saw that even Hazaras of status, commanders and clergymen, were trying to leave. He saw people he believed could be governors and ministers skulking away to drive taxis and clean toilets in the West. He believed that what he saw was a surrender. He believed his people were collapsing in on themselves.

But he also believed he was in a unique position to do something about it.

In the 1980s, as a fifteen-year-old holy warrior, he was given the nickname "Teacher." He had no formal education past the fifth grade, but he had been a curious child and by the time he was a teenager he'd read so many books on so many different subjects that he could challenge the elders fighting alongside him at the front. When they quartered in villages, Aziz taught the kids. He thought himself rather a natural at it. Then the 1980s ended, the Soviet army retreated, a vaunted moment came and passed, civil war began, and by 1994 he saw his people cowering in Pakistan. Aziz watched as a generation was lost. So when another Hazara refugee had the idea of holding classes in his basement, Aziz embraced it for reasons that had as much to do with tribal pride as anything else.

Word of the school began to spread through the camps. The Teacher dispatched his little brother to the dimly lit rooms where refugees wove carpets because there wasn't much else they could do for money. And he pried children away with the promise of return on investment. *Don't worry*, he told them. Fewer hands on the loom today would be made up tenfold by cultivated minds later. Sometimes it worked, sometimes it didn't, but soon they had a dozen students.

The school itself wasn't anything to look at. Not in the beginning, and not for most of its history. It was one room, a few sorry-looking chairs, a chalkboard leaning against a wall. But they made do with what they had, and word began to spread among refugees in other cities, because there was nothing else like it. A place refugees could learn to read and write between shifts at the loom, where they would not be barred entry for lack of citizenship.

Then one autumn evening during the school's seventh year, while the Teacher was outside washing his family's carpets, his oldest daughter came running out of the house with her face wrenched up. "America is on fire! Come look, it's on the TV, there is a war in America!"

The Teacher did not know immediately what the 9/11 attacks meant for him and his people. But as it became clear that it was an attack launched from Afghanistan, by a man named Usama bin Laden and that the Taliban government was refusing to give him up, Aziz saw the next steps unfold before him. The Americans would come to dispense with the Taliban and make it safe to return. He began to plan. Just after the U.S.–led invasion, Aziz was ready. He moved his school home to Afghanistan.

Home, for the very first time.

Even after the small educational center called Marefat had earned a reputation throughout the refugee camps, it actually had so little to its name that the entire thing could be moved across the border by students. Some chairs and books, an endowment of $550, in Pakistan rupees. Marefat was still mostly an idea.

The supplies were divided, given to the students' families, taken across the border, and reassembled in a rundown three-room apartment Aziz rented in Kabul. His family crowded into one room, and the other two became the Marefat School. It was still just a few dozen students, and only up to the fourth grade. Aziz knew nothing about building a curriculum. What he knew was that he'd seen his country destroyed by men who spoke and expected people to take what they said for granted. And by people who did. He wanted students to *interrogate* ideas.

People were pouring back into Afghanistan, and word spread among Hazaras of the little school in the apartment. Aziz's reputation helped. He wasn't loved by all Hazaras, but he was known by many for his former role at the top of the prominent faction of holy warriors. Marefat's students also helped. As people began to rebuild their lives in the new Kabul, they ran into Marefat students, who, even in those early days, tended to have a quality Hazaras still weren't accustomed to: confidence. They spoke forcefully, they argued, and they would correct you about a political or historical matter if you were mistaken. People were surprised. Students recruited other students without even trying.

They also impressed the occasional foreign visitor. Marefat would grow without the help of any foreign government, but occasionally foreigners would come across the students, and they were always moved. Frances D'Souza, a scholar from England visiting the country on behalf of a democracy-building organization soon after the Taliban fell, found her way to this school in a rundown apartment building. She raised £2,000 almost immediately, and she kept returning. On one trip, she brought her daughter Christa, a *British Vogue* contributing editor, who was also moved to help; on another, she came with £6,500 pounds and an idea: Why not have your very own building?

Already, after less than a year in Afghanistan, there were too many students for the little apartment, so Aziz took D'Souza's advice. He bought land in the middle of a wheat field so far out of town that it was almost free. It was to the west of downtown Kabul, in an all-Hazara area aptly called the Desert of Barchi—if you stood in front of the school and looked in any direction you had to strain to see another building. The students got to work digging and mixing and building. When they finished, it was just a few mud-brick classrooms around a dirt courtyard, and when the farmers irrigated their crops, the students had to walk through a bog to get to class. It wasn't much, but it would do. The Hazaras had a school.

It was the first private school in Afghanistan, and it soon became one of the most successful schools in the whole country. Within six years, it was right at the top in student performance on college entrance exams, so the best school in the country was funded almost exclusively from the tuition dollars of the country's poorest people.

Hazara students graduated from Marefat and won scholarships to the finest universities all over the world: Brown, Harvard, Tufts, Northwestern, Sciences Po in France and the South Asian University in India, the American University of Central Asia in Bishkek, and the Asian University for Women in Bangladesh. And Marefat became more than a school, it became an epicenter of Hazara politics and culture. Students volunteered for political candidates; they went home and convinced their parents to oppose the ideas of certain religious figures and instead follow leaders with more liberal ideas. They broadcast their opinions on a radio station and sold provocative art to foreigners. They became more visible probably than they should have, and there were confrontations, some serious ones. They made enemies. People were threatened by Marefat, and sometimes they threatened it back. The school's ideas—about girls and humanism and critical thinking even about religion—were often attacked. Sometimes the students were, too. But Marefat endured, and it thrived, for a while at least. It kept growing and attracting more students, drawing people in from other parts of the country, and even back from exile abroad. It became a place where the innumerable stories of war—the long impossible journeys of people and families, the growth and decay of community, the destruction of cities and the rebuilding in their place—would converge.

This, then, is the story of a school. But it is also story of the Hazaras, a people whose history has been defined by tragedy but whose future has, for a decade, held a glimmer of hope. It's the story of the one institution that has, as much as any other, allowed for that hope to grow. And it's the story of what happens to that place when it's confronted by imminent danger.

Most of all, this is the story of the individual journeys that have intersected at this special school, in the unlikeliest of places. It's the story of the people who have shaped Marefat, and the lives that Marefat, in turn, has shaped. Including my own.

Before any of it it could happen—before Marefat could begin in a Pakistani refugee camp, before it could be brought to Afghanistan and built up there, before it could even be named Marefat—Aziz had to experience bloodshed. He had to develop the desire to lead people away from it, and the drive to do so even if it meant risking his own life and the lives of those closest to him. For that he had to see violence so close it changed him physically, chemically, from the scars on his body to changes in his brain, what his mind did at night. For Marefat to exist, Aziz had to see war.

3

TWENTY-ONE YEARS LEFT

Kabul, Afshar District, February 10, 1993

It began at about four thirty in the morning.

With first light, Aziz could see the earth coughing up jets of smoke and dust. It was a windless winter morning, so the thick billows just hung there, frozen in place. He was confused; he thought he was seeing smoke signals. *They're talking to each other.*

Then he realized: artillery shells. He couldn't tell where they were coming from, but he thought they might be coming from everywhere. He had the sense then that a lot of people were going to die.

Aziz was a holy warrior back then, fighting for the Unity Party, the party that brought all the different Hazara factions under one banner. He carried a machine gun all the time; like a good soldier he treated his weapon as an extension of himself, his own body, which he couldn't leave behind. Though he hardly ever shot it. He was always close to the front line but rarely at it, because even back then, starting at age fifteen, he was known as Teacher. He became a spokesman for Grandfather Mazari, the Hazara's beloved commander, a messenger between Mazari and the people. His words reached Pakistan, Iran, Saudi Arabia; by the time he was twenty he had admirers in countries all across the continent and by the time he was twenty-five he had bounties on his head in most of them. He learned to argue long before he learned when not to. He surpassed his father's education so quickly that there wasn't anybody comfortable trying to discipline the boy. Or to caution him: to teach him there was valor in knowing when not to fight.

The Unity Party was encamped in a town of Hazara civilians, a warren of houses tucked into the joint where the hills met the flatland. The army held most of the posts on the ridgeline above, and a faction led by an Ayatollah guarded the others. In the years to come, Aziz and this Ayatollah would never see eye to eye, though they were at that moment allies of convenience.

Or so Aziz thought. Aziz did not know that the Ayatollah had sold them out. When an alliance of rival parties planned a surprise attack, the Ayatollah cut a deal, and before dawn, his men simply let the attackers through. The other checkpoints were either compromised or overrun. The mountains overlooking the village were taken before the villagers woke up. Before anyone even knew an attack had started, the enemy had taken positions looking down on them from the west, northwest, and east.

Afshar had been transformed into a gauntlet.

In the only video that survived, Aziz and Pike, a friend who had the job of documenting the civil war for the Unity Party, are in the background speaking to each other quietly as the attack begins, like they've woken to find wildlife in the yard and don't want to startle it. Their voices sound casual, they don't know they're watching the beginning of a massacre. They stand together near the window of the Polytechnic University building, which the Unity Party has converted into a barracks.

"They've started attacking the houses," Aziz says to Pike, to no one. Aziz hawks and spits. The highest peak the Unity Party holds is now on fire. Artillery comes from the east, a hill the Ayatollah's men were supposed to be protecting—*is the Ayatollah firing at us?* A commander radios Aziz and orders him out to the Desert for help: *gather as many people as you can to come and fight.* The commander could tell even then they were in trouble. They were going to need reinforcements, anyone who could fight or help in any way. The party's finance officer had a Russian jeep he wasn't using, so Aziz took it and a driver and set off on the nine kilometers toward the Desert, while behind him, Afshar started to burn.

He got to the Desert and drove west, yelling through a megaphone that Hazaras were under attack at Afshar, they needed fighters, medics, anyone who could help. All the way past Dry Bridge, past the wheat field that his school would occupy two decades later, stopping along the way to wait for people to come out. No one did.

Nobody even came out of their houses; he turned and headed back to Afshar. He reported to the commander that he hadn't found anyone in the Desert willing to help, but the commander refused to believe it. "Go back," he said, "try again." Again, Aziz rode the nine kilometers out to the Desert, again he yelled through the megaphone, "Come help your brothers and sisters who are in trouble at Afshar!" and again, no one came to help.

Only this time he turned at the end of the road to head back, and a group of Hazaras stood in the street, blocking his way. A rocket had just landed—*Are all Hazara areas under attack?*—and the people wanted his vehicle to ferry the dead and wounded to the Red Cross hospital. He was outnumbered, so he gave up the jeep and set off to make the trip back to Afshar on foot.

The attack hadn't let up. By the time he found the commander and explained that he'd failed again, it was hopeless. "Afshar is falling," the commander said, "it's too late." A sedan slipped by as they spoke, and Aziz heard the commander say, "That's Grandfather Mazari." The Hazara's highest commander, fleeing.

"You need to leave now," the commander said. "Don't stay."

"What about you?"

"My family's in there. I have to get them out, and then I'm leaving. You leave now."

Aziz didn't speak, just listened to the artillery shells landing, still growing louder. He couldn't tell which were new mortars and which were echoes, so the effect was one long, pulsing roar, the whole valley protesting. Then the fog in his mind thinned for a moment and he realized: it wasn't just the shells landing that was getting louder;

the crack of them being fired was getting louder too. That meant they were being fired from closer. The attackers were moving down off the ridgeline toward the village, a pincer operation coming in from three sides.

Aziz found Pike filming from the roof of the dormitories and told him it was time to get out. Together they ran down to the front gate of the Polytechnic. They had cover near the archway, but the moment they stepped beyond, they would be totally exposed for a hundred yards until they reached a cluster of small houses with alleyways running between.

Aziz looked at Pike. Behind them, fighters moved down the hills and filtered into homes. Aziz and Pike had already wasted critical minutes. They had to move before the soldiers reached them, but moving meant running the length of a soccer field with no cover, and artillery was coming from 180 degrees. One of the factions rolled two tanks into the traffic circle in front of the Polytechnic with barrels pointed away from Afshar to battle back the reinforcements that never came, but the effect was of weapons and fire going in every direction with no sense or order. Rounds snapped overhead, dusting the walls next to them; red tracers flashed above them, heated metal flying in every possible direction. There was no order in it, and Aziz felt fear giving way to a tremendous, hulking weariness.

"Are you ready?"

"I'm ready," Pike said. "Are *you* ready?"

And they ran. They ran off the asphalt because the side of the road felt less conspicuous, but bullets kept whizzing by, closer and closer as they moved toward the houses. The roadside led them through a garden, and before they got to the alleys for cover the dirt gave way to mud. Even the ground wasn't cooperating. Moving became an incredible effort. Aziz was close to giving up. He felt hollowed, all the power leaking out of him. His legs no longer listened to the rest of him; he was having a hard time locating the focus he needed to take back control. He had the feeling of being in a nightmare; his killer getting closer and closer, but when he willed his legs to move they didn't listen. Adrenaline was gone, used up, an engine red-lining for a hundred miles and now coasting to a stop. He was nearly paralyzed. With Pike alongside, he dragged himself to an alley and collapsed against a wall. He looked at Pike. They just stared at each other. Aziz tried to convey sympathy.

"Everything is—it's just zero."

When they could summon some strength, they crawled across the street to where a stream of villagers had begun filing out. It had taken too long for them to leave—for people living amidst civil war, sporadic shooting wasn't cause enough to abandon their houses. They seemed so foolish, but it took hours, as the attack intensified, for people to understand that this was not just fighting going on around them, but an attack intended *for* them. When Aziz and Pike caught up, a maniacal commander screamed, "Get back! Get back and fight! It's not lost yet! You have guns, go back and fight!"

A frantic girl came to Aziz, crying hysterically, she had been moving back and forth between a man and a woman. The man was on a crude kind of wheelbarrow, a flat plank, maybe a door, attached to two car tires and an axel. He had no legs. The woman was crumpled in a pile in the middle of the street. "Please help me" the girl said, "my mother is hit." Aziz was woozy, but he tried. Again he summoned what energy he had and reached around the girl's mother to lift her off the ground. He felt something wet and recoiled. He looked at his hands; they were covered in urine and blood. He steeled himself and tried again. He managed to get her a few meters over, at least so she wasn't in the middle of the street, in the tank's direct line of sight. Another fighter came down and saw Aziz with his gun, and began shouting. "Leave her, soldiers, go back! Go and fight! You're just using this girl as an excuse not to fight!"

"It's fallen," Aziz said, "Mazari is gone." He was too tired to argue, so he went quiet until the commander's fury carried him off to another deserter.

They found their way to a friend's house, then another, then another, finally a place to stay for the night, but Aziz couldn't sleep. He'd walked or run twenty kilometers, back and forth across the city, but he couldn't push from his mind the image of the family he'd seen on Silk Road, inching away from the massacre, a girl moving her father, then her mother, a little at a time. When he finally nodded off, he dreamt of a tank barrel coming toward him, but he couldn't move, he was cemented to the street as it got closer and closer, and as he wondered why it hadn't already fired, he jolted awake.

He got up and went to the window, which looked over the neighbors' rooftops toward the hills, and he could see Afshar. Still, even in the middle of the night, he could hear sporadic gunshots. Not machine-gun bursts, not artillery, just one or two shots at a time. There was a calmness to it. There was no resistance. He knew no one was left to protect the people. He knew the gunshots he heard were not from fighting, that they were instead executions. Every few minutes, he'd hear another. His imagination filled the space between them. All the things the attackers were free to do to the civilians now that he and the other fighters had fled, he imagined.

As Pike slept, Aziz stayed at the window for most of the night, affixed to it as if by a sense of duty to bear witness. For the rest of his life, this time of night would be when his mind ran fastest; the time of that sickening calm. When he couldn't see his people, but could hear them being eliminated. The time when his mind switched on and conjured in the dark, filling in the blanks.

In the morning, he decided he was going to the front. He was not a teacher anymore. He would shoot at the people who had attacked, hopefully he'd kill one, hopefully he'd kill more.

It would be a suicide mission, he was not deceiving himself about that. It was not a desire to die that had taken him over, just weariness. Dying was a kind of revenge for him. His people had failed him. No one in the Desert came to help. He went all the way out there twice, and they just left their brothers and sisters to crawl away from the massacre alone. They'd given up, so he was giving up on them. He went to Burnt Bridge where the Unity Party had an office and asked for permission to go the front.

No one bothered trying to talk him down. By now the fighting was condensed around a few square miles in the capital, so whether or not he had anyone's approval, he could walk right up to it if he chose. He was valuable, the kind of person you didn't want risking his life to shoot and be shot at, but he was still only twenty, thin but strong and vital, and the Party was in chaos, in no position to turn away fighters. Two friends came forward and said, "If he goes to fight, he will not go without us."

The fighting had stalled out near a big grain silo the Soviets had built during the communist era: a glen of houses that had once lodged the luckier civil servants surrounded it. Now they were abandoned. The Unity Party still held one side of the silo, but to the east and south were hills held by enemies. The fighting had reached its equilibrium there: artillery fire would come down from positions on the hills, and Hazara soldiers would shoot back up at them, but no one was making any progress. Aziz arrived where a group of Hazara fighters were lined up against a wall, waiting for instructions. He could hear bullets occasionally hitting walls nearby. He walked right past them into an abandoned house. People followed him in. He didn't feel brave. He didn't feel like a leader. He felt abandon.

They started clearing houses. Making sure one was empty, moving on to another. The first was a two-story house with a large empty room on the second floor. No sign of life: the furniture was all gone, the glass was shot out, dust rose and swirled through an uncovered window. Aziz was drawn to it, because looking out over the front line, up at the mountains, toward Afshar, was like looking at a monument. It already felt like a place where something determinative had happened a long time ago, its place in history solidified. It was a strange sensation to see a part of a city with so many homes and no life, and he stood there gazing out, transfixed, for a moment too long, still just staring when a burst of machine-gun fire hit the wall outside and sprinted toward the window. Aziz ducked too late and felt electricity in his abdomen.

He was on the ground, and his friend was saying, "Get up, Aziz, this isn't funny." But he felt something, pressure, radiating out from his chest, his stomach.

"No, I'm hit!" He ran his hand under his ammunition vest and moved it around and then he could feel it was wet, he pulled it out and held it out to his friend. The man's face changed.

"Teacher Aziz has been hit! Someone come get him," he yelled. "Someone come get him to the hospital!"

His shirt being unbuttoned. Ammo being stripped off him. His surroundings have changed. *Where am I?* It takes a moment to register that he's in the same house but a different floor. He's losing his understanding of time. There is motion all around him and then no one is there, he is alone, a boy is coming toward him. *How fat this boy is!* he thinks. Then he is on the boy's back, and they're out in the open with the wind whistling past his ears.

He can't feel pain anymore, just extreme fatigue; all this motion is draining him even more. *I need to stop moving.* He wants to lie down, to be still and just watch the sky for a moment. "Can you stop, please. I need to lie down," he asks the boy. When did he ask the boy this? Did he ask the boy or just imagine asking? The boy is not slowing down, houses bounce by. Aziz wraps his hands around the boy's neck, tries to summon strength from somewhere to strangle him, maybe then the boy will stop. Aziz can't remember how to send instructions to his fingers, and he passes out.

He is on the ground.

He is being carried again. The need to lie down is even stronger now, again hands around the boy's neck, groping for an Adam's apple, trying again to make him stop, but this time he doesn't. Did they stop once before? Now he can't remember. Buildings trotting by.

The hospital: a brief moment of heightened awareness. A female voice, English, an Outsider. He hears the word "scissors." He feels the individual fibers of his clothing pulling apart, air against skin.

Aziz is in the hospital for eighteen days. He misses one of the most important speeches of the civil war, when Grandfather Mazari confronts his people with shame rather than sympathy. It will be the first time anyone has ever seen Mazari cry. It will be the only reason anyone believes that Grandfather is capable of crying. The entire crowd will cry with him, his own shame contagious in that moment, a whole room of grown men wailing like children. Mazari will quote Imam Ali, the story of a Jew woman whose jewels were stripped from her by a thief, and Ali had said, "Shame on me that I couldn't protect this woman. Even for this to happen to a Jew, I am shamed."

Aziz misses all of this. The doctors tell him that the same person who brought him to the hospital stayed and gave his own blood to save Aziz. "You were five minutes from bleeding to death, and the bullet was a millimeter from your spinal cord. Who was the boy?"

Aziz doesn't know. They don't know either. They ask him to recount the story, what he remembers of it. "You were shot over by the silo?" From there to the Red Cross Hospital was more than a mile. "On a man's back?" They exchange glances. "Tell us again."

Later they say that the bullet went through his liver. Had he been standing straight up, it would have hit his spine. They say he was so close to dying that if not for the boy who carried him to the hospital, stayed to give blood, and then disappeared, he would have died. When he leaves the hospital, he is affirmed. He no longer doubts his people. That he doesn't know who the boy was means he can look at Hazaras and imagine his salvation anywhere among them.

Aziz never got over Afshar. It imprinted itself on him, changed pathways in his brain. Afshar was a culmination of sights and sounds and smells from a lifetime of violence and extremism stacked one on top of another. It wasn't just Afshar, but the things that came before: a flower-patterned sundress in the rubble, from a young girl he'd seen moments ago, alive and laughing, in the back of a lorry that had rounded a bend and been hit by a Russian bomber. The stories he heard of the infamous prison in East Kabul where wardens pushed counterrevolutionaries into ditches, covered them with dirt, and ran them over with steamrollers, back and forth, until the earth spat up blood like it was punched in the gut. The screams of a man Aziz had seen dying from wounds he'd given himself, while mourning the death of Imam Hussein—seven hundred years before.

Aziz was determined to never experience these things again, and he was determined to see that his people never did either. These things

he'd seen in Afghanistan, in Pakistan, on the paths he traveled between them: they were an atlas of suffering, with Afshar at its center.
He would lead his people from it. He would march them away from
Afshar. It's why when his friend suggested the school commemorate
those dead and wounded, Aziz reacted viscerally. "It will *not* be called
Afshar!" He nearly screamed it. It will not be backward looking, it will
be forward looking. Our minds are poisoned with corpses; remem-
bering them does not require effort of us. No matter where we look,
we will always see them in the fringes of our vision. It is time we try
to see other things. It's time we try to know other things.

4

_____

THE SCHOOL

Aziz proposed the name be a single word that carried many things: wisdom, enlightenment, knowledge, gnosis, spiritual awareness, understanding deriving from experience. *Marefat*. Three syllables that contained a menu of all the things a person could provide for herself, regardless of where she was or what had happened to her parents in the war.

Marefat grew. After the Outsiders came and cleared the land of the Taliban, and Marefat came home for the first time, it took on a pace of its own. From a few dozen kids, none beyond fourth grade, into a two-story center of enlightenment in the middle of the Desert.

Soon it was not just a school, it was a forward operating base from which Aziz nudged his community toward his own hopeful way of thinking. He met with the students' parents, who were often illiterate, so they would gain from their children's education and be brought into the community. The kids published bulletins with news from the school, put out a magazine with poetry and editorials, and Aziz helped them organize political demonstrations. When President Karzai first came to visit the Desert in 2004—a significant moment, this Pashtun leader coming to see a Hazara slum—it was Marefat that left the greatest impression. The students lined up on either side of the street, waving Afghan flags and photos of the president in perfect synchronization. When the country had its first elections since the fall of the Taliban, a Hazara challenged Karzai and the students organized on the new candidate's behalf, establishing the school not just as an educational and cultural force, but as a political one as well.

Despite his nickname, Aziz had no formal training as a teacher, so he was winging it. He built a curriculum based on his concept of humanism. He predicted resistance, so he hid it within a Trojan horse of religion, cherry-picking ideas from the holy book that best fed the mind-set he wanted for his students. "Look at the holy Quran," he said in class, "here, here, and here. It says 'A human being is the Caliph of God.' Here it says 'The human being is the Bearer of God's Soul,' and here it says the human being is 'Entitled to Dignity and Freedom of Choice.'"

His trick was using reverence for the holy book to teach irreverence in general. Irreverence was the end goal. With Afshar always on his mind, he wanted students who were incapable of participating in such a thing. If they believed that humans had value because they were humans, not because of money or religion or a family name, it would be harder for them to kill. They would be less easily swayed by the war cries of powerful men. The government schools were focused mostly on memorization; Aziz didn't care about that. He didn't want students who could recite passages of the Quran. He wanted students who, the next time a tribal leader or a cleric or a warlord said, "Fight," answered, "But why?"

The government had textbooks, and Marefat mostly ignored them. They were outdated and riddled with religion, and they missed the point. Aziz wanted his students to study subjects that made them think, not memorize. So he wrote his own. Marefat published textbooks on civic education, human rights, democracy, ethics, and philosophy. The school even made its own books for the basics; Aziz printed language and economics textbooks. It was his way of stacking the deck, giving a generation of Hazaras the ability to think for themselves, and then, critically, the confidence to go out and spread their own ideas. Marefat was a living contradiction: a strong community held together by the dedicated practice of individuality.

It was coeducational: on this Aziz was adamant. Boys and girls

in the "New Afghanistan," as he began to call this country the Outsiders were ushering in, should be comfortable with one another. Boys
at Marefat wouldn't view girls as strange things to fear or punish; girls
wouldn't think of boys as overseers. No one would kneel. Literally—
when parents pressured Aziz to build a prayer room, he held firm.
"This is a school," he said, "not a mosque." The students could pray
if they wanted, but not here. Here, God was in the individual; the
muscle that softened when you knelt before God was the one that
could make you stand up and challenge a cleric. Or even a teacher:
Aziz instituted a student parliament. Every month, students gathered
to appraise their teachers' performance in public meetings. No one
got to exert status, unchallenged, over anyone else.

Class discussions were like master's thesis study groups. The contrast
between what it looked like—barren concrete walls and floors—and
the energy in the classrooms was striking. They were the poorest students in Kabul, many of whom would never leave this part of this
city, and they spoke as if they'd traveled the world and knew all the
important books to have read.

I've seen them debate whether racism in Afghanistan is worse
than in countries they will never see but whose histories they understand. I heard a young girl in class say "Racism is worse here because
other countries made it worse," invoking the long history of foreign
powers picking favorites among the ethnic groups in Afghanistan.
Another girl disagreed: "Imagine Afghanistan was an island and no
one could reach it. You don't think there would still be racism? Of
course there would still be racism."

"It's natural for people," another said, "to want to be better than
other people."

These were girls once banned from school. Out in the city's
poorest slum, and in just a few years, they'd gone from illiteracy to
deploying Socratic thought experiments in the service of classroom
debates about the country's most taboo issues.

They criticized their country, for its segregated cities, for corruption, its weak democracy. They were so critical I worried they were
erasing their own cause for hope, so I argued with them too. "Your

country has come a long way in a short period of time," I said. "In America, we're only on our first black head of state, but Afghanistan is a new democracy and already has a minority vice president."

"But sir, we can't compare America's democracy at the beginning to Afghanistan's democracy at the beginning," a student said. "There are hundreds of other democracies now. Back when America started, it was the only one."

This is how students at Marefat would talk. Their opinions were unpredictable, which was perhaps the best testament to the fact that Aziz was succeeding in making them think independently. They engaged according to no prescribed system of thinking. Instead, like Aziz, they did so according to a constellation of ideas and arguments they picked up from a hundred different sources and synthesized on their own.

To see Aziz in class was to see someone genuinely curious about what these young minds might produce. He liked to see if they had ideas about how he should tackle problems he was facing. A water shortage in the Desert; the need for a new well the school couldn't afford. "How do you think we should pay for this? Should we let our neighbors use our well? What if it means there's not enough water for you?"

He brought these predicaments up and then, often with no agenda, pushed the students to give him ideas for how to resolve them. I watched school administrators grow frustrated because when Aziz taught, he quickly forgot the subject he was supposed to be teaching, lost any notion of a lesson plan, and instead simply asked children about things he was interested in. He probed, teased, took a student's argument and turned it back against itself to see if she could escape from the trap he'd set for her. When it came time for exams, after Aziz had spent a semester teaching nothing measurable, he simply asked questions he wanted to know the answer to, had them write what they thought, grading them according to whether he found their opinions interesting.

When he wasn't teaching his own civic education class, he stalked the halls, walking into classrooms in which a teacher was trying desperately to get through a curriculum on time. The teacher would slink off to the corner while Aziz took over, usually by starting an argument with the students. He'd pick a shy one and get her to disagree with him about a fact of science, the qualifications of a foreign head of state. He'd put her on the spot, and continue engaging with just her until class was over and the students stampeded through the halls, while the sidelined teacher tried to hide his panic over the lost day and the shy student realized she just successfully held off the most famous person she knew in front of the whole class.

Aziz was loyal to nothing. No idea, no schedule. Loyalty was not a value he put a lot of stock in: it was too close to reverence. For him, nothing was exempt from interrogation. A children's book might end one way, but when he read to students, or to his own children, he closed the book halfway in and told them they had to dream up the rest on their own. I saw him walk into a class of third-grade girls and tell them that he's *sure* one of them was going to become president. "You have twenty-nine years to be ready, because there is only one restriction keeping you from being president: you have to be at least forty years old. But I will be a campaign manager for you! And a speechwriter. So today, write in your diary," he said, "that you plan to be president. And write down a reminder to say a prayer for me, so that I'll be alive then." As a parting shot, before leaving the classroom, he said, "You know, you *have* to be president, because I can't. There is no law that says a woman can't be president. But there *is* a law that says someone like me, who is not educated past the fifth grade, can't be president. You're more qualified than I am. Get ready! you are going to be my boss."

As a child, Aziz, like the first generation of Talibs, had very little exposure to girls. Since being forced by war to leave school in fifth grade, he'd lived on the run, away from the women in his family. He was surrounded entirely by men. He lived and worked in Pakistan, surrounded by men. He fought surrounded by men. It was not preordained that Aziz would became so adamant about educating girls, rather than containing them, like so many others whose lives were so similar to his.

His attitude about women derives, like so much else, from the fact that he always had a fiercely independent mind. He was not loyal to any single ideology. To escape the grueling work he did as a child on the run, in sweatshops, for abusive bosses, he picked up books and devoured them. He tried on philosophies, strutted around in them, showed them off in conversations with elders, and put them down. He considered himself a Maoist, then by turns a devotee of Pakistani cinema, Russian literature, Iranian literature, Steinbeck, Hemingway, Victor Hugo. Each held for him an entire way of thinking, something close to religion. He became a recognized expert in the holy Quran. These were not casual assignations with philosophies; he dove into them, but if an idea did not hold up to questioning after a month, or a year, or a decade—it didn't matter how long—he went looking for another.

Each way of thinking deposited something on his psyche, small barnacles that built up over time, until in the end he had his own ideology. By the time he'd gone from his exile in Pakistan to fighting at the front in Afghanistan, and back to exile in Pakistan, he believed principally in one thing: himself. His own ability to interpret the world, without anyone else's manual. He had suffered abuse from and seen destruction by people who claimed authority over those who never questioned it. He'd come to identify with the poor and abused, not just because abuse was written across the history of the Hazaras, but because he had experienced such a prodigious amount of it in his own life. When he began building Marefat in the refugee camps of Pakistan he saw two trends that he believed were related: his own country was devouring itself in violence that expanded at an ever-growing rate, and his country was becoming every day more male-dominated.

He figured this couldn't be a coincidence. So the solution to the problem couldn't be teaching boys. Boys would always carry in their hearts the lessons from their fathers' lives; they would always be at risk of following in their fathers' footsteps. It had to come from girls.

So Aziz, whose childhood was rearranged by war in the same way as the Talibs who were most brutal to women, came to consider women his country's last best hope.

That boys and girls can sometimes still be found in the same room at Marefat is due to no small amount of courage, and perhaps some foolishness. Aziz is taking a big risk. For its first four years in Afghanistan the school was entirely coeducational, and Aziz believed this to be the most impactful thing he did. Boys and girls became comfortable around one another. Boys didn't fear girls, and did not find it shameful to be corrected by a girl in the classroom. Visitors to the school were stunned whenever they saw it happen. It was so impossibly soon after Taliban rule, a period during which women couldn't study at all, and here was a place where girls debated with boys so naturally it was as if it had always been that way.

Then Marefat became a victim of its own success. As the school continued to grow and students went barreling through Aziz's makeshift curriculum, two or three "grades" per year, he ran into a problem. In 2002, when the school first moved to Afghanistan, the most advanced students had been in fourth grade. By 2006 Marefat had its first graduating class.

In order to get into university, the students would have to take the national entrance exams. In order to take the national entrance exams, Marefat needed to register with the Ministry of Education. This presented the problem.

The Ministry of Education regarded coeducation as illegal and would not recognize the school unless it was segregated. Aziz had to decide: give his students the chance to go to college or keep boys and girls together. He felt he didn't have a choice.

It was the first major blow; others would follow. On the day he told the school that coeducation was over, many of the girls he talked to were humiliated. *Why is someone else coming to tell me "I have to protect you from the eyes of nasty boys?"*

After that, Aziz looked for little ways to get boys and girls together. When they were young enough no one would care, so he put first, second, and third graders back. For older kids he started extracurricular activities, reading groups, art classes, anything boys and girls could do outside of their standard classes. If someone stopped by to check, they would all be in trouble, but it was a risk Aziz believed he had to take.

There were other changes, too, that the ministry demanded. A major shift in the curriculum began, and government textbooks re-

placed the ones Aziz and his friends had written, which were rele-
gated mostly to the afterschool reading groups. Marefat's revolutionary
curriculum took a blow.

As devastating as it was to separate boys and girls, there's reason to
believe it was the right choice. Marefat's very first graduating class
passed the college entrance exams with flying colors. Not a single student failed. So began a winning streak, during which Marefat out-
performed every other school in the country, posting a near-perfect
passing rate every single year. The country's universities were about
to see an invasion of Hazara students. And Marefat students started
winning scholarships to colleges in countries all over the world. Girls
from illiterate families in this slum of west Kabul won full scholarships to universities in the United States, Europe, Australia, India,
Bangladesh.

    Often these scholarships required immense work on Aziz's part.
Girls would come in to his office devastated because their fathers
refused to let them travel on their own. Aziz took on the roll of me-
diator, going into homes, spending hours talking to fathers, whittling
away the risks and concerns of apostasy, until families, given Aziz's
personal assurance, relented. Then he would stay in close touch with
the girls when they left, calling and emailing, so they never felt alone
in their strange new surroundings. But the real reason he kept tabs
on the girls after they left Marefat was because if a single girl slipped
up—if she was photographed without a headscarf, or with alcohol in
the frame, or being too cozy with boys—it would be a setback for
every future Marefat student hoping to study abroad. It felt to the
girls like support, but it was as much about policing from afar.

Despite the end of coeducation, and the slowly growing scrutiny, Aziz
continued to build new programs. The school launched a radio station, broadcasting civic education programming around the Desert.
It held art shows around the city and sent musicians out to perform.
And Aziz continued to write provocative opinion columns and go
on TV to argue with politicians.

    He decided that even though the new building would house the library, most of the offices, more classrooms, the science labs, and one day maybe even computers—things even students would want to use and all were paying tuition for—it would be the girl's building. Boys would be able to use the facilities in the new building, but they would do so as guests of the girls. It was imperative that the girls feel comfortable and in charge, because it was the girls he was readying to go out and change the country.

5

THE STUDENT

Najiba arrives fully thirty minutes before any other students.

She thinks about sitting in the first row.

The first is too close to the board, she decides. Looking up might hurt her neck, so she chooses the second. Close, but not too close. She settles herself down in a chair by the window, adjusts her head scarf, pulls it back from her forehead so that she feels air against the dome of her hair, then pushes it forward again. Then she takes it off and rewraps it. She puts her purse on the floor, nudges it under the chair with a heel. And she begins to weep.

There are kids at home. She had her first at sixteen, then she had another, then one more, then twins. She was embarrassed the first time she was pregnant; she would hide behind the walls in her village when she went out so that people wouldn't see her changing body. She wore the loosest garments she could for cover. "This is natural," her husband told her. "There's no need for shame." But he was ten years older than her, maybe more. His words were kind but unhelpful.

That first baby was born in winter, a girl. The men took the child into a separate room, where they read verses from the holy book and named her daughter Benazir, like the president of the country next door.

Najiba was just a girl herself then. She wasn't a mother, not really. This thing had arrived to torment her, first to shame her while it was inside, then to come out and remind her about the ugly parts of her. She had no idea what to do with a baby. It would cry and remind her of her own pain, so to quiet the girl she put blankets over its mouth and then went wandering in the fields where she couldn't hear it. Her husband scolded her: "You will hurt the child! Take her in your arms," he said. "You should hug her more." He didn't understand that she wasn't at all prepared for any of this.

Still, her marriage had been liberation. She was fifteen when an aunt told her that the youngest son from a good family across the river had come to ask for her. She wasn't afraid. She heard the man was kind, and her childhood had been a hell. Her father was a tyrant: he beat her, he beat her mother, and her happiest moments were when he went away to settle land disputes. He beat her with whatever was nearby; his fists, sometimes a lamp with a weighted base, and no one protected her. Not even her mother, who once tried and was so ferociously beaten herself she never intervened again, just knelt in a corner and cried quietly when Najiba was punished.

But she was a village girl, stout and strong. Abuse was part of discipline, something she learned to handle. The draft animals were hit, too, and they were watered and sheltered. It was part of the deal.

Her father filled his house with books and knowledge and kept it all away from her. For her brothers, he had brought in private tutors because the schools weren't good. He brought them special books. But when she asked her brothers to tell her what they were learning, they rolled their eyes. "Leave us alone, you're not supposed to be here." They yelled at her when she tried to sneak in to their tutoring sessions. But they always left their studies early and ran out beyond the walls to play.

The boys weren't serious about their studies, so she would flip through their books, looking at the pictures. Her father brought new books from faraway places, from the capital, from a holy country next door. When he left to visit friends in the village or walk the farm with his workers, she told her mother she would clean his room and then she would move as quickly through the tasks as she could, neatening and restacking his papers, squatting down to sweep the carpet, washing and folding his clothes, and after everything was done and she was out of breath, her reward: she took the books down, opened them up, and began her studies.

She knew three letters. Her mother taught them to her from the holy book, so mostly she scanned the pages for the designs she recognized, looking for familiar faces on a crowded street. The letters were little doses of fulfillment for her, *her* three letters, just enough reward, when she saw them, to pull her along. And when she was sure she'd found where all of those letters were hiding, she studied the pictures to see if she could divine some sort of meaning, as if by trying hard enough she might force the book to relent and give up its meaning.

She didn't get much, but she learned to partition her mind. She imagined splitting it in two, one half assigned to the task of interrogating the book before her, the other half on alert for someone coming, a vibration on the floor, the sound of footsteps, anything that might tip her off that someone was climbing the stairs.

Still, those stolen moments with half her mind looking for three letters were formative. They solidified something in her, locked in her a desire to decode. And eventually a frustration began to bloom, a kind of poison really, because she knew it was a desire that would never be satisfied. In those moments, she swore that she would be happy if just one sentence let her in and revealed its meaning. If just one idea would open up to her, she'd use it as a key to open the next sentence and the next; the book's defenses would collapse before her and she would step into its world.

She learned to recognize her name and her brothers' names. She discovered her father's copy of the holy book, with names inscribed in the back, and next to the names, other markings, which she later learned were their birthdays—by writing a child's name and birth date in the holy book, you ask God's words to protect the child whose name is written.

She felt a thrill finding the book and understanding this code. So she looked for the arrangement of scribbles she knew to be her own name. But when she flipped the pages back and forth, when she checked, double-checked, and triple-checked, it wasn't there. Her father had chosen to spare her the blessing.

"Oh girl, where *are* you!" Her mother's call, her oldest daughter gone too long and the house too big to clean alone. "You're wasting your time, keeping yourself busy with something that's no use for you," her mother would say—the words of a woman who means to protect her child but can't, and so instead tries to keep the child from bringing harm on herself.

It was on a night when Najiba's father threw a big party and she was in the kitchen serving the guests, that her journey began. It had been an exhausting event, vats of rice and whole lambs to stew; her father's parties kept her in the kitchen for hours. As the evening wound down and she was heating water to serve the guests their tea, and washing the last of dishes, her aunt came in. "Najiba, dear, do you know what this party was for tonight?" She didn't.

"Oh, my dear. It was your engagement."

"This? Tonight was my engagement?" Najiba thought it was a joke. But her aunt insisted, and her mother came in and confirmed it.

And so it was. Everything happened quickly after that. Arrangements were made, and it felt like only days later the village gathered for her wedding and she saw her husband for the first time. Although on that night, just his legs: she spent the whole wedding celebration behind a veil, and all she could see all night were people's shoes. Her husband's pants were made of light-colored cloth, and that's what she had to judge him by.

She was happy for the marriage; it meant leaving her father's house and moving in with her husband's family, a large brood of eight brothers, their mother, and all their wives and children. There was joy in being free from her father's reach, and in being an adult.

But it was short-lived. Her in-laws proved to be as hard as her own father; her husband's oldest brother, Ahmad, lorded over the brood like a tyrant, and when she sought to commiserate with the other wives, she found the women divided by their own petty jealousies. When she became pregnant, she was given no advice, though there were eight other mothers in the household. The honeymoon, such as it was, didn't last.

★ ★ ★

Then there was a bigger change.

Her village, Waras, was along a main route, so as the Knowledge Seekers pushed farther and farther north, a procession of people fleeing them passed through. Some stopped and sought shelter. First it was three trucks from Yakawlang, a Hazara village like her own, with old men, women, young children. They all piled into the mosque, and then, mostly, they cried. She cooked for them because it was the Muslim thing to do, and she heard their stories, of houses burnt to the ground, people slaughtered, summary executions for transgressions people had committed without ever knowing it. The people from Yakawlang spoke of a whole new system of rules, the punishment for breaking them severe, even if you could never possibly know what all of them were. She knew that she'd eventually see for herself. The Knowledge Seekers would keep coming—she could tell from the stories that they had a momentum, an appetite. More people arrived with stories. The district governor finally admitted what he knew, that the Knowledge Seekers were coming closer, that they were making their way to Waras and that it would happen soon.

Najiba paid attention to the men listening on the radio for the Knowledge Seekers' progress, she watched them shaking their heads, and she knew the moment was close. She talked to women coming from the village center, asked them for the latest news of how far the Knowledge Seekers had gone today, what they'd done.

And then one day, they showed up.

There wasn't much warning. They arrived in the district center first, and as the district center was half an hour from Waras, she knew the Knowledge Seekers were coming only a half hour before they arrived.

The governor sent out a message: put up a white flag like the Knowledge Seekers have, so they know you support them. The men were running around getting their weapons together and burying them in a straw-covered pit they'd dug in the barn. No one knew what might set a Knowledge Seeker off, but if they went searching door to door and found guns and bullets, maybe they'd think the people meant to resist, and raze the whole village to make an example.

The men worried that hiding the guns wasn't enough, that maybe even showing themselves might seem like a confrontation to the Knowledge Seekers: how could you know? They'd heard what happened in Yakawlang, how they took all the young men out of their houses, and then they tied their hands behind their backs, and then shot each one of them, careful to use just one bullet in the forehead. They say Grandfather Mazari's troops were mostly from there, so maybe that was why the Knowledge Seekers had been so cruel. But maybe that's what they did to all men. No one knew.

So the first impact of the Knowledge Seekers' arrival was not women hiding themselves, but men. They all scurried into holes like spooked squirrels, and for a moment, it was completely quiet. Peaceful even. The women left their chores, dried their hands on rags, and went to the little porthole windows on the second floor to watch what happened next.

Najiba had the best view in the village. The house was up on a hill, so she saw them before anyone else. First, she saw the dust rising like a little storm gathering in the distance, then she could make out a Toyota, a Datsun pickup truck, then more trucks, a fifth, a sixth, up over the rise. Then she could make out the white flags on the trucks, and then there were ten trucks, all bouncing toward them, and then the whole convoy *turned toward her house*, heading for an open field just two hundred meters in front.

The trucks stopped. She saw the men get out, and even from a distance she was struck by the sight of them, so tall and thin and severe-looking.

They began calling, yelling toward her house, and then she saw one of the family's workers standing there, a kind old man, totally exposed. He'd gone out for his morning chores like any other day, he was hard of hearing—*Had he not heard they were coming? Oh God, did we forget to tell him?* Inside, the women looked at each other in horror, then back out as the Knowledge Seekers cupped their hands and yelled, and she could hear their voices calling toward the old worker, demanding that he come present himself to them.

She watched the old man move slowly toward them, head down, his body hunched. He was already a small man, but it looked to her as if he'd shrunk, compressed by his fear. He moved cautiously, and out in the field the men put their hands to their mouths again and called for him to hurry.

By now the sun was up and it was full light; she could see clearly from the second floor as he moved toward them. It felt like such an impossibly long time, a long drawn-out silence before the inevitable. She wished for him to turn and run, to run away from them, or even to run toward them so that at least the moment could be over. She wished for it to be quick—she couldn't bear the idea of hearing the old man screaming. But he just kept moving slowly, and then she saw he wasn't going straight toward them, he was taking so long because he was working his way carefully around the maze of wheat. In his final moment, he was making sure not to damage his master's crop. She could see that the men were getting impatient. It was a full fifteen minutes later that he reached them, his head barely up to their chests.

One of the Knowledge Seekers leaned close to him, and she watched from her window as he lifted the old man right up off the ground and swung him around like a father who's just come home to his favorite son.

This was how the Taliban began their occupation of her village.

They went on in the same strange fashion. The Knowledge Seekers moved through the village, finding farmers and commoners who hadn't hid, hugging them, saying kind things, and offering each the same message: "Don't worry, we have no problems with you. We're not going to hurt anyone here." And so life under the Taliban began. They were long, monotonous years. She was frightened all the time, but it was a remote fear, one she didn't believe she would ever have to face. What she had to face was closer: her husband's oldest brother, who ruled over the house with as much violence as her father had. His eruptions became even more violent, and her husband was powerless to stop them; soon he didn't even try. The pressure they were under from the Knowledge Seekers occupying their province all seemed to be channeled onto the women in the house, and life was such an ongoing sadness that when complications arose in her third pregnancy, and she was sent away to the capital to see it through, it felt like a relief.

Kabul didn't feel at all like her country. It felt like something huge and from the future. There were so many vehicles, and the vehicles were so *small*, for just a few people, almost like everyone had their own. Until the pickups and SUVS driven by the Taliban, she'd only ever seen trucks and busses, but now there were even smaller automobiles wherever she looked, hundreds of them flying around the streets. When she rode in them they turned her stomach and her head would hurt, but it was exciting, having a machine to move only you.

There were huge buildings wherever she looked, and even though they bore the signs of war, and many were destroyed, they were big and tall and *everywhere*. So much had been built here. And there was so much writing everywhere. Written signs on every building. Back home, everyone knew where everything was; people didn't need signs. Here in the capital, people must go to new places every day. A whole big place full of things announcing to her what they were, and still she could not follow. It was a world trying to explain itself to her, but which she could not understand. When she went to the doctor, she was humiliated; first to not be able to read the signs in the halls, and then because in order to ask strangers for help, she had to tell them what kind of doctor she needed.

There was a massive trove of information at her fingertips, but in a different language. It was inspiring, exciting, overwhelming.

The Knowledge Seekers were different here, too. There were many more of them; they had infiltrated every aspect of life, even the homes.

She found them to be impressive-looking, colorfully dressed and proud, fancy exotic birds. They were crueler here than in her village, but the women in the capital seemed fearless. Hidden under burkas, they were constantly reminded that they were living under occupation; she never saw a woman's face outside. But they spoke so boldly—they were clear, they expressed themselves so intelligently. She watched women berate the Knowledge Seekers as if they were scolding their own children.

Once, when she was riding a bus across the city, the bus stopped suddenly, the curtain separating the women's section slid opened, and there appeared a tall handsome man in a big black turban and a bright purple shawl. He carried a whip, just like one that her father used to use on her, and began to yell at the bus driver because the curtains covering the windows in the women's section weren't completely closed. He yelled and clenched his jaw, insulting each of the women, and then, from behind her, Najiba heard a woman get up and interrupt him.

"Take out your dirty face from us! Don't look at us, *you* are looking at us, and asking us not to be seen by the others!" Najiba was stunned. "You son of a dog! This is not your business, why do you care that we would be seen by the others, take care of your own business and get the hell out of here!"

And he did. He left, went back to the front of the bus, gave a feeble warning to the driver, and then he was gone. Najiba was thrilled.

Then there was the time she and some other Hazaras were washing clothes in the water by a mosque, when she noticed that a Knowledge Seeker was staring at them. She didn't have her head covered—none of them did—because she was washing. But she felt at fault anyway because she relished any chance to get rid of the burka. She found it to be a strange and constricting thing. It was hard to breathe in it, and she had a hard time seeing out of the tiny holes. Especially to the sides. When she crossed the street, cars were effectively invisible to her until they were right on top of her, so walking in the city was terrifying. She'd been dropped into a world with tiny vehicles flying around in every direction, and then made to walk around in it nearly blind. So she liked having the burka off, and she knew that at that moment, as she washed her clothes, she was in defiance of the law. She was guilty.

But the man seemed to be enjoying watching them. Then he approached, and he stood in front of one of the girls, the tallest and most beautiful of them all. He unwrapped his turban and put it in her hands. "Wash this for me," he said. She looked him right in the eye and held his stare, and then she bunched his turban up into a ball and threw it in the dirt. "No way I'm going to wash that for you." He came back with candies, handed them out to all the women, and then asked her again. The girl threw the turban down again. "I'm not going to wash that filthy thing you have on your filthy head!" In the light of day they were buffoons, afraid of a woman who raised her voice.

At the house she stayed in, she heard all sorts of things. She heard that women were spying for the Taliban. She heard that the Knowledge Seekers hated people who had money, that they hated people who had links to other factions of holy warriors. And every night, around the time she was settling down for bed, she heard *them*. She never saw them at night, she just heard the sounds. Gunshots, just one or two at a time. The images that came to mind were not of fighting, but of punishment.

And screams, every night. From far away, from just next door, a kind of call and response all around her. Every night, she went to bed with her mind racing through the things she'd done that might have been against the rules, and that might get her killed or tortured.

And then in the morning, the women sat together washing rice and accused each other of spying. Under the Taliban Najiba found that women had free time. It was a gift at first, but she soon found herself sitting in circles of women who spent most of it gossiping in ugly ways, accusing friends and neighbors of spying for the Taliban.

She was eager to leave the capital and return to the village. But when she did, after the birth of her child, she felt a tie severed. In the capital her life had changed, it had become wider—this was the only way she could understand it—and the village squeezed her back up. She'd lived seven months surrounded by cars, people, words, and ideas, in a place that mattered in the world, and now it was gone; a beam of light that had lit up a part of her mind was now switched off. She had to keep that part of herself alive: she felt it as an animal need. And there was another thing too. What happened during the night in the capital—the screams of unseen people suffering—these things still haunted her. It was a great, ongoing tragedy she didn't understand, and she needed to know what was going on, how it all ended. It was like witnessing a disaster, a car crash receding in your rearview mirror—and not knowing if in the end, everyone ended up okay.

Again she looked toward books, but they still kept their own communion, not letting her in. She found an old transistor radio her husband kept in a closet, took it out, dusted it off, and used it to tether herself to the people outside. She'd been for a moment in a place where important things happened, where women were tall and loud and a million tiny vehicles zoomed around all over the place like ideas. There was suffering there, she knew it, she'd seen it and felt it, but it was important suffering. For-a-purpose suffering, suffering *about* something. Suffering that was an escape from her own.

She did it in secret. It was embarrassing; like a base desire she should be able to resist but couldn't. "Who are you," the other women said when they found her with her radio, "the wife of someone important?" So she waited until the men had gone to work the fields and the women were occupied with other chores, then she switched it on and caught the news before frivolous things came on for the rest of the day. She learned that in other places, men and women didn't live the same way they lived here. The tone and timbre of their voices, when they spoke together wherever they were speaking, let her know this. When the women spoke, the men were quiet.

Her husband tried to tolerate her habit; most of the time he was patient with her. One day he came in frustrated about something else and saw her with the radio. He grabbed it and yelled at her, "Don't you do anything else? Don't you have any other work besides listening to that radio all the time? Always occupied with that radio?" Other times, when she made a mistake baking the bread, he would blame her new habit. He also took in the violence around him, and sometimes he beat her as well.

So she hid it from him too. The news was just an hour, and if the men were moving slowly in the morning it would be over before she got to it, replaced for the whole day by music and talk shows about trivial things she didn't care about.

When her husband went to take a UNICEF training course in giving vaccines near the province's central town, she listened more. When he'd been gone for a month she began to hear about something she couldn't believe.

The world was mourning something that was happening very close to her. People in England and the United States were talking about a place nearby, the giant statues that looked like her people in the cliffs. The Knowledge Seekers were talking about destroying them, and she didn't understand why or how it mattered, but she could tell from the voices on the radio that the world was sad about it, so she started to be sad about it too. She felt something else along with it, a swell of excitement. She was being seen. She had wanted to connect to the world, and now it was reaching back to her. It was thrilling, really, when the people on the radio so many miles away knew about her little province.

She sat and listened every day for a month and learned that the Knowledge Seekers were attacking the Buddhas, shooting at them, using grenades, unable to destroy them until they scrambled up the statues and put dynamite in the fissures. And then the Buddhas, after their month of peaceful resistance, finally succumbed: an electric flash rippling through them, the staccato cracks of timed explosives sounding around the valley. The mighty Buddhas roared, coughed up a storm of dust and sandstone, and then laid themselves down.

It was from the little transistor radio that she learned of other new rumblings in the world. The Knowledge Seekers, the tall handsome men in Toyotas and Datsuns, had somehow made it to America and attacked there; an extraordinary thing, her little village in the middle of nowhere, more than a day's drive in the nimblest car from a real city, had, in the space of a year, *twice* shared with the world a common tormentor. It was like growing up in a slum and learning the same man who stole your chickens also stole the king's. It was the strangest thing: when she—in a tiny place, living a life she now understood to be small—looked out of the window even from the high floors of her home, all she could see was wheat. But now she felt the king saw her.

She took extra long now when bringing the men their tea and bread, checking what the radio told her with what she overheard them say, running little cross-references in her head until they shooed her away. "This is about the Knowledge Seekers," her oldest brother-in-law said. "It doesn't concern women."

But even *he* was excited—she could see that they all were. She knew, she could tell, there were big changes coming. America was *here,* they were more powerful even than she imagined. She heard of exciting, mythical things: the Knowledge Seekers on the first floor of a tall building when a U.S. helicopter came and killed every single one of the Knowledge Seekers there, the men said, and hadn't broken even a window on any other floor. She felt a breathlessness, as if all this time she had been submerged beneath a big heavy ocean but now it had moved around and let her up, and a great big swell was carrying her along. Americans were here to turn her country into one that looked like theirs.

With the spirit of freedom all around, Najiba's husband had an idea: why not plan their own liberation?

It would have to be a big one. They wouldn't be able to just get their own house in the village. His oldest brother, responsible for all eight sons from his father's two wives—and responsible for the families each of those sons produced— would never allow this kind of secession. It would be a slap across his face. Not just a sign of ingratitude but a threat to the authority he needed to keep the whole enterprise functioning. Najiba had lived in those little fiefdoms long enough to understand that a man can't keep a peaceful kingdom if his subjects all think independence is an option.

If Najiba and her husband were going to break away from his parade of older brothers, and from his mother, the arbiter of family honor, they would have to go far enough away that no one would see their treason. They would have to disappear. And nature conspired to give them the cover: the village was in the throes of a drought that year, the water through the irrigation channels reduced to a trickle, and soon the family's mills stopped turning. Without water, they couldn't turn wheat into flour. When the idea of getting electrical mills came up, Najiba's husband volunteered to travel down to the capital to get one. While there, he told her, he would lay the groundwork for their escape.

It took months, and by the time word came back, summer had turned to fall, fall to winter, and the weather threatened the kind of oppressive winter the highlands put down on its people as if to remind them that they were just victims of nature.

Her husband sent a letter with a man who made the drive back and forth between the city and Panjaow, he gave it to someone who made the drive between Panjaow and her village; he in turn gave it to a cousin of her brother, who gave it to a brother of her husband, who, finally, gave it to Ahmad.

Ahmad knew exactly what had happened. He reacted exactly the way she thought he would. "This little boy! Now he thinks he is a man and he can just disobey my rules! Trying to separate from me." He threw the letter to the ground and turned to face her. "You!" he yelled, "I know it's you, you tempted him, didn't you! You *made* him do this! This woman finally finished her plot, to take my brother from the family. And I tell you you're mistaken if you think I'm going to give you money to go to him in the city. Don't you dare ask me for any help. I won't give you *anything*. I hope you die on the way! I hope you crash! And if you do, I won't even pay for your corpses to come back and be buried! I will teach you a lesson about trying to divide this family. You will pay the price!"

She was terrified, but she knew they'd won. Because with her husband already gone, Ahmad would be compelled by custom to provide for her and the kids. If he forced her to stay, he'd have to bear the burden himself, to clothe and feed them, with no support coming from her own husband. With the mills stalled and the farm not producing, that would be worse than just letting her take the kids and go. They had used tradition as a weapon against him and he knew it.

Najiba was in the capital for the second time in her life. This time to stay.

Now it was a city just liberated from the Taliban, a place full of Outsiders—Americans, French, Germans, Italians, British, Australians—all of them there to make her country a place like theirs. She could hardly believe it was the same place she'd been to three years before. She'd remembered the cars, but still, now there seemed to be motion *everywhere*. It took her a day before she understood why that was: there were no longer so many rules to follow. She saw women outside, out on the street, without their faces covered. Children played on the street, people were arguing over prices at market stalls. Everywhere, everyone was *excited*. There was no fear. And at night, there were no screams. No one spoke of spying or being spied on, no one suspected anyone else. On her first trip to the market, she found a crowd of people standing and watching while one of the Outsider's army trucks drove into a dead end. She watched a door open and a woman step out, a soldier, with a long braid of sun-colored hair swinging down from beneath her cap. Najiba watched the soldier move with such confidence, found her beautiful, a woman in an army uniform with a handgun at her waist. She was so thin, she looked so *smart*. The people around Najiba were making fun of the woman, "Look at this lady! No scarf on! A woman working in a truck!" But Najiba just felt a sudden sadness overtake her. It was a tragedy that this woman was right here, and there were so many things to tell her and to ask of her, but there was no way. Again she felt so close to something she wanted intensely, but it was just beyond her reach. In that moment, she wished as hard as she could that she could somehow speak the soldier's language or that the soldier could speak hers.

The woman soldier didn't notice her and seemed to be hurrying on to get clear of the crowd. She climbed back up into the truck, and drove away.

The population had swollen in the capital. The Taliban were gone, the Outsiders were here, and people from this country who had left were coming home. There'd been so many empty houses when she'd been here before; now they were all occupied. And people were building even more. Even out in the Desert, with all the returning Hazaras, and where her husband found a cheap place to rent, there was a new energy.

She felt as though she had been an object moored to the earth as things happened around her, and now she was free to drift, detached from her husband's family, her country liberated from its own patriarch. She was feeling something she'd never felt before. It was a kind of excitement, pressure, too—something she couldn't define, but it was thrilling. Later she understood it as agency. She had never before had any control over what was happening around her or *to* her. She had never thought more than a day into the future. There was nothing she'd have been able to do about it anyway. The chores had always needed to be done tomorrow, and tomorrow she still wouldn't be able to read. There'd never been a way to make tomorrow any different, so she'd never tried.

Now she felt she could. Now she *should*. Now she looked at her daughter and had another new feeling. She felt free, she felt her children were free, and suddenly there were choices you had to make for them. There was the sense of building something. When the Outsiders had come and lifted a big weight right off the country, it was as if they said directly to her, "It's yours now. You have your country back, now do something with it."

She went out to find a literacy class for herself. She went downtown to the city department of education and asked if they had any programs for adult women, but they paid no attention to her. She heard about a course near her neighborhood, but when she went it was full of kids, and they all teased her. *Oh, look, Aunty came to read and study!* She spent two weeks there. The teacher would write on the blackboard, Najiba wouldn't understand, and when she asked, the students all clapped and shouted. "Again she doesn't know! She doesn't understand *anything*!" They had fresher minds, she decided. They didn't have life to distract them like she did. They were cruel, and it was embarrassing to try to keep up with kids. She couldn't learn like this, so she quit. She waited; she thought maybe the kids would get older, or the school might start to enact some kind of discipline, but she came back once more, and it was the same. She gave up.

Two houses down there lived a mason who did some work at a private school and sent his daughter there. Najiba began to notice that this young girl had a confidence about her that her own daughter didn't. Najiba watched the girl write, listened to her speak, and was impressed. The adults asked the girl questions to show her off, and she'd answer with such force that Najiba decided she ought to do something about her own daughter. She asked her neighbor where his daughter was getting her education. He was very happy with the school, especially with how strict it was, and with the education for girls. Not all of the men were happy to have their daughters going to school, but the headmaster had a way of convincing them that it would be good for the family. They could be married better, he said, if they had an education.

Najiba decided she wanted her own kids to be part of it. Her husband had found work in a clinic, so Najiba went herself to ask the mason where this school was and then set off to find it. It was early spring and the roads had all turned to mud. She went the wrong way first, so when she finally arrived at Marefat she was exhausted, freezing, and filthy.

She was given a pitying look when she asked about enrollment and brought to an office to wait with teachers and students; it seemed less a man's place of work than a waiting room—everyone had a question for this person. When he arrived—a short man walking quickly with a stack of papers tucked beneath his arm—everyone began calling for him "Mr. Aziz! Teacher Aziz!" She walked right past them and asked that man to enroll her daughter.

"There is no room," he said. "We cannot enroll anyone else now." Hazaras were pouring into the city. Thousands upon thousands of returning refugees, so many of them going to Kabul, all of them looking to take from the surplus of hopefulness for their own families. Word of Marefat moved through the Desert and out through west Kabul, and the school couldn't keep up with demand. There weren't enough teachers, there wasn't enough room, they were short on books, there wasn't space or material for even a single extra student, Aziz said. The enrollment period had been three months ago anyway, and, he said, the school year was now in full swing. Then he left the office.

She stood for a moment, stunned. So, she would need to be persistent. She could do that.

"Take my daughter! Just one girl!"

"No, we don't have any room, Auntie. Don't waste my time. Please go and stop bothering me."

He went into a meeting, and she stood and waited outside the door until it was over. "My daughter is only one person and it won't create any problem and you can fit her in one of the classes. I know there's room here!"

"I said go and don't waste my time! This is not the time to enroll your daughter, we *don't* have the room, we're already full. Come back next year during the enrollment time."

"There might be some girls who might not come to school on some days. Or who drop out, so you can give one of those spaces to my daughter when they don't show up."

"No!"

She'd marched all through the Desert, dirtied her nicest clothes, she was wet and freezing, and this man she'd pictured as some kind of savior wouldn't even look at her.

So she waited for nine more months, and returned. And this time, Benazir became a student at Marefat.

She had to take an entrance exam first, and though she was old enough for seventh grade her scores placed her in second. But neither she nor her mother was upset. Benazir quickly found second grade to be more challenging than any of her studies before. It took half a year for her to feel comfortable with the work, and then only barely. But her complaints pleased Najiba; it made her happy to see her daughter's mind challenged.

Najiba's other children followed Benazir to Marefat. Soon Najiba's brothers came to the city because they wanted to study more, too, and they brought their own kids, who also went to school. Everyone was studying but her. She sat with her brothers and their children, talking about the things they were learning in their various classes, and she'd try and talk too. "Najiba, you should be quiet. You're embarrassing yourself, you don't know anything about these issues, stop talking about things you don't know about. These issues are much higher than you have the talent to understand." So when Benazir came home from Marefat one day and said that some students were planning a protest because the Ayatollah had proposed a law that was going to make it legal for men to rape their wives, Najiba decided she had a chance to show she wouldn't shut up. She snuck out early the morning of the protest. She was the first one there. And she was the oldest.

6

FOUR YEARS LEFT

There is a bad man across the city, a man with dark features and a bright white beard who calls himself an Ayatollah, but who, for the school, is a villainous figure, beady-eyed and austere. A man who, it seems possible, has never once smiled in his entire life but emerged from the womb with a scowl. To Aziz, he will always be a rival. Even before the Afshar massacre, when the Ayatollah sold out and let attackers through, Aziz didn't trust this man. To Marefat students, he is an institution, it's as if he's been issuing proclamations from his madrassa forever. He is a Shia, like Aziz, like all the Marefat students. For years, Aziz and the Ayatollah have been fighting with one another over who represents this minority, the Hazaras. They sometimes settle into a kind of détente, tensions cool, and Aziz resolves to allow the Ayatollah his following among older Shias, while Aziz takes the younger generation. But it is an unfair fight: this Ayatollah has a wealthy benefactor. While Marefat struggles to make payroll in the slums, the Ayatollah has millions and millions of dollars from Iran to spend on construction in a nice part of the city, on a television station, on patronage. He's made it his mission to torment Marefat, especially Aziz, and has used the apostasy out in the Desert as a rallying cry to his own righteous flock. He preaches often about the obscene girls at Marefat who don't know their place, and the impotent men

who can't control their women. He has been Aziz's rival ever since
Aziz was a big-mouthed holy warrior during the Soviet occupation,
and it intensified during the civil war that followed. Aziz and the Ayatollah offered competing paths for their people.

But seven years after the Outsiders arrived the Ayatollah finally
went after the kids.

The Ayatollah has just convinced President Karzai to pass a law specifically for the Shia minority, based on their own Shia religious principles. It was a way for Shias to have more recognition in a country
that was so heavily influenced by Sunni dogma.

Many Shias were proud. At Marefat, they were not. They read
the law closely, and there were problems with it. Among them: it allowed Shia men to rape their wives.

The day the Ayatollah's wrath came down on girls as young as
fourteen was a cool, overcast spring day. There was an electricity in
the air the girls felt as excitement. The girls who planned to protest
were charged with the energy of doing something independent and
daring, and maybe outside the approval of their fathers, and also
with that whole-body calm that comes from doing something you
know is right and worthwhile. Fathers were distracted as they walked
and drove their children to school; some didn't notice their daughters
weren't wearing their school uniforms. Some of the girls told their
fathers what they planned to do that day. One, an eighth grader
named Fatima, was having a hard time summoning the courage.
She was worried he would yell at her, or worse, forbid her from
going. She knew he had a powerful instinct to protect her. Fatima
was, after all, a waify little thing, barely seventy pounds and so pale
she seemed spectral, but with a hidden store of energy, a wit, and
rectitude—she was the kind of person you probably wouldn't notice
in a crowded room, but if you did, you'd be unable to pay attention
to anyone else.

When she had finally, reluctantly, told her father what she
planned to do that day, he began to speak, stopped himself, and then
told her, "If this law passes, it is you it will affect, not me. I am a man
and it is not my right to tell you not to do this." Fatima was so moved

she nearly cried. At that point she had no idea what the day would bring.

It was cool and cloudy then, the girls in parkas, before it started to rain—to rain first insults and stones and spit, and then real rain, real cleansing rain, which made her think *even God is crying at this*. But right now all the girls knew was the excitement of being with other girls they admired and who admired them back. They were brave, and smart, and more than smart, they were *wise*, except perhaps there was one way in which they were not wise, in which they were actually dangerously naïve, for they were going to take on a powerful Ayatollah and once they got together with their friends and sisters, absent from all of the emotions they felt was the one that was probably the most appropriate one, which of course was fear.

And it was not because they were brave, although they were that, as they would soon demonstrate to the world: they didn't fear because they didn't know there was anything to be afraid of. They knew the cause they stood for was just, and they believed that when what you're doing is good, higher powers line up to make sure you get what you ask for. Teachers, God, police, the government.

The first sign that something was wrong went unregistered by the girls. As they left the school that morning—six girls in Fatima's group, plus a teacher—boys were lurking in the curves and alleys wielding crude weapons, sticks, and fist-sized stones. But this was just boys being boys; what was strange, but only in retrospect, is that when the girls took a different route to avoid the boys, the boys never showed up again. Every boy from this part of the Desert knew every alley; it shouldn't have been so easy to lose them. How come those boys hadn't shown up to bother them again? Only later did Fatima understand this was a sign she had missed: that the reason those boys didn't know the alleys was because they weren't from this neighborhood. They had come from someplace else.

Shopkeepers and bus drivers on the way out of the Desert were giving them queer looks and asking them intrusive questions: "Where are you girls going?" "You don't know what you're doing." The girls weren't scared; at first they were confused, then they were offended. A man said, "You're being used by politicians."

"*You* are not my father," Fatima said, with venom. "It's not *your* right to tell me anything."

When they realized that traveling as a large group of girls was drawing stares, Fatima suggested they split up into smaller groups and reconvene at the scene of protest. Not because they were worried, but because they were a large group of girls out in public in a place where large groups of girls out in public was uncommon and being stared at becomes tiresome after a while.

Why men were quizzing them, why buses were not stopping for them, why shopkeepers were squinting at them—these things didn't register as worrying signs, just as curiosities.

The idea that a powerful Ayatollah might mobilize his masses against young girls wouldn't have made sense. The law was dumb and crude and insulting. It was the product of simple minds, certainly not of Islamic scholarship. Anyone with a head on her shoulders could see that this law was foolish and un-Islamic. The Ayatollah was someone Fatima hadn't learned to fear yet. Teacher Aziz had made her feel she didn't need to fear him, or anyone else for that matter. She knew that terrible things occasionally happened to girls in her country, but *other* girls, in other places. At Marefat, the idea of girls getting acid thrown in their faces for attending school or stoned for adultery—these things were entirely foreign. They were cruel and devastating, but so far removed from what she had experienced in Marefat's safe haven that they hardly factored into Fatima's thinking; they were instead novelties on the news. What *she* understood was that girls were precious and powerful, not to be guarded but to be thrust forward, to be given not the same rights as men but *more* rights to make up for lost time, and because they knew what to do with them better than anyone else. She was the vessel of change, first in her family, then in the whole country. That's what Teacher Aziz said. So it was her *right* to question authority, her *responsibility* not to kneel to men or even to grownups just because they were men or grownups. She believed herself to be a guardian of virtue, because that's what Teacher Aziz had told her. She had not considered the possibility that his ideas might not stand her in good stead.

The Ayatollah's followers were, most of all, what the girls hadn't counted on. And they were everywhere. He had masses to mobilize at his command, and he also had a direct line into homes. He had a television station, which Marefat girls never watched, since it felt so dissonant, like watching a news channel partial to a rival political party. So Fatima and the other girls didn't know that all night the Ayatollah's channel had been broadcasting a banner on its programming with a warning: "Tomorrow, some young naïve girls will be used against their will by foreign powers. They do not know what they are doing. These poor things are being manipulated by the communist, Teacher Aziz, and the infidels who support him." Finally, a law just for them, winning them a place of influence in the government. And some naïve brainwashed girls were trying to undo it.

The girls had split up into small groups before arriving at the protest site, to avoid calling too much attention to themselves, and for the older girls to arrive first—including the oldest of all of them, an adult woman someone said was Benazir's mother, who followed the girls because she couldn't read the street signs. Then the younger ones would arrive next, and the even younger ones after them. That way, everyone who wanted to participate could, but the younger girls could stay behind the older ones, who would handle the press and any unsympathetic parties they might encounter.

But the plan began to unravel almost immediately. The older girls ran into more resistance on their route than Fatima and the younger girls had. Which meant that when Fatima and her friends arrived at the Ayatollah's compound, the older girls weren't there yet.

To Fatima it didn't seem too important at that point. She was thrilled the moment she first saw the compound, a giant building with spires that reached all the way up to the sky, covered in an intricate skin of minutely arranged tiles. The complex was something out of a dream, massive and beautiful, with perfectly manicured lawns, an artist's idea of heaven. She took it in, and it brought her to tears. *My God,* she thought. *What if we could all pray in this mosque? It's definitely big enough for all of us, and if all the Muslim people come together for praying and spending time with one another, and young people can get to know each other . . .* Her spirits were lifted even higher when they marched around the corner of the giant seminary to join their sisters, and saw not just their sisters but a huge mass of men assembled, too, well-dressed and educated-looking, a turnout that was so unexpected and so validating that she felt she might just float right up off the ground. For the first time she felt a pride in her country, because look what her country was saying to the world: *We aren't a country of cavemen. We're educated, and all of us, even the men, will stand up against anything that takes us backward.* Fatima hurried toward the men, almost laughing, ready to join them and march from the madrassa to Parliament where they would all together demand this stupid law be rescinded. She felt like the army had assembled, an even bigger army than they'd planned for, and at that moment everyone knew they were all going to be okay.

"Wait, hold on," said one of their teachers, who'd just arrived. Fatima slowed. "Read the signs."

And, yes, now, this was curious. The men were holding signs, even better and bigger ones than the girls had brought to the protest. But the words on the signs were not quite right; and now that she noticed it, the expressions on the men's faces didn't seem quite right either. They didn't fit with what she was feeling, this pride, gratitude, hope, all those things. Fatima was now close enough to make out a word on one of the signs: INFIDEL.

Her stomach turned. She saw another sign: FIGHTING WITH THIS LAW MEANS FIGHTING WITH GOD.

By the time she realized that the mob wasn't there to support her, she was ten yards away.

"Girls," the teacher said. "*Run.*"

They were chased by grown men cursing and spitting and hurling rocks. The girls tried to outrun them, but they weren't used to running. They were in a part of the city they'd never been to before. Its twisting avenues led them away and then directly back toward their pursuers, the neighborhood confused and dispersed them. They became separated, terrified, suddenly alone, and very far from home. And then the men chasing them were gone. It was like a nightmare, to be chased by someone who hates you for a reason you don't at all comprehend, then to have them suddenly slip away, so you don't know where they might rematerialize. The girls didn't know then that the men had been instructed to take the fight straight to where it would hurt most, so that while the girls tried to find one another in a strange new neighborhood, the men were headed to their home base. The mob had peeled off to join the crowd already assembling at Marefat.

Back at the school, Aziz stood on the roof of his home where the crowd couldn't see him, and he listened to them chanting.

"Death to Teacher Aziz!"

"God is great!"

"Teacher Aziz is a communist!"

He looked across at the school, where students had barricaded themselves; the Ayatollah's followers were now trying to beat down the door and throwing rocks through the windows. Aziz could hear the younger boys inside, screaming. Behind the walls, the bravest boys had lined up to lean against the gate; together, they were using their bodies to keep the mob from pushing it open. Some of the boys trapped inside had taken off their blue shirts and hid them in backpacks, so that they could pretend they weren't Marefat students if the mob got in. Some of the boys fainted.

Outside, the mob roiled and swayed, its energy feeding on itself. *These people will burn the school down*, Aziz thought. *They will burn it with those boys inside.* They would find him on the roof and drag him down and put him against a wall and shoot him. Maybe they'd beat him with stones. They'd kill him, thinking they were doing God's good work. He would die watching the faces of his assailants, wrenched in righteous rage, and behind them, glimpses of his school burning, with the boys barricaded inside.

But worst of all, he seemed to have no one defending him. Where were the Hazaras he'd built this school for? They were going to let this mob destroy it.

Aziz had a phone in his hand, and he was trying to focus on giving updates to the one important man on his side, a Pashtun official who controlled the Afghan army and the police, a man he respected. Aziz wasn't sure he could depend on the official, but didn't feel he had a choice. The man promised Aziz that help was on its way. "Just stay on the phone," he said. "Keep calling me and keep me updated about what's happening."

Aziz was not hopeful.

Another stone went through a window in the school, and Aziz heard the boys inside scream. A cheer bubbled up and released itself from the crowd. He couldn't tell exactly who was who. The crowd swelled and pushed against itself: Hazaras shoved Hazaras, not everyone was in agreement, but all he could tell was that far more people were attacking the school than defending it. He felt bile rising inside him. *Where are my friends? Where are Marefat supporters? Where are the Outsiders? Why has no one come to safeguard us?*

Here he was, standing on top of his house like a treed cat, while a mob yelled for his head, and no one yelled back.

Fatima finally found her way onto a bus, but some of the girls she was running with had been hit by stones. They helped each other on board, and passengers gasped. "What did you do? Who are those men? Why are they running after you?"

No one else answered, so Fatima did. "I don't *know* what we did! We did nothing! They just were running after us!" Now she was disoriented, she'd lost her ability to determine who around her was friendly and who wasn't. Maybe no one was. Maybe the Ayatollah had got to all of them. She thought again of the men chasing, the rage on their faces. *My people can be so hard,* she thought. *When my people are attacking, they turn into such bad people.*

Suddenly one of the girls screamed. "Teacher Aziz has been killed!" The girl had managed to get through to family back at Marefat. "There's a mob there and they've killed Teacher Aziz!"

Fatima felt a wave of terror soar through her. *What have I done? What have we sparked?*

If there was an attack at Marefat . . . her two younger sisters were there now, she had no way of knowing whether they were alright. After she'd lost patience with the barely moving bus, inching along toward the Desert, she got off and ran toward home, weeping as she went, her face soaked because it had started to pour. She saw a shopkeeper she went to every day for groceries and snacks after school. "Sir," she said through her tears, "have you seen my sisters?"

He was unmoved by her concern. "What happened at that school of yours today? What mischief are you up to? There were gunshots."

Was he accusing her? Did the Ayatollah get to him, too? She left him and ran home, but her house was empty, and then she remembered: her mother was sick, so her father might be at the hospital with her—but what about her sisters? She ran through the mud to her uncle's house and found his wife.

"Have you seen my sisters?"

"No, they're not back yet. What's going on out there?"

She tried to decide where to begin, but she couldn't and she didn't know, and the notion that Aziz was dead choked the air out of her. "I can't—" And she collapsed.

Finally, she was called for. Her whole family had been at the hospital, the girls were fine, and they were all home. She heard that the crowd had chanted for Aziz's life, but no one could confirm that he was actually dead. Once the rumor spread, everyone tried to call him, so nobody could get through.

By that point no one could get to the school; the streets had been choked to a standstill. Police didn't know who was coming to attack and who was coming to help, so they were stopping everyone.

The crowd had calmed briefly, then gathered again with renewed vigor and prepared to attack once more. A police commander who had finally arrived with a few dozen special forces told Aziz, "We aren't going to be able to protect you. You need to leave here. Go into the city tonight and hide."

He was frightened and embarrassed. *I shouldn't need you to protect me,* he thought. *Where are my people?*

In front of the school, policemen raised their weapons and fired into the air; the crowd compressed. It roiled, then began to leak bodies as if punctured, floodwater receding. An hour later, the boys stepped out from behind the gates.

All night and into the morning people fanned out in the Desert to pass around leaflets for the Ayatollah. MAREFAT IS A CENTER OF ESPIONAGE; MAREFAT TEACHES PROSTITUTION. So when Aziz finally got through to his board members on the phone, it was clear that the only thing to do was to close the school indefinitely.

Already the damage was significant. Most of the windows had been broken. At least one of the Ayatollah's men had been shot in a confrontation with the police, and the Ayatollah's TV station was reporting that he'd died. The Ayatollah's followers could be counted on to avenge the loss of one of their own. Who would Marefat be staying open for? Who would send their kids to the school? Now that the Ayatollah forbade it and had shown he was willing to bring his full wrath down upon Marefat, who would take the risk?

One board member dissented.

"If even a single student wants to come to school tomorrow," he said, "the school should be open."

"Maybe," another said. "But tomorrow is too soon."

"No, listen: the final defeat would be if a child shows up for school and finds our doors closed."

Aziz felt so defeated he didn't have the energy to weigh in one way or another. It was decided that as a symbolic gesture, the school would stay open, even if not a single student showed.

The next day, before the 6:30 a.m. lineup, three students from the same family arrived on schedule. Aziz watched them filing in. It seemed, at first, not much different than any other day, save for the broken windows. He looked down the dirt road leading up to the school and saw students in the pale blue and white Marefat uniforms making their way toward him, some with parents holding their hands. He looked back to the courtyard and thought there might be a few dozen students today. And then back out to the dirt road, where the stream of approaching students still hadn't slowed. Students kept coming, and by three minutes to morning assembly time, the courtyard was filling almost as fast it usually did.

My god, Aziz thought, *the story isn't over yet.*

This day was as dangerous a day to be part of the Marefat community as there had ever been, and parents were putting their kids in harm's way. They were defying the Ayatollah's messages, pumped out through his TV station and through the leaflets spread all night. They were bringing their kids to the center of communist Christian prostitution.

Aziz would later find that attendance on that day, the day after the Ayatollah attacked Marefat, was 95 percent. In all, only three families permanently pulled their children from Marefat. The rest decided to send their children back into Aziz's charge, come what may.

When she returned from the hospital, Fatima's mother was so shocked to learn that the school had been attacked, and that her eighth-grade daughter had been part of the protest that sparked it, that she begged the child to stay home.

Fatima, already feeling guilty at having caused her sick mother distress, decided she'd argued enough for now. She agreed to stay home.

For one day.

On the second day, she was back in class, along with all the girls she'd protested next to, even the ones with welts on their heads from the rocks.

7

THE STUDENT

It was not just the kids that showed up. Najiba arrived, brimming with the previous day's excitement, looking for a copy of the law they'd all been protesting. Even if she couldn't read it, she wanted to hold it in her hands as proof that she knew what she was fighting for.

To Aziz, there was something in that. Of all the things that had unsettled him about yesterday's attack, what stuck with him more than anything was how many women had come out so rabidly against Marefat. Against their own rights. They were surely being used by their husbands or fathers, or just by the Ayatollah. Clearly, women could have an impact, but if they didn't have access to information, what would their impact be? The women fighting on behalf of the Ayatollah showed that just because a woman was politically active didn't mean she understood what she was being active about.

Many had never been educated. Even for those lucky enough to have fathers and husbands and brothers inclined to let them, study had been forbidden during the Taliban years, so many were illiterate.

But there were women like Najiba, coming to school just because she wanted to prove she knew what she had been protesting about. She *wanted* information. What if it was just a little easier? What if it didn't take Najiba's extraordinary stubbornness in order for an uneducated woman to access information?

When he turned it over in his mind, the solution began to seem obvious. Adults were the population Marefat had skipped. What do you do if a bunch of adults come out arguing against you when you're trying to defend their rights?

You *educate* them.

He'd have to design a program that made adult women comfortable at school, even if they were traditional. That meant classes for just women. No men, no kids. It meant it had to be accelerated, several grades completed in the course of one year, because the women were going to have to do more in less time. And you couldn't expect women to be away from home for more than an hour or two a day, so those hours had to be packed. It had to be timed just right so they didn't have to move through the hordes of children every day; that meant beginning classes in the afternoon, after all the kids had left, but before a mother would need to be home to prepare dinner. It meant making it affordable: it was harder to justify the value-add of educating a grown woman than a girl; for grown woman it meant time away from childcare and domestic tasks, and Aziz's property manager argument wouldn't work for already married women. Aziz asked the board to fund tuition for his new adult learning program. Though there wasn't money to pay for all of it, they settled on covering 85 percent now and figuring out how to pay for it later.

So it was settled. Marefat's counterattack against the Ayatollah would be a literacy program for adult women.

Najiba didn't know anything about Aziz's plans for retaliation against the Ayatollah. What she knew was that one spring day a few months after the protest, she came to Marefat to pay her children's tuition and saw a new banner hanging against the wall. She knew by the colors and the size that it announced something important and new, so she asked a boy nearby to read it. As he did, her eyes welled. She walked home as fast as she could, almost running, and told her husband about the new adult literacy program at Marefat, begging him to let her join.

"Oh yes," he said, "I've seen those posters. If you want to go, that's fine. It's your own business."

On the day classes begin, Najiba is the first one there, a half hour before the other students. She's overcome even before another student arrives, but she's early enough that she has time to wipe her eyes and compose herself.

Her first days of homework are exciting, seeing a whole world she'd never seen before. At first, she is occupied mostly with copying letters from the alphabet. She picks it up quickly. She waits until the kids are asleep, and then she takes her books into her bedroom and stays up as long as she can. Other times her excitement overwhelms her; she'll be cleaning dishes or cooking with a problem from an assignment dangling in her mind, and a solution will present itself. So she'll leave the dishes in a gale of energy and run to consult her notebooks. Then back to her household tasks, then back to the books—it becomes a frantic commute across the house that makes the kids giggle. Numbers are harder than letters. No logic reveals itself, one number has nothing to do with the next, and math doesn't flow naturally like the course of a day. Sweep the carpets, sweep the halls, clean the pots, begin dinner. Each thing in its place, each thing with an order and a relation to the next that explains itself. The logic with the numbers is different, the way they interact is backwards, sideways, they twist, they loop around and come back to the beginning, tangling her up in knots and leaving her exhausted.

Still, she begins to feel a power almost immediately. Now she is drawn to the bazaars and markets, she lingers to listen while stall keepers talk politics. She can't contribute anything yet, she wouldn't feel comfortable, but she can hear a language that has been foreign to her now opening up and inviting her in.

She ventures out more, she spends more time around people who aren't her family. She spends more time around men. She listens to the drivers talking about politicians, mostly insulting them, as they drive up and down the Desert. She goes to speeches. She's often the only woman, or at least the only woman who isn't a smartly dressed university student or some expensively turned-out returning émigré, but it feels right to be around these kinds of minds. Her family sees this in her too, and they begin to report to her about goings-on around them. "The minister is giving a speech tomorrow at the mosque: Najiba, dear, do you want to go?"

All these ideas she is coming close to fill up her head in the day and calm her at night, the intense pressure in her chest has withered, replaced by a milder anxiety about homework still unfinished. School pours through her whole body. She is with other women who are learning, other people who want *her* to learn, and by some strange but certain mechanism, it feels like school has somehow cured the things that hurt most.

8

THE AMERICAN

It is March 1971 and Michael Metrinko is in Afghanistan for the very
first time. He is high as a kite and confused. He is in the west of the
country, and right now, it just feels like the West: women wearing
long colorful dresses, ribbons in their hair, berries and seeds in their
jewelry. Liberated-looking women. Well, it's the seventies, even here.
This is Afghanistan before the communist coup, before the Soviet
Army invaded, before the holy warriors fought back, then fought each
other; before one faction emerged stronger than the rest and took the
country over; before an international terrorist group called Al Qa-
eda set up shop here and brought the wrath of the world down upon
their heads.

This was before all that, when Afghanistan was a stop on the
hippie trail. A place with good strong dope, friendly people, and a
long history of cultures that had come marching through it, deposit-
ing their art as they went. You could almost hear the history echoing
around you. Especially if you were high. You looked up and there
was a castle built by Alexander the Great. Rumi wrote about it; the
Timurids called it their capital. It was sacked by Genghis Khan.

Metrinko is in Afghanistan for spring break.

He is in the Peace Corps, teaching in remote villages in Turkey
and Iran, but no place has drugs like Afghanistan. So he'd traveled

from his village to Tehran, where the festivities had begun sooner than expected. A friend's wife was so happy to see Metrinko that she laced the chicken parm, and then they all went to a party where Metrinko understood too late that the punch had been laced as well. Heroin, maybe, or LSD? He thought both, but either way, before they'd even left Iran he was flapping his palms and flying laps around the Eiffel Tower. He woke up the next day expecting a hangover, but he was still flying, and even after they boarded a rickety old bus and crossed into Afghanistan he still hadn't come down. He spent two weeks stoned, two weeks of drugs and diarrhea. Decades later he would tell the military folks trying to cut off the Taliban's poppy revenue that he knew all there was to know about drugs there. He'd gone to Afghanistan once on a drug eradication project, he explained. He'd tried a novel approach, which he called "personal consumption."

It hadn't worked, so he'd given up. He advised them to do the same.

Eight years later, when the Soviets invaded Afghanistan, Metrinko was next door in Tehran. He'd gone from the Peace Corps to the Foreign Service, and was serving as a political officer at the U.S. embassy in Iran. In those days he felt an occasional thrill that came from standing near a pivot point in history, even if he wasn't quite at it: In Afghanistan, a revolution had just put a communist government in power. In Afghanistan, political prisoners were being killed and disappeared by the thousands. In Afghanistan, the cold war was getting hot. The country held his interest, as a place where history was happening, a place he'd been to briefly, and a place whose art drew him in. There were rumblings in Iran where he stood, but of a different order. The CIA had looked at Iran and said it wasn't close to revolution. Not even prerevolutionary, the agency had reported.

Maybe not prerevolutionary, maybe not Afghanistan, but still fun. Metrinko brought his Peace Corps approach to the Foreign Service; he walked out of the comfortable American compound and threw himself into Iran. He knew the language, and that helped; he liked to party, and that had helped too. There were always great parties in countries passing through political change, political movements produced and thrived on excitement. It was after one of those parties that he was sitting in his embassy office one morning, earlier than he would have preferred given the previous night's revelry, and heard chanting outside. He waited for it to pass, but it didn't; it grew louder, and then stalled in front of the embassy gate. While the crowd of protesters swelled, inside the embassy staff members looked at one another with concern. Then the crowd broke through the gates and started to stream into the embassy compound and Metrinko had the bizarre realization that he was now under attack. He called the Iranian friend he was supposed to meet at the embassy that morning, and the friend's bodyguard answered. "He won't talk to you, Michael."

"Do you know what's happened?"

"Yes, we know," he said. And then, "I personally am very sorry."

So his friend had set him up—had made sure Metrinko would be at the embassy. He never saw it coming.

As the mob moved in and the violence began, Michael Metrinko went through a series of calculations.

First, he identified the attackers as mostly students.

Second, because they were students, he was at risk of sympathizing with them. Also because in a way, they were underdogs and he was partial to underdogs.

Third, in order to avoid sympathizing with his captors, and to protect himself psychologically, he was going to have to make sure that *they* didn't like *him*. He was going to have to be an asshole. He hardened. As his captivity began, he showed the captors his anger, and he tried to elicit theirs. He tried to get them to beat him so that he could hate them, and the chance for any bond to build between them would be spoiled before it could set. He cursed them, they hit him, tormented him, dragged him out and put him against a wall and aimed guns at him so that he thought he was being executed. He insulted their mothers with the coarsest words in their language. He spent a year that way, careful not to say anything cordial to his captors.

1979 turned into 1980.

1980 turned into 1981.

And finally, 444 days after he was taken hostage, a deal was made. At the very moment Ronald Reagan completed his inaugural address, Michael Metrinko and fifty-one other American hostages were released.

It is September 2001 and Michael Metrinko is on the phone with his doctor. "I have to get this cast removed."

"What are you talking about?"

"I have to have it removed—it's an emergency." Confusion on the other end of the line. *What the hell kind of emergency requires you to take off a cast?* "Look, I have a meeting this afternoon, okay? I need it off. Can you do that?"

Metrinko had just been summoned to Foggy Bottom. "We're going to open the embassy in Kabul. Can you come in for a meeting?" He didn't know what they wanted him for, but if there was a chance it had anything to do with sending him to Afghanistan, a cast and crutches were the kind of thing that would make the suits at the State Department uncomfortable. That State was even calling him in was a sign that something was up; he'd been retired for five years. Desperation? Were they scrambling to figure out what to do in Afghanistan now that the whole U.S. government was hurtling toward a military adventure there? This was his movie character moment: *Rip the cast off, Doc. They need me.*

He'd first called in to State as soon as he'd seen the planes hit the towers. *I'm retired, but if you need someone to go . . .* And when the call from State came weeks later, it was three days after Metrinko had undergone a long-planned foot surgery. He knew how it would play out if they saw him on crutches. "Well, actually, no thank you." As a career Foreign Service officer who'd worked in the region and knew the language, he had no doubt of his value to them.

But State could sometimes act as one big stumbling herd of amateurs, and if there was an excuse *not* to do something that made sense, they'd find it.

The doctor relented, made him sign a waiver, and cut the cast off. Metrinko jammed his foot into a dress shoe and went on down to Foggy Bottom.

"Look, Michael. We're opening the embassy back up."

This he already knew. "Okay," he said, "Well, I'd be happy to help prepare the group going over with whatever orientation you have planned for them."

"What do you mean?"

"At the Foreign Service Institute? I assume you're bringing people together to get them ready to go . . ."

"No —we're not doing that." There would be no orientation. They wanted him on the ground, getting the embassy up and running. It had been closed for twelve years; now they were going to cut the chains off and open for business. Metrinko was to land, get the major departments started, and be back home in a month.

That's what they said: one month. He had a sense that this project was going to last longer. And at the same time, that it couldn't last forever.

The city was like nothing he'd ever seen.

It was an empty place, sad and hollowed out. "Desolate ruin" was what came to mind, over and over. It was winter. The people who hadn't escaped to some country of refuge were burning things to keep warm. A thick shroud of smoke hung over the city, and the effect was apocalyptic: a city that looked as if it had just now been decimated, abandoned, and was still smoldering. He had in his career seen cities under siege. He'd seen the consulate in Aleppo after it had been burnt, the staff scrambling out a back window. He'd seen Iran, of course. But never anything like this. Such a big, empty space, where the only buildings that stood were themselves monuments to war, roofs slanted in, walls so freckled from gun and mortar fire that they seemed insubstantial, one gust away from giving up and collapsing. He had the sense of walking into a photograph from World War II. Dresden, after the firebombing. Hiroshima.

Shops were shuttered. Streets were deserted. There was no traffic.

He met men so slight they seemed to have no shoulders, and their hands, when he went to shake them, felt brittle in his, like chicken bones. He didn't know all the recent history of the country yet, who the power brokers were, the particular grievances and triumphs of the different tribes. There had been a civil war: he didn't know who'd won, but it was hard to see how anybody had. By the time the Americans got there, it seemed like everyone had lost.

That was the most difficult thing to process: people had done this to their own city. To themselves. Now, they had to start from nothing.

But even as the view was tragic, it was energizing too. This desolate ruin presented itself to him as an overture. When there's nothing left, anything can happen.

He was fifty-five years old, but when he landed in Afghanistan, he felt like he was twenty-one again. He felt the way you feel when you're young and adventurous and in a new country where no one knows you and you know no one and you can be anyone. All his senses received the same stimuli they had felt when he was a kid just out of college serving in the Peace Corps. He was speaking the same language he'd spoken then; he might as well have been looking at the same people; so many Afghans looked like they could have been Iranian, the same dark hair, the same Alexandrian features—he hadn't met many Hazaras yet. In Virginia, Metrinko's mother had lived with him until she died, less than two years before. She'd been old and immobile for most of that time, dragging an oxygen tank around and leaning on a cane on her good days, sitting in a wheelchair on bad ones. Metrinko had begun to feel old just being around her; now he'd shaken that feeling.

Now, he was surrounded by young Marines who were occupying the whole bottom floor of the embassy. Vital young men, inclined to act on impulse. Twenty-one years old, or maybe nineteen. He began to act like them. He did whatever he wanted. He found, in those early days, that he could get away with it, going out on his own as long as he was a little vague with the security people about what he was doing. He went out, he visited the restaurants that were starting to open up, he watched the city come awake. He walked down alleys by himself and felt he was not just seeing things he hadn't seen before, he was seeing things *nobody* had seen before. It felt like he was discovering a new world no one had ever laid eyes on. If he walked into a shop, there was a good chance he was the first American the shopkeeper had ever met.

He felt like he was at the center of the universe. The whole world was watching Afghanistan, and somehow, here he was, one of the most senior Americans on the scene. It was exhilarating, really. To be the person for the job—a job everyone believed should be done. He was the consul, he was representing America's diplomatic presence in the country. He *was* the American diplomatic presence. He led the consular section and the political section, each of which had only one other staffer, and he led the economic section, which was only him. His job was just supposed to be getting the embassy up and running again, but there was an entire country to fix, and the embassy was as good a command center as any. It was building something new, with billions of people standing behind him, cheering.

And in Afghanistan, people behaved as if a new king had arrived. The Outsiders were here now—first the United States and England, eventually almost sixty countries—and Metrinko was at the head of the table. There was enough energy that he could, in the beginning, overlook the mistakes being made around him. Though in retrospect, those mistakes were grave. And in retrospect, he'd seen them almost immediately after he landed.

There were discomforts, of course. The embassy hadn't been occupied in more than a decade, and the building they were living in had been built for offices, not residences. There was one shower for the whole civilian staff, down in the bomb shelter where the pots and pans were cleaned. He bathed with cookware around him, and did it quickly because there was always a line and hot water was in short supply.

But there were small joys, too. Wandering around the embassy, Metrinko discovered an old toilet no one knew about, in a building that had been mostly demolished. The toilet worked, it was clean, more or less, and had a door, rare privacy. He decided not to share the discovery.

In the basement, they found a fleet of beat-up Volkswagens the staff must have used before the embassy closed, and when they put batteries back in, the cars all ran. Metrinko began driving himself around the city. With thirty-year-old cars you could park anywhere and no one would notice, because they looked like they belonged there. So he went out, and he began meeting people, listening to them, hearing how the language was spoken here. Dari, it was called, a patois of the Iranian Farsi he already spoke. It took some getting used to; it was like coming from the suburbs and hearing English in the inner city. Words half pronounced, slang he'd never heard before. But the same language. He understood almost all of it, but it sounded rough, hard-edged.

The main chancery of the embassy had been sealed off and chained. He'd heard that just before he arrived, when the American soldiers cut the chain and went in, the walls were hung with artwork, antique weapons, and handmade carpets that had been given to the embassy as gifts before it had closed, which no one had bothered to remove. By the time Metrinko got there—by the end of the first day it was open, he heard—the walls were bare. It had been entirely looted, by our own people. *Well, that's what people do in war*, he thought. *They loot.*

There was no television, no Internet. There wasn't even radio. The country had had an old Chinese switch telephone system, but even so, nobody he met had a handset. There were no cell towers, so there were no cell phones. Metrinko had to send messengers in person to communicate with ministries, and if people had business with the embassy, they just came to the embassy. There were no big barriers, just a cream-colored stone wall between the embassy and the street that he found pleasant and inviting. A few weeks after his arrival, a shipment of satellite phones arrived, and they were handed out to ministers and the important ambassadors. So, for the first time, it was possible to call ahead, as long as the person you wanted to speak to was *the* minister, or Karzai himself. But watching people in the government begin to communicate with one another—even just getting paper and pencils to the ministries—was thrilling. To watch a government start to form in real time, and to be there, helping it along. He got to know the power brokers here; one of his tasks was helping the country prepare for the first Grand Meeting which would gather hundreds of political and tribal leaders together to decide on the country's new constitution. He went to the palace and saw the country's new, post-Taliban flag raised for the first time. And he pushed to get schools up and running by that spring, just months after the U.S. arrival. He came from a family of educators. He had begun his career as a teacher, and had always, even in the foreign service, considered himself a teacher (save for the year and a half when he was held captive by students). For Metrinko, getting schools open in time for the first spring since the foreign invasion was as much of a high as anything he'd experienced at any point in his career. Hundreds of thousands of books needed to be printed, and then distributed all around the country, but they'd done it. He saw girls going to school for the first time in their lives. They weren't good schools; he had no illusions about that. The schools would need to get better, much better, and very quickly, or the swell of optimism would be lost. Kids could only go to schools in dilapidated buildings with insufficient supplies for so long before their hope would run thin. Still, Metrinko felt inspired.

But there were other problems he knew would doom this whole big enterprise if they weren't corrected immediately. Already, just two months after opening the embassy's doors and inaugurating the State Department's presence, the whole thing was threatening to go tumbling off in the wrong direction.

He was summoned one day down to the embassy gate to meet a group of Pashtun elders. It was early, just months after the invasion had begun: bin Laden was slipping away through the mountains in the east. To Metrinko the U.S. military seemed to be flailing around like a child in a tantrum, picking up suspected militants indiscriminately.

Metrinko welcomed the elders as they filed in to a room at the embassy. They were thin and asymmetrical men, missing legs, an eye, their backs stooped. They were old, biblical-looking, and he asked around the room who was the oldest. He was. The men with the ravaged, weathered faces were rarely beyond their early fifties; many were in their thirties. He contained his surprise, took out his cigarettes, and passed them around. He should have been serving tea, he knew that, but there was no way to get the water hot, so he passed out bottled water. The men sat drinking water and smoking cigarettes, and when an appropriate interval had passed, Metrinko commenced the business.

"Welcome to the embassy of the United States of America. What can I do for you?"

One spoke up. "We are here because your soldiers arrested our schoolteacher, and we would like him back."

"Okay. Well, what is his name?"

One of the men gave a name. Metrinko switched his face to sympathetic.

"I don't know if he's been arrested or not by our soldiers," he said. "I can find out. But if he has been detained, it's because the soldiers thought he was doing something wrong, and there will be an investigation. Once the investigation is over, if he hasn't done anything bad, he'll be set free. If he has done something bad, he may have a trial, or he may have to stay longer in prison. But I will try to find out for you."

The man who replied was firm: "No. Sir, you don't understand. *We* are the elders. We are the clan representatives and it is *our* job to decide if he has done something wrong. It's our duty, and if he has done something wrong, we will guarantee to you that he will never do it again, or anything like it. We will stand as guarantor of his good behavior." There was some movement, a conferring among the men, and then one approached Metrinko.

"Here are the thumbprints of three hundred men from our clan. All of us guaranteeing that if this man has done anything, he will never do it again."

Metrinko accepted the document with ceremony, with as much grace as he could muster. He understood that he was dealing with something important here, a kind of organization that was important but fragile, and it struck him immediately as something he should defer to. It had suffered a blow, and if he wasn't gentle, it might crumble further.

"I don't know where he is," Metrinko said. "I will have to find out. And as soon as I find out, I promise, I will tell you."

They smoked more cigarettes, they drank more bottled water, and they kissed, and Metrinko could see that the men were happy that he had heard them and would deliver on his promise, and he knew immediately that he never would. The military wouldn't tell him anything, and as far as he could tell, they had no idea who they had anyway.

It kept happening. Groups of men came to see him, warm and gracious in those early days, grateful even, with this one small request: give him back, and we will punish him if that's what is required. The meetings played out so frequently in such a similar manner that it began to feel like a Japanese tea ceremony. But he saw that there was not really any point, and he knew it was only a matter of time before they realized it, too. So, in these meetings, he saw the fuse being lit for a bomb that would eventually go off. Here were elders, who had always been in control of their villages and who no longer had much to offer. As the old-looking men in the meetings became more desperate, Metrinko grew more concerned. *We're making them look silly.* He'd seen this happen before, in his classrooms in rural Iran and Turkey. When his students saw there was no reason to do what he said, they walked all over him. *This* is how you lose control. Right about now, down in those villages, people would be wondering what purpose their elders really served. It would become less and less clear why anyone should pay attention to them. Those little village administrations would break. That was a problem. The one rule Metrinko believed always held true, wherever he was serving, was that things always change. Right now, they like us, mostly. But they did in Iran, too, in 1978, 1979. A beautiful embassy, thousands of Americans, three big consulates, a status of forces agreement, a close relationship with the country's leader—and then suddenly mobs were storming the gates and putting diplomats in prison.

Things *always* change.

Back in those villages the elders had traveled from, people are happy with us. But when that changed—and at some point, for some reason or another, it *would* change—those elders would be the only way to control the people. And right now, we are neutering those elders. They won't be there when we need them.

He tried to explain this to the military, via every avenue he could think of. He explained it to the defense attaché, he went over to the American military at Camp Eggars to explain it to the generals, he went to the airbase up at Bagram. He got nowhere; he couldn't get anyone to listen. *Metrinko's gone native.* That's what they said behind his back, he was sure of it. "He speaks the language, he likes the art, he goes and has dinner with them, he sits on the floor like them and eats their food. He carries those prayer beads."

When he begged the military to pay settlements when errant bombs destroyed homes or killed relatives, he was talking himself right into the assumption they had of him: "He's compromised. At best, he's naïve, and he's forgotten he works for the Americans, not the Afghans." And for those who knew his past, there was a suggestion that he might be damaged goods. After all, how could you go through a year and a half as a hostage and come out whole?

The excitement of building something gave way to the chaos of not having anything there to build on. He was part of a big lurching herd of Americans, each telling the new President Hamid Karzai, "I'm the one you need to talk to. I'm in charge." The CIA station chief thought that he was king, the American generals thought they were, the chargé d'affaires at the embassy thought he was. The reality was, it wasn't just Karzai—nobody really knew who was in charge. Nobody was in charge. Or else, everybody was, even though the various representatives of the U.S. government never talked to one another.

To Metrinko, the U.S. military was especially imperious, and as far as Metrinko could gather, Karzai was in the dark about what the military was doing. There was a military occupation beginning in his country, and as president he had nothing to say about it. The generals would go and see him occasionally, but they never told the embassy what happened when they did. The CIA saw Karzai every

day, but they never told the embassy what went on in those meetings. When Metrinko met Karzai, he didn't bother to tell the military,
the CIA, or any of the other Americans what he was doing. America
was presenting itself to Karzai as parents whose messages never aligned.
Metrinko didn't know who was in charge. How could Karzai?

And then, just when he began losing hope, something came along to
restore it.

There was a commander, a man Metrinko had been flying up
to the highlands to meet. It was an inconvenience, but he didn't
mind— when he was up there, he got to see the giant Buddhas. Or at
least, the giant, gaping craters in the sandstone where they'd been—
only months before the Taliban had taken it upon themselves to tear
the statues down with dynamite and grenades. Seeing the place
now was less looking at art than at an empty picture frame, but it
was still impressive: giant-sized arcs in the sandstone, like a mon-
ster's missing teeth. The damage was done, the dynamite had long
since gone silent, but still, they cast an aura over the valley, and it felt
like if you could get there soon enough, maybe you'd witness something that hadn't quite expired yet.

It was in his meetings with this tall, Asiatic-featured man, with
narrow eyes and a flat face, that Metrinko began to learn who the
Hazaras were. From the commander he understood that the Hazaras,
through some historical paradox, were Shia, even though just about
everyone else in the country was Sunni. And once he knew they were
different, it was easy to pay special attention to them, since they *looked*
different from everyone else.

Metrinko found the commander tolerable. A whiner, but then,
everyone was a whiner. Everyone wanted special treatment from the
Americans for his own tribe. Khalili held forth about how poor the
Hazaras were, how free of guilt. Their long history of persecution
continued right up until now, right up until yesterday, when a poor
Hazara farmer was attacked or mistreated or taken advantage of by a
Pashtun or a Tajik. Metrinko abided it, because part of his charge was
getting to know the various power players in this country. Com
mander Khalili was one of them.

When a friend of Khalili's convinced the commander to come down to the capital—to come and really be a part of this new country being built—Metrinko's job became easier. He went across the city every few weeks to pay the commander a visit, to keep himself apprised of the Hazara side of things, and, more importantly, to keep them assured of America's interest. Best not to let anyone think we don't care. Best not to give anyone a reason not to like us.

But abiding these sessions was the extent of Metrinko's commitment. He went and listened, but his mind wandered and he didn't try to stop it. Khalili was a man of status, clearly, perhaps the most powerful Hazara in the country. But he did not seem particularly sophisticated. He was a man who wielded power, but was out of touch with those over whom he wielded it. The kind of man who would perhaps have a role at the beginning of the new country, but would eventually walk himself right into irrelevance without even realizing it. The only hold on power he had was ethnic politics, and if people began to get along, as Metrinko hoped they would, he'd be of little use to anyone. He bored Metrinko. During one visit, Metrinko's eyes scanned the room. He listened for inconsistencies in the translation and tried to pick up the idiosyncrasies in this new dialect of a language he spoke. And he noticed one of Khalili's aides.

He was a man who seemed to have no status. He was a full foot shorter than the commander and dressed like a skinny kid who'd raided his father's closet. He wore a suit that was too big and too boxy, and looked comical next to the commander—the little man trying hard to look professional, next to the regally appointed vicar in his finery, robes upon robes and a complicated-looking head covering like a big linen beehive perched atop of his head. An odd couple, certainly, except that they shared the same Asiatic appearance. The tall one's features were more pronounced, a stately Kublai Khan; the smaller one less so, with features you might not identify as Hazara if you weren't looking closely. He was translating for the commander, and—here was what interested Metrinko—as far as he could tell, the man wasn't one of these Afghans who'd lived in the United States or Europe for a while. He was a real Afghan, who'd never left the region.

So when this man spoke English, almost flawlessly, it was jarring. Like a pet you'd assumed to be mute suddenly asking you to be let out.

Metrinko could identify with him. Metrinko had played organ monkey, too. He had come to enjoy the confusion on people's faces here when he spoke Farsi. They blinked, and then they were silent, suspecting they were objects of a prank, or were beholding some bizarre sort of miracle, a dog riding by on a bicycle. "Are you Iranian?" This was a question he received almost daily.

"No, I'm not Iranian. I'm an American."

This was not accepted. "Don't be ashamed of your Iranian heritage, be proud of it."

So he found himself paying more attention to the small man in the suit than the tall commander he was supposed to be meeting with. *Where was he educated? How did he learn to speak English?* He was intelligent, Metrinko could tell. He struck Metrinko as worth talking to, the kind of person who might have an interesting take on things So Metrinko cornered the commander's interpreter after one of these meetings.

"Aziz," the man said his name was. "Some call me Teacher."

He was pleasant, outgoing even. He was interesting, and he had an obvious mischievous streak—Metrinko could see it on his face, which sometimes cracked into a thin smile, like he knew something Metrinko didn't. It drew him in. This was a man from a downtrodden people, who didn't seem interested in whining. He was confident, a little cocky even.

The next time the embassy went to meet with the commander, Metrinko made sure to take the small interpreter aside and speak to him. He wanted to find some art to bring home, and it occurred to him that this Aziz probably knew the right places to look.

"Actually," Aziz said, "I have a school, and we have an art teacher who comes sometimes. Come visit, as my guest."

The school wasn't much to look at then. Not the building, not the place. It was in Dasht-e-Barchi, and while he knew *dasht* meant "desert," it didn't occur to him that it would actually *be* a desert. When he crossed into the Desert, it was a punch in the gut. He was not new to conflict zones, and he'd seen neighborhoods weighted under the kind of poverty that pulls you down and holds you there. This was both. It was big, flat, and dry, and the only disruptions to the terrain were hovels people made of mud and straw, mounds of earth that could have just as easily been shaped by wind.

He'd thought all of Kabul was a ruin, but the Desert, was, incredibly, worse. This was where the Hazaras lived.

Aziz's school wasn't anything to look at either. It wasn't even a school, really. It was thirty kids squeezed into two rooms Aziz had rented in someone else's home, and a third room where Aziz's family lived. One single room for his wife, his three kids, two parents, two brothers, himself.

The rooms were alive. The students were . . . "serious" was the word that occurred to him. They didn't waste time. They attended with an eagerness that wasn't all that far from desperation but was somehow still inspiring. Many had been in refugee camps just months before, living in tents in another country. But they didn't have the resignation he often saw in refugees, that resignation which he found to be not unlike laziness, and which made it harder to sympathize with people. Metrinko knew he was sometimes seen as someone who went native too quickly, as too easily swayed by the locals, as a sympathizer. But that wasn't quite right. He didn't give anyone a pass just because he was a foreign service officer and they were foreign. He regarded people as a teacher regards his students. Disappointed when they don't achieve, satisfied only when they do, on their own. When Metrinko saw these students, he was instantly moved.

He hadn't ever been much of a champion for women's rights, but he found himself registering it as special that there were girls here. It was 2002, less than a year since the collapse of the Taliban, and it struck him immediately that there were girls here studying next to the boys. They argued with each other. They corrected each other. A girl sauntered over to a boy, draped herself across his desk, and showed him where he'd made an error in his workbook. They weren't intimidated by one another. Metrinko didn't know whether the way they interacted was something purposeful Aziz was doing or just an issue of space. The school was so small they likely couldn't have kept boys and girls separate even if they wanted to.

Still, Metrinko knew that bringing boys and girls together couldn't have been easy for Aziz. Many people still didn't see their daughters as anything other than property. Something that costs money to maintain, something which, if its integrity is somehow compromised, is a setback to your own worth, but for which you might get something in return when you give it away, if it is intact. Rather than fight the notion of girls as property, Aziz tried to convince fathers that he could make their property more valuable. An educated girl can be married better, he said, so give me your girls and I'll make them more valuable. He didn't go into homes as a proselytizer; he went in as an investment manager.

By the time Metrinko first saw the school, there were girls bold enough to look a foreign man in the eye, there were girls speaking over boys, girls speaking over him. And as a man who was an educator at heart, he decided he'd found his cause. He'd come out of retirement into the midst of a mess and he'd stumbled upon this school—even if it was only two classrooms—that was on to something.

Aziz introduced Metrinko to the art teacher, Sher Ali, a man smaller even than Aziz, a fragile, barely-there kind of person. He spoke softly; he seemed to have no age. He projected no energy. His expression—an indifferent smile, eyes creased—never changed. It was hard to get any kind of read on him. He seemed to be elsewhere.

But Metrinko was astounded by his art. His paintings were as faithful as photographs—on which many of them were based—but he had a way of ratcheting up the way they made you feel. Whether through color or texture or shadow, this man had a way of making his paintings emote.

His students' art was impressive as well. Metrinko was drawn to the front of the room where the canvases leaned against the wall. He was pulled in by an oil on canvas of a man pouring tea, deep lines in a face that expressed a dignified kind of sadness. "This is a superb piece," he said. "Are these for sale?"

Sher Ali's eyes widened. He looked at Aziz, standing across the room, giving no signal, and then back to Metrinko. "I don't know," he said. "We never thought about that."

"Well. *Could* it be for sale?"

"I guess it could be."

"Okay, how about this: *If* it were for sale, how much would you ask for it?"

"I don't know. We've never thought about putting a price on them." The class had gone silent, and Metrinko was aware that he was now performing.

"Would a hundred dollars be a good price for this piece?" Sher Ali did a series of rapid blinks, like he'd just been awoken by a door slamming. One hundred dollars was a month's salary. More, out here in the Desert.

"That would be a *great* price for this!" And then he snapped into action, called the student up to the front of the class, Metrinko unfolded a hundred dollar bill and handed it to the boy, who stared at it.

"I want you to take this money," Metrinko said, still on stage. "Take it home, and give it to your mother. Not your father. Tell your mother it's for her." The students began clapping and whooping, thrilled with the American's largesse, in on a joke Metrinko himself wasn't aware of—that the nine-year-old boy was Abuzar, Aziz's son. But Metrinko's mind was elsewhere. As the class clapped, he had an idea: if Marefat was willing to sell student art, he knew where to find buyers. The U.S. embassy in Kabul was full of more and more officers with fewer and fewer opportunities to go out. Why not bring some culture to them? He consulted Aziz; he ran the idea by some colleagues at the embassy. In short order the school was holding an art show at the U.S. embassy, and the students sold almost thirty pieces in a day. Sher Ali took the money from each painting, gave half the purchase price to the kid, and took the other half to remodel the art room. Metrinko allowed himself a sense of accomplishment.

The next time he went to the school, Aziz said just about half the school had tried to join the art class. Art was no longer trivial; it had become something Americans would pay for. Something they could have pride in. Metrinko counted this a battle won.

He wanted to keep going back to Marefat. But the embassy's Regional Security Officer had become an obstacle. The Desert was far away and the security service had finally wrested control of comings and goings at the embassy. Marefat was unknown to them, and it had nothing to do with Metrinko's portfolio here. So he signed a waiver of responsibility for the ambassador and he launched a charm offensive with the RSOs. "Look," he told them. "I'm not going to go near any crowds. If I see a situation that's threatening, I'll be the first one out of there, trust me. I speak the language, I'm not crazy, and I know how to deal with situations like this." And he threw in a sweetener. "You need somebody out there on the streets anyway. I can be an asset." After he went out, he came back to the security officer and filled him in on what was going on out beyond the wire. "That part of the city was quiet last night," he would say, "everything was okay." Or, "Things don't look good in the western sector." He quickly made himself valuable to them, because of his movement around the city, rather than in spite of it. He tried to be the first to alert them to a holiday coming up or a demonstration that was being planned, situations where "it would probably be better if people from the embassy didn't go out into the city for the next couple of days."

By helping security lock everyone else down, he freed himself. He went to the school whenever he could. And whenever he could pass Aziz off as an expert on something, he brought Aziz to the embassy.

Metrinko wanted it to look like Aziz and his school were protected by the Americans. It was a mafia mentality, but Metrinko had a feeling it would work here: make it look like the school had a guardian angel lurking in the background. But he wanted to throttle it carefully. He would not give Marefat money, or even let it *look* like the Americans were giving it money, because if people thought Aziz had a cash flow from the Americans, they'd try to take it. He wanted it to look like the school had a protector to discourage attacks, not a benefactor, which might attract them. That meant just the right number of cars going down to Marefat when Metrinko went to visit, and just the right number of meetings at the embassy for Aziz.

In the meantime, Metrinko was growing more attached to the school.

After seven months in Kabul, he left the embassy in Kabul to do a short stint in Yemen, and then came back to Afghanistan—to Herat, the city he'd first seen during his drug-fueled holiday thirty-five years before. Seven months later, he made it back to Kabul, this time working for an organization helping politicians get ready for another Grand Meeting, where they would discuss the new constitution. The organization put him up in a hotel, and on his first day back in the city he took a taxi to the embassy. Nothing looked familiar. He was sure these roads were new. There were big walls and HESCO barriers rising up on either side of the road; he was driving in shadows. He leaned forward. "Where are we? What is all that?"

"That? That's where the American soldiers live. They have all those walls," the driver said, "because the American soldiers are cowards."

Everything had changed. The United States had only been in Afghanistan for two years, but Kabul had become a place he couldn't recognize. Hearing the taxi driver's insult, Metrinko recalled a chilling conversation he'd had a year before, when the U.S. embassy was just beginning to creep in all directions. A security officer had decided the wall around the embassy wasn't sufficient, so the Americans pushed it out and took over the sidewalk. Metrinko doubted the embassy bothered to ask anybody for permission. They just took over something that didn't belong to them and declared it theirs, swallowing up a sidewalk and nudging Afghans out onto the street. It had been a minor issue in the grand scheme of things, trivial compared to the other problems he was beginning to see. When an Afghan general summoned Metrinko to a meeting to discuss the wall, he went as a courtesy.

"Listen," the general said. "You're putting up that big wall around the embassy?"

"Yeah, we are."

"Don't do it. Because if you do it, everyone in Kabul will

think you're afraid. Once they think you're afraid, you're finished." Metrinko had sat politely but hadn't engaged. "The Soviets never did that when they were here," the general said. "They didn't have to. Once you put up that wall, people will lose their respect for you."

A year later, as the taxi snaked through a series of tunnel-like roads sunk beneath HESCO containers and sandbags, Metrinko worried that the general was right. The embassy had become a fortress, concertina wire climbing up and along the walls like vines, and massive, institutional cinderblock gates keeping the Americans and the locals farther and farther apart from one another. Metrinko felt a chill.

Even Maretat was changing.

After Metrinko returned, Aziz asked him out to the Desert, for the beginning of construction on their first building. They'd moved from two rooms in one rented house to two slightly bigger rooms in an only slightly bigger rented house, and they finally had some money, thanks to a donation from Francis D'Souza, to begin their own building. Just one floor, a few rooms made of dried mud lined up around an open courtyard, built by the students and teachers themselves.

The site was so far out Metrinko wasn't sure they were still in Kabul. You couldn't even *see* another building. "The land here was very cheap," Aziz said. But of course it was. It was *nowhere*. Metrinko imagined Genghis Khan galloping over the horizon with his hordes, he pictured wolves coming to surround the building at night. "Remote" didn't do it justice.

Aziz offered a shovel, in the spirit of cooperation between their two nations. Metrinko didn't take it. He lit a cigarette.

Aziz looked confused, then insulted, his eyes following Metrinko as he walked off to the side, where he stood well clear of the digging and made a show of watching the Afghans sweat over their new school, like a colonial master.

(Later, Metrinko smiles mischievously at the memory. "Did I do that? Well. Sometimes I do things for dramatic effect.")

Metrinko was, by that point, alarmed. *Because they're cowards.* The taxi driver's words lingered. He was alarmed by the massive building up of the embassy, the thousands and thousands of foreigners who'd poured into the country and sent real estate rates skyrocketing. He was alarmed by the fortifications rising on all sides of every building foreigners occupied, and by how rarely foreigners left them. Two separate worlds were forming, the foreigners occupying an archipelago of self-contained compounds reaching through the city.

Aziz was still constantly asking for help. He wondered aloud why he couldn't get any money out of Metrinko. All the building and the wave of foreigners coming into the country only made it harder for Metrinko to convince him that this mission was going to end, sooner or later.

"Look, Aziz, you need to look forward to a time we're not here. It's going to change. Everything changes, relationships change, governments change, the way we interact with other governments, with other countries—it all changes. We go to war, we go out of war. It's always been that way. One day we're dropping the A-bomb on a country, and three weeks later our GIs are marrying girls from there. One day we have a beautiful embassy and consulates and everything is fine and the head of the country is our best friend, and the next day, mobs are storming our gates and putting our diplomats in prison."

Aziz's expression remained fixed.

"*I know* the level of attention that an American can give to a foreign problem. It doesn't last very long. It's impossible to keep an American occupied for that long of a period. We've *never* had it, with any place."

Still, it didn't seem to register.

"There's nothing here for us! Realistically speaking, there is nothing in Afghanistan to attract us. It has no natural resources that we can use, period. We don't need the copper. We don't need anything that comes out of there. And besides that, it's far away. It's difficult to get to. We have nothing whatsoever in common with the culture! And you know as well as I the neighborhood is not our kind of neighborhood."

But everything he was trying to tell Aziz was inconsistent with everything Aziz saw around him. There were more and more people coming from foreign countries every day, spending money, giving money, starting projects, opening offices. The country was safer than it had ever been. There were more foreign troops fanning out to more parts of the country, and the U.S. embassy was growing bigger by the minute, sprouting cranes and spilling onto the sidewalk, subsuming more and more land around it. The idea that the foreigners would turn around and leave contradicted all the evidence.

Metrinko heard himself sounding alarmist. He knew his warnings applied too far into the future to be impactful now. Marefat had never planned much further than a few days ahead; there'd never been any reason to. There weren't good schools or jobs or prospects for Hazaras worth planning for. So many had been in exile in a country where their rights as refugees were limited. There was no way to change their lives, even by planning ahead, so few did. The future was tomorrow; a year from now was incomprehensible. Metrinko might as well have been warning about an asteroid centuries away. And by then his flair for the dramatic was known to Aziz. He heard himself sounding like he was making excuses for offering no help, apart from the big American bills in exchange for souvenirs.

"You're responsible for your own relationships," he told Aziz. "With different ethnic groups, you know, and with neighboring countries. Period. We're not. We have our own neighborhood to deal with."

Aziz wanted American money. Metrinko had shown he could deliver it. He had shown he was a person of influence with the Americans. Aziz wanted his help, and couldn't be convinced he shouldn't have it.

"You can't become dependent on us. If you do, it won't last. Because *we* won't last. The only way you can make this thing of yours survive is if your people support it. The money has to come from them."

It was a tall order, Metrinko knew. How many times had he been out to the Desert? And each time it struck him as it had the first time—how little there was, how poor the people were. But he held firm. "No money from me, Aziz. No money from the Americans. Make it work on your own."

9

TWO YEARS LEFT

Exactly one year before General Allen's speech, in which he claimed Marefat students as family, soldiers at an airbase north of the capital discovered that Taliban prisoners had been passing messages back and forth in the pages of Qurans they'd borrowed from the prison library. This communication naturally needed to be stopped, so the soldiers set out to destroy the vessel containing the secret messages. They made a crucial misjudgment though, because rather than locking the books away or otherwise disposing of them quietly, they took the holy texts out to a trash heap where the rest of the base's garbage was being incinerated, and threw them in.

A few locals happened to see what was happening and their account quickly became public. The optics were unfortunate, this burning of Islam's holy text by American servicemen. It looked like oppression, a deliberate taunt. The qualifying details of prisoners and surreptitious messages and compromised security were all whittled away by the streamlining effect of a story taking flight, and what was left was one startling offense: the foreigners have pissed on our religion.

There is a kind of political man for whom an offense to a shared sensibility is a godsend. Here were these men whose power was derived solely from religion, people whose base was the faithful, the followers of Islam who follow nothing else. For that kind of men, especially those whose influence had waned, a grievous offense to Islam was a gift, a thing to react violently against, and in so doing build up one's own relevance.

So it was in Afghanistan. There was a mostly irrelevant body of clerics, the Supreme Council of the Islamic Clergy, whose job it was, theoretically, to keep President Karzai's dealings in line with the Prophet's teachings. It was a body the president had regarded with only the limpest of interest, a council that had, until then, been mostly ignored.

But when word got out that Americans had burned Islam's holy book, the Council was immediately relevant again, suddenly so suffused with influence it was like someone had turned on a fire hose and the elders had only to hold on, the rage aiming itself. The wrath of the uberfaithful spread from the American servicemen who had done the deed to the entire U.S. military, and then to the government back in the United States that had made this offense happen, to the entire foreign presence, and then, finally to the most offensive examples of that foreign presence: the Muslims who had accepted it

Who was worse than the Muslims who had given up their principles and sided with the foreigners, for their own selfish ends? Who had reveled in the intervention—these traitors who had adopted the foreigners' ideas and in so doing threatened to undermine the country's very foundation in Islam? So it was that the full force of this revulsion against the West found a perfect target: a little school out in the slums whose teachers and students had accepted the kind of men who would piss on Islam.

"They've banned our civic education!" was the subject of Aziz's frantic message. In the six years I'd known him, it was the first time I'd seen him lose his composure. The full force of his country's political elite was bearing down on his school. Drunk with righteous rage and flailing for targets, the Council had set its sights on Marefat. They had collected the textbooks Aziz had written for his students and then cherry-picked from them to find examples of how the school was anti-Islamic, pagan, secular, atheist. They'd charged Marefat with "preaching Christianity, Darwinism, and Protestantism," and condemned it as a place where "historical issues contrary to the

Islamic views" were discussed, as well as "human rights issues contrary to the Islamic belief." Aziz was guilty of "creating suspicion and doubt over monotheism," of "calling for religious pluralism," of "profane and immoral expressions about religious issues," and, most richly, of entertaining "complicated philosophical issues beyond the level of understanding."

The books were banned. The classes in which they were read and discussed were canceled. Coeducational activities, even extracurricular ones, were stopped immediately, until further notice.

Worse, Aziz had no recourse. The Americans, having ignited the wildfire, were in no position to intervene on the school's behalf; doing so would only fan the flames. A stance in defense of the school's values might spread the fervor more, and at least for now the radicals seemed content to focus their wrath only on the one school. The damage, in other words, could be confined to Aziz and his students, and as long as that was the case, no one would risk making the situation worse.

Nor could Aziz himself appeal to the Council. "They will not waste their time to hear me," he said. "They already know that my profane words will spoil their ears." The school was in the wilderness, their foreign protectors rendered impotent. This is what it felt like to be dispensable, to be abandoned by the people whose side you chose. Aziz was frantic because he knew the pressure would not stop here. This was just a preview of what would happen after the foreign forces left.

"I am worried about a civil war," he wrote, in the wake of the crackdown. "About the minorities who would suffer, and especially the women who will be brutally suppressed and, of course, in particular my own lovely optimistic students who have been too lovely to be forgotten."

The banning of books had been a grave setback, the beginning of the crisis Aziz had tried to will out of existence.

"Now, I have fourteen hundred girl students currently in the classes and hundreds more out of the school who all look at me asking what is going on, and what is to be done."

Aziz fell into an uncharacteristic depression, a period in which he wavered between a despair he had to hide from everyone around him and a frustration with the foreigners who, he now had to accept, would at some point—perhaps soon—abandon him after all. They would break their covenant, leave a job unfinished, and he and his students would suffer. "Should we all just escape the country now, while we can?" he asked. There was no obvious path forward.

But as Aziz says, in times of distress, when God gives you a locked door, be grateful it's not a wall. And as he struggled alone, unable to seek solace because his own put-on optimism was a beacon keeping the community from panic, he began to stumble toward a realization, a new clarity about the situation he faced, and maybe—just maybe—a way forward.

He began to see that as the withdrawal of foreign forces began, the clouds forming on the horizon warned of a coming political storm: that the oppression the Hazaras and the school were beginning to feel was a re-Talibanization but with one important distinction. Back then, extremists directed their rage against the government. Now, they were also directing their rage *through* it. There were extremists who weren't opposing the established political order, but were actually using it.

As the withdrawal began and fundamentalists became more emboldened, they would continue the process they'd just begun, of using the government as the rifle barrel with which to menace Aziz and the students, and anyone else whose sensibilities might be incompatible with their own. They'd use the government to bring Aziz and the students to their knees.

Maybe, then, they had to fight fire with fire. If the first battlefield was going to be a political one, then Aziz knew how to mobilize. He was a civil society leader, after all, who'd conjured an improbably successful school out of whole cloth, and in doing so he had launched his people on a crash course of social growth. Through sheer force of will and charisma the little man had propelled his people a few generations forward in less than the time it took one girl to go from kindergarten to college. If he could push an entire ethnic group to accept women's rights and fund a school when they hardly had enough money for food (or guns), than certainly he could manipulate the political system, too.

Yes, now he was on to something. His task came into focus: it was "vital to shift a little bit toward the political side of my work." He began thinking of "creating a network of like-minded friends." Yes, here it was, here was what he would do. He pulled together his council, and together they began to dream up their last stand, a kind of political O.K. Corral, where they would reach more young, active, energetic people than the fundamentalists could. To show that his ideas were better, what more evidence did one need than his students?

His students, though, were also his soft spot. If he became more visible, they would, too, and they would be exposed.

He would just have to find a way to make sure his students weren't more vulnerable as he took more risks.

He would make a last stand, one in time for the presidential election, scheduled for the year the foreign forces left.

He would become a politician.

10

THE MECHANIC

From the very beginning, he saw people like machines and machines like people.

When he got the job of dropping liquid into their mouths, he learned the exact place on a child's face that worked like a button: a little sudden pressure, just there, right below the pointy part of the jaw, would shock the child's mouth open. Then you could force the droplets in before the face could react.

If that didn't work, he learned how on a small enough face, you could use your two free fingers to press the child's nostrils closed, and if you held it there, the kid's eyes would bulge and its mouth would pop open to gulp at air, and you could get the drops in that way.

It was a cruel thing to do to kids, and he suspected that's why the doctor always made him leave his own village to do the work. Because if he came across children he knew, he might be inclined to spare them this punishment.

It's not that he didn't have a conscience. He was a harsh person, quick to anger, but he felt sorry for the kids. Even so, he had a family to support. He was a man now, already thirteen and too old to shy away from a job just because it was unpleasant. He had his own parents to worry about, and a brother who'd begun smoking the plant you were only supposed to use to soothe sickness.

He got the job of putting liquid into kids because he could read and he knew numbers. Which meant he could put the marks above the door of the houses he went into, etching them into the wood high enough that no one would see them if they weren't looking and a mischievous child couldn't reach the marks to mess up the fractions. That's how the people who came after him knew whether all the children in each house had received their punishment yet.

Not that learning numbers had been easy. No one went to schools, except once or twice a year when the people in foreign clothes came from the capital to do their audits. Then, all the parents sent all the kids to school and pretended that's what they always did.

Really, the only place to learn was the small mosque where the old man smacked you across the face if you forgot a verse.

He learned anyway. He was small and angry and had something to prove, so he went into the hills with the doctor whenever the doctor came around looking for henchmen. The doctor was so eager to get to all the kids in all the villages that Nasir assumed he harbored some kind of personal hatred for kids. Or maybe the doctor's bosses did. They were named "Yunos and Asef," or at least, that's what their names sounded like. Maybe they were business partners of some kind. Maybe they owned a company that made chemicals. Or maybe this was the name of a government organization, or even a country, although Nasir hadn't heard of any countries named after people.

Anyway, whoever it was Nasir was really working for, the job suited him. Even though he didn't like manhandling the faces, it was an outlet for the anger that had begun rising in him since he'd become a man. The elders picked on him because he was small and because he was different in some incalculable but certain way. They sensed it and he did, too: he didn't *belong* here. He'd been in the same village his whole life but felt like a foreigner. He hated being confined, by the hills on all sides and a community of uncurious people. He hated that there wasn't any connection to anything beyond the valley, and he hated that they didn't have real teachers.

Once, he marched all the way down to the provincial center to complain about the school, how they never had classes except when the men came from the capital, but no one took him seriously. He hated it all and had only the kids to take out his rage on. That was one thing he had some control over, a child's jaw.

Later, a shipment came in from Yunos and Asef. The doctor summoned all his henchmen and handed out light blue tank tops with dark lettering in a foreign script. "These are your uniforms," the doctor said. "This is 'Yunos and Asef,' in English." A foreign language, then—a connection to the world. Nasir studied the shirt until he could make out each individual letter, and place them together in his mind when he closed his eyes. He didn't know what it meant, only that it was the company he worked for. It wasn't quite "Yunos and Asef," just "Yunos Sef. U-N-I-C-E-F was how it was spelled in English. It was one word, but a connection to a different place, and like the first taste of a wonderful new drug, he wanted more of the thrill.

The shipment had come with illustrated booklets, and the doctor talked them through what it all meant. For the first time, Nasir understood what he had been doing all this time. These pictures are of bugs, the doctor explained. Tiny ones you couldn't see, but that could steal the movement from a child. And the drops you are forcing into kids are weapons against these bugs. This was pleasing to Nasir: fighting a tiny war against an enemy you could never see. It was a relief to learn there was good in this man he had thought so cruel. Good in himself, too, good he'd never before seen, but now knew was there.

He learned the mechanisms by which a person might be convinced that this small torture had a purpose. When he went into a house where there were more children than the parents were presenting, he could explain as convincingly as anyone how they were trying to fight a tiny bug that would hurt the child, and hurt his parents, too, because it was so hard to take care of a child who couldn't move.

When the Taliban reached his village, they saw the vaccines the way Nasir had first seen them, as the senseless tormenting of children. They saw more, too. The people carrying out this cruelty were not just tormenters of children but spies. The Taliban couldn't be convinced that it was a good thing for the people. The books with the pictures of the tiny bug didn't move them. They wanted to put a stop to it, and when the doctor tried to defy them and do it in secret, they responded without mercy. Nasir ached when he heard that people he'd worked with had been killed. The doctor, who for so long Nasir had thought was a cruel and spiteful old man, but who he now understood had driven himself to exhaustion protecting children, was taken away, and never returned. No one knew what happened to him.

The Talibs kept getting more violent, and soon he began to hate life under them more than he had hated life under the simpleminded elders who'd been in charge before.

When they left, piling into Datsuns and driving off into the hills, Americans came to replace them. They gave out jobs building roads, and he got work on a team manning the stone drill. It was a good fit for a boy with his mechanical instincts. If he needed proof, he got it on the first day, when the equipment broke down. The team was paid per kilometer, so they were working faster and longer than the drill was meant to run, and now with every second it stood idle, everyone lost money. A worker banged on it, another peered importantly around its corners and then gave up. They were all resigned to wait for some other authority to come and tell them what to do.

Nasir decided to try. He walked over to the drill, the first engine he'd ever seen. He found a seam in the metal and traced his finger along it—it was a kind of lid. He pried it off, and the machine opened up to him like it was confessing. In his imagination it was saying *I need to breathe*, and though he didn't then know what any of the parts were, he could see there was a screen full of fine stone dust. It looked like a filter that should allow air through but was blocked, and he imagined a person with a scarf pulled too tight over his nose and mouth. He thought of the children: if you covered one way for air to get in, another one opened up because if there was no way for air to get in, the child would die. Everything worked in the same way, he thought, people or machines. He reached in and wiped the filter off and then put all the pieces back in their correct order. He asked the foreman to try it again; the machine coughed and chugged and rumbled back to life.

He could handle any machine, he decided, anywhere.

He got a wife. He couldn't resist anymore. His parents needed help in the house and his sisters had all married and moved in with their husbands. But his wife had friends down in the city, so he decided that marriage was his chance to get out of this place. He tried to convince his family to stop worrying themselves with so many petty land disputes and instead sell everything and come with him, but they held firm. And he was relieved. Money from selling the land would have helped get him on his feet, but caring for his whole family in a new city was a daunting prospect. With them at home, at least he only needed to worry about himself and his wife. And that would be hard enough. Two years after the Americans came, he moved with his wife to Kabul.

Renting a house came first. They had almost no money, just what Nasir had been able to save working the drill for the Americans. And with all the foreigners pouring into the city, landlords had more demand than they knew what to do with. Nasir was small, he spoke like he was forcing air through a teakettle, and he looked like a boy. At sixteen years old he *was* a boy. Landlords dismissed him; they said he was probably a runaway. He walked with a bounce that looked like a swagger if you didn't know better, so he came off as a hothead who'd taken a girl for love and made off for the city. He swallowed his pride and moved in with his wife's family. Still, he needed cash, and he asked around until a cousin who'd been living in the capital for a few years already came up with something. "There's a well we're digging at a school out near Dry Bridge," he said. "It's way out in the Desert though and it's hard work, it might be too much for you." Nasir showed up the next day at dawn.

The work site was in the middle of nowhere, far out in the Desert where there was nothing as far as he could see. It looked like a mistake. Why would anyone build this far away from everything? There was a handwritten poster on the wall of the only building for a mile in any direction: IN THE NAME OF GOD, OF KNOWLEDGE, FREE-DOM AND EQUALITY. This was not how he'd learned about God in his village.

There was a contrast, though, that struck him immediately: the building was no more impressive than what they'd had in the village—nothing but a few low-slung mud-brick rooms arranged around a courtyard that hadn't been cleaned or paved. But the students were a perfect picture of order. It was striking: they stood bolt-straight in neat lines and conveyed a seriousness he'd never seen in a student be-fore, let alone hundreds of them.

"Dig, boy!" His cousin yelled. He tried to work but couldn't stop staring. He'd never in his life seen anything so choreographed be-fore. So many people, doing the exact same thing. He'd never seen so many people in one place, period.

As he dug, a teacher took the podium and faced the students, and the whole assembly, nearly a thousand students, began singing. An anthem of some sort, but not a national anthem—it was about learning, as far as he could understand, but the words didn't much matter to him anyway. Hearing hundreds of voices in unison—it stirred him. In that moment, as he was digging the well and listen-ing to the students sing, he felt something inside him shift, and he decided he never wanted to leave this place.

Nasir saw another man walk to the front to face the students, a short man with a close-cropped, jet-black beard.

"Welcome, sir," the students said. And then, in perfect unison, "May you not be tired." When the short man addressed the students, he spoke in a way Nasir had never heard a teacher address students before. There was no anger in his voice. He was soft. Later, Nasir watched him in a classroom with the smallest kids, teaching them word by word and waiting patiently until they understood. That whole day, Nasir didn't see a teacher hit a student. He listened to a geography lesson in a room near the well. The teacher was an old man in a big white turban, hard of hearing so that when he tried to whisper, he spoke; when he tried to speak, he yelled. As Nasir dug outside, he could hear every word the teacher said inside the classroom.

When the students filed past him on their way home, he braced.

They were surely wealthy kids and he was just a worker, so he prepared for their ridicule. He'd have to contain himself. He was quick to anger, and yelling at a student would cost him a job he held only tenuously. But every child who walked by smiled at him. Even the small boys greeted him and called him sir. He'd never seen anything like it.

It took a week—a week in which the well was finished and he convinced the workers to let him stay on and help with the sewer—before he realized that all along, boys and girls had been together. The girls, even with their headscarves, didn't look like girls in the village. Here, they wore pants and shirts that went down around their knees, so at the morning lineup, he'd always just assumed it was boys on one side, and differently dressed boys on the other. Boys wearing untucked shirts and head covers, for warmth, maybe.

He had a lot to learn about life in this new city.

At Marefat no one seemed to tell anyone else what to do. The students lined up in perfect rows, without anyone he could see instructing them.

There were big kids, too. One looked like an adult, lined up with the second graders, so when Nasir had the chance, he asked. The man said he was twenty years old, Asef was his name. Like Yunos and Asef. He'd been in Pakistan for most of the war years and the Taliban times, too, he said, so he was going to school for the first time since the war years began. He was a quiet man, but didn't seem at all ashamed to be with the kids

There was a Pashtun teacher in the midst of all these Hazaras, and no one appeared to be bothered by this. Back in the village, he'd hardly seen Pashtuns, except for the Taliban. Every time Pashtuns came up in conversation, everyone seemed angry, so he swore he'd kill them when he grew up. What he knew of Pashtuns from the village is that they believed themselves to be better than Hazaras, and that they all believed Hazaras were worthy only of being slaves. But here was a Pashtun, gentle and kind and content, it seemed, to be surrounded by Hazaras. Working for Hazaras. Not just working for Hazaras, but for Hazara children.

Later, after he had worked at Marefat for a year, he resolved that when he had his own kids they should not know that they were Hazara. Not until they'd lived long enough without race that the very idea would feel distant and pointless. They should not know what religion they were either, because that way, they wouldn't care that it was different from others. They would grow up to think that when people killed each other over these things—when people felt the way their father had—it was very sad, but also very stupid.

The short man with the jet-black beard came by to check on the progress of the sewer. He was engaged by the project, he lingered with the look of a proud parent watching a child, and Nasir decided to seize the moment. "Sir, I'd like a job here." His cousin glared. The teacher cocked his head sideways and took Nasir in.

"You're a boy. You'll hurt yourself if you do this work all the time."

"No, I'm a man. I'm strong. I'll have children soon."

"You should do some easy jobs, soft jobs. We will find a way to pay you a little."

So Nasir found ways to make himself useful. He carried water from a public well to fill water tanks for the students. He became a watchman, keeping an eye on bicycles the students rode to school. He cleaned the classrooms at the end of the day, and he made himself an apprentice to the man in charge of the school's generator, a machine bigger even than the stone drill back in the village. He was scared of it in the beginning, but he closely watched what the man in charge was doing, so when that man left for another job two months later, Nasir was ready to take over.

After the generator, it was the copy machines that fascinated him most. Whenever he finished his chores, he stood behind them and watched the lights moving back and forth inside. One day, Aziz's brother was making copies and saw Nasir standing there. "I'm in a rush," he said. "Do you think you could do me a favor and finish these copies for me?"

So he did. When another teacher came, Nasir offered to handle his copies, too. Soon he was offering to handle copies for every teacher who came by. It fulfilled a sense of mission in him. Teachers were busy with the important tasks, they should be spending their time with children, not making copies.

And when the copier broke, he learned to fix it, so the school no longer needed to spend money and lose time taking it downtown. Soon he was fixing everything at the school. He was a small but important piece of the machine, taking the load from other parts so the whole thing could move better.

11

NINE MONTHS LEFT

Late in the morning of May 1, 2013, a 747-400 jumbo jet lifted off from an airfield just north of the capital into a thick cloud cover, as a thunderstorm threatened. Four pilots were on board, along with two mechanics and a loadmaster.

Shortly after takeoff, the plane's nose pitched up sharply. This was not an uncommon maneuver at this airfield, where pilots used steep angles to avoid rockets from shoulder-mounted launchers. But this jet's angle was especially severe, and the plane began a rapid loss of airspeed without correcting.

When it stalled, it seemed, for a moment, to hang weightless in the air. Then it nodded gently to its left, overcorrected to the right, and fell from the sky.

To those on the ground, the last six seconds before it crashed were a small eternity, enough time for the plane to right itself just before impact, yawing its wings back into perfect alignment with the ground before slamming down and erupting in a giant fireball, shock orange, then ink black as billows of burning jet fuel unspooled over the crash site. The Taliban immediately claimed responsibility. The timing was perfect; they had just announced the beginning of their "spring offensive," an annual ritual in which they promised to ac-

celerate the tempo of attacks, as the spring thaw opened roads that had been impassable for months.

But the plane crash hadn't been because of a rocket strike or any kind of bomb planted on board. The way the plane had pitched up suddenly, then stalled, betrayed what really happened: a sudden shift in the center of gravity, as if the rear of the plane suddenly became much heavier, like a large person falling into the back of a canoe. It didn't take long before investigators confirmed the cause of the crash: the plane was brought down not by an attack at all but by the cargo it was removing from the country, five military vehicles with heavy armor plating had come loose and rolled toward the back. It had been a self-inflicted wound, a symbolic beginning to the Outsiders' departure. A spectacular confirmation, just as the Taliban announced their offensive was beginning, that the Outsiders were really leaving.

In the aftermath of this spectacle the school had a crisis of a more minor sort: a group of boys and girls were seen spending an afternoon together in a part of the city people went to for picnics. A student uninvited on this particular outing saw the group fraternizing and reported back to the school. The teachers met and decided that this was just the kind of breakdown in decorum that, these days, could endanger students, so Aziz summoned them into a meeting and came down hard. He forbade them from ever again spending time together outside of school, and to show he was serious, he stripped one of the boys of his seat on the student council.

One of the girls erupted: "You have no right to do this! You don't have any legal authority over us when we're not in school, and we weren't even wearing our school uniforms. You can't just police all of our lives!"

Aziz turned his attention to the girls. "Remember, when you do something like this, it harms your own reputation." It was a cheap shot, but he had to demand more restraint from the girls than the boys, and "reputation" was the quickest way to remind them. "It doesn't just harm your own reputation," he said. "It harms your family's honor and it puts the school at risk."

"It's hypocritical, sir," the girl said. "You can't tell us who we

can be with and punish us for what we do on our own time. *You* always tell us how important our free choice is, how it's the most important thing for us to have free choice—"

"No," Aziz interrupted. "That's wrong." The girl recoiled. "The first priority for you girls is being safe. If free choice causes problems with that, then free choice is no good."

The girl became quiet. This was a seismic shift they were witnessing. For as long as they'd been at this school, Aziz had been an emancipator. He'd shown that they should be independent and never let anyone tell them otherwise. Now *he* was telling them otherwise. He was reaching into their lives and holding them back himself.

Aziz knew that he was taking the pressure mounting outside the walls of Marefat and channeling it onto the girls. He had no other choice. The foreign forces were really leaving—that had just been made spectacularly clear. At first he hadn't believed that they ever would, or that they'd leave behind an enemy still growing in strength, one with a grudge against collaborators like him and his students. Then he'd tried feebly to forestall it, begging every American he could reach to reconsider this departure. But one man alone shouts only so long with no reply before he must accept that no one is listening. While he was venturing out to try to make alliances with the country's political leaders, he had to prepare his students for what came next: a world without protectors. For the students, that preparation would have to mean retreat. Especially for the girls. If he was going to walk out onto the battlefield of national politics, he had to push the girls back into their seats, even though he had always been the one pushing them to stand up and yell.

It was a movement that started as many movements do: a long, simmering frustration that could have been set off by anything, so that the spark that finally ignited it was almost arbitrary.

At the county's biggest university, Hazaras were angry. For years they'd been punished by discriminatory policies, low grades, professors ridiculing them in class. Hazara girls reported being harassed, brought into their instructors' offices and threatened with expulsion if they didn't submit to sexual advances. Hazaras, both male and fe-

male, felt that they were being punished for their ambition, that their professors were trying to open up more seats for other ethnic groups by making college so miserable for Hazaras that they'd simply drop out.

For Hazaras, the experience of going to college had become deflating. Aside from the punishment they received for just being Hazara, the professors often used no textbooks, and instead printed Web pages, or recycled essays from other students, or from their own days as students. Many of the professors were utterly unqualified to teach anything, let alone be university professors. The library was sparse. The Internet never worked.

College was supposed to be a culmination of years of studying for ultra-competitive exams. Instead, they had left home, traveled to the capital, many of them for the first time, and then found, as their reward at the end of this journey, homemade "textbooks" and racist professors.

Aziz had always been sad about how poor the country's universities were, and how demoralizing attending them was for his students. It's what had made the task he'd taken on seem so insurmountable: even if Marefat managed to turn a generation of Hazaras into confident young men and women, when they graduated, they would run into a wall. Marefat graduates complained about Kabul University all the time. He watched some of his favorite students graduate full of vigor and return pallid and aged, ready to quit. This was why he'd begun dreaming of Marefat University—a university out in the slums for the poorest people. Not a project he could take on anytime soon, but a fantasy he entertained every time a Marefat alum came to him and said she'd been called a flat-nose or a mouse-eater in class.

For these circumstances, he had no good advice. If he told the students to confront the professors, he knew what the professors would say: "So, child, if you don't like it, why don't you leave?"

It was the most intense kind of frustration for the Hazara students. When there is no higher authority to complain to—when higher authority itself is pulling against you—then either you're defeated, or you resort to something extreme. So after the April exam period, when an improbably high proportion of Hazara students were given failing grades, they snapped.

There were eighty-eight of them at first. They crowded between university buildings holding up signs printed out on copy paper. NO TO PREJUDICE and NO TO DISCRIMINATION, in large type. The signs were unimpressive, but together, in three different languages—Farsi, Pashto, and English—they made for a compelling optic.

They were announcing to the country that they were fed up and they had specific demands: The removal of the dean of the social sciences department—the students called him an unrepentant racist with a vendetta against Hazaras. The removal of a lecturer who had harassed Hazara girls and failed Hazara students without justification. An improved Internet connection. An improved library.

As the students began to protest, the minister of higher education put out a statement: "I'm sorry the students are upset that they failed but you can't improve your scores, no matter how long you protest."

One of the protesters fired back: "Forty out of seventy students, that's 60 percent of the class," he told a local newspaper, "all of them from one ethnic group, were told they failed an examination. That can't be anything other than intentional discrimination by the professor during the calculation of grades."

So they marched and chanted, and they gathered in front of Parliament yelling out their demands. Then they took it one step further: if there was no way to make anyone feel their pain, they would make their own pain more visible. They put down carpets in front of Parliament and declared themselves on hunger strike. They wouldn't eat until their concerns had been addressed and the offending professors had been fired.

The first offer from the government made its way through the students: suspend the professor for ten days. The students rejected it immediately. They remained, out in the heat, for two days, then three, without any indication that anybody was taking them seriously. They'd planned to have tents, but security personnel said the tents presented a security risk. The students saw that as a negotiating tactic, since it was upward of 90 degrees each day and someone must have figured that without shade, the students wouldn't last as long.

Then another blow: a separate group of students staged a counterprotest in order to undermine the Hazaras. They said that the strikers were just lazy ethnocentric students who blamed professors for their own shortcomings, that the university was already overrun with Hazaras, and they didn't want any more. Some had signs with slogans calling the Hazara students puppets of Iran.

Three days into the hunger strike, they were isolated, and their demands were still being ignored. It looked like a handful of Hazaras trying to take on the whole country. But they knew that no matter who turned against them, they had at least one important person on their side. If there was one person whose support they could count on, it was Aziz Royesh. Indeed, Aziz was soon to arrive on the scene.

With precisely the opposite of the message they expected.

On the sixth day, Aziz saw on the news that some of the students' health had taken a grave turn. Some of the kids had blood in their urine; others had lost consciousness and were taken to the hospital, where, they later reported, they were denied treatment or charged exorbitant fees.

It was clear now that the students were serious. They intended to stay out there until their demands were met, or until they died.

Aziz worried. Just as the foreign forces were leaving, this demonstration was calling attention to the kind of emotionally charged issue that could put them all on a path to disaster. If just one student fell into a coma or died, which now seemed possible, even imminent, the narrative would be a Hazara student dying because of mistreatment by another ethnic group. There were Hazara leaders looking to exploit just that kind of opportunity. If ethnic tensions boiled over and his people felt threatened, they were liable to rally behind their strongmen—he'd seen it before. There were Hazara leaders who thrived when Hazaras were scared or humiliated, leaders who offered bravado, and legacies of violence, and the prospect of pride. These people would do their best to inflame tensions. But Aziz was sure these leaders couldn't actually protect Hazaras. Hazaras had disarmed, and the foreigners who once had their backs were leaving. These leaders were capable of leading Hazaras to war, but not of actually fighting. The students believed that they were safe because all they were doing was standing up for the rights they'd been told to stand up for since the Americans first came. Aziz saw that clearly. And he knew they were wrong. If the students sparked a fire, they would burn.

So when he went to see them, he did not tell them what they wanted to hear.

"Your life is the most important thing," he said. "You're foolish to endanger that, for *anything*. Look, at college, you are studying so that you can make your life better. Why would you risk that with this foolish action?"

The students couldn't believe what they were hearing. Their own most radical activist advising them to conform. "There are two red lines," Aziz said. "Don't ask me to support you if you are crossing any one of these lines. One is your life. The other is your studies. I will not help you if you are endangering either of these two things." For the second time in a month, students stared at Aziz like they no longer recognized him.

He knew they were right, though. The only way to finally change how Hazara students were treated was by doing something extreme. But if he gave them the encouragement they wanted, he'd be walking them into a disaster that might be impossible to contain. When a group of defenseless people believe moral authority is cleaved entirely from actual authority, they've entered a dangerous place. "Look at the price you're paying," Aziz said. "You might harm your body, and already you aren't well-nourished people. We Hazaras are still poor, we are not well nourished to begin with, now you are starving yourselves. If one of you dies here it will spark fighting, and it will be catastrophe for our people."

He had a vision of himself at their age, twenty years before. Aziz had emerged from the civil war with guns still blazing. Even though he was in Pakistan and the fighting was in Afghanistan, he regarded everyone he encountered as an enemy, and honor was in firing at all of them, his own well-being be damned. Even his family's safety hadn't merited a second thought after he'd brought them across the border. The civil war had destroyed his country, it had destroyed many of his friends, and his mentor, Grandfather Mazeri, had died a violent death as a prisoner of the Taliban. And as the Taliban took over the country, he was forced to flee next door and cower with his wife and children.

He was angry, hurt, embarrassed. For all of it—all the cursed things that had happened around him during the war—he blamed religious people. All of them: he didn't discriminate, they were all fanatics. Everything that had happened was the fault of believers; it was the fault of *belief*. He took to rebuking religion just as fervently as he'd once taken to mastering it. He'd once poured himself into the holy book so that he could call himself a scholar of it, but in exile with his family in Pakistan, he used all that knowledge to knock the legs out from under the clerics. He published a periodical and wrote articles in which he lobbed insults at Iran, the Ayatollah, Pashtuns, even other Hazaras who were too consumed with foolish superstitions.

"I'll pay $50,000 to anyone who kills Teacher Aziz." That's what a Hazara warlord had said—an important man not known for making idle threats, a man as shrouded in the mythology of wartime exploits as he was actually shrouded in the layered robes he wore to show off his status. He was just now making the rounds through the striking college students, looking for ways to inflame the tensions even more. Back in his exile years, Aziz would have been happy to be martyred if that was the fate throwing stones at giants brought him. So he threw stones at giants. He was angry all the time, and his only salve was in attack. Back then it felt like success, to make so many people so angry, and even though he had no clear purpose in doing it, he had no doubt he was doing right.

But now, he saw all of it as wasted energy, wasted time. He looked back at himself and thought, "I was not even a good person." He had believed that if you risked your life doing something, it made that thing worth doing, rather than the other way around. It was a perverse way to carry himself, especially because there was family involved. It made him shudder to think how stupidly lucky he'd been to not have been killed, to not have had one of his children killed. Simple stupid fragile fucking luck. He had emboldened old enemies and made himself new ones, and he hadn't changed anyone's mind about anything, because he wasn't actually doing anything for his own people by lobbing grenades at others.

Until finally he understood: you can aim at enemies hundreds of miles away, but if you don't change the people right there in front of you, nothing, nothing, ever changes. There was a saying he'd hear later, after he'd come full circle. A warning about "the man who wages war against the whole kingdom, when he doesn't have any wheat at home." His own people, Hazaras, were in exile and they were hurting, while he was busy with an ill-aimed offensive, attacking religion wherever he detected it. So when another exile came to him with the idea of a small tutoring center for other refugees, it may have saved Aziz. He was finally ready to look inward, having exhausted himself attacking. That's when he began to regard his nickname as a sacred charge, to be adhered to with devotion; to be taken literally. *Teacher Aziz.*

In the midst of a hundred Hazara students starving themselves, he's becoming Teacher again.

As he answers the questions the students ask of him, he finds he's answering questions for himself, too. He doesn't want to be an activist, a revolutionary, a writer, a provocateur. Though he's been all those things and still is, it's not what he wants, not really.

Really, what he wants is just to teach.

And he knows it's hypocritical to tell the students that putting themselves at risk for their beliefs is foolish, but he's frightened for them. They're not as indestructible as they think they are. Just as he wasn't. And he's not as revolutionary as he used to be. Because now he understands that it's not just their own lives they're putting on the line, just as he finally understands that it was never only his.

He leaves the group of protest leaders, after having issued his instructions to them, and as he leaves, he hears behind him an aide to one of the Hazara warlords saying to the students, "Teacher Aziz is a traitor. Don't listen to him, he's trying to stop your protest because he's working for the fascist Pashtuns."

Well, so be it. If he could get these kids to avoid a fight they would lose, maybe being called a traitor was an acceptable price. He is satisfied he'd gotten his message through, however difficult it had been for them to hear.

He hadn't. After his intervention, the college students raised the stakes even more. "If our demands aren't met," they said in a statement, "we will burn ourselves in front of the Ministry of Higher Education."

Aziz immediately got a message to the protest's leaders: "Make no mistake," he said. "This kind of suicide attack won't be any different from the Taliban."

The Hazara students had become zealots. No one was going to walk them back. *The only way this won't end in disaster,* he thought, *is if somehow, by some miracle, they get what they want.* He didn't see how that could possibly happen. He needed help.

There is a group of leaders Aziz has been meeting with for several months now. This group prefers to be a shadowy agglomeration of people from each ethnic group and all religions, bound by a loosely defined but unquestioned need for secrecy. Not quite secret handshakes and passwords, but close. Membership is by a special nomination process Aziz has only recently completed. He's come to be hopeful about this group of people, because they are all educated, or at least, they are intellectuals, all people he considers deep thinkers. He was surprised, when he was first asked to come and speak to them, that something like it had existed right under his nose without his knowledge. The G-72 they call themselves, as in the G-8 or the G-9: in this case, seventy-two Afghan civil society leaders.

There aren't yet seventy-two of them, still closer to fifty or so, but Aziz has come to regard the people in the G-72 as potentially invaluable for Marefat's security. He just didn't realize he'd need to call on them so soon.

He called the member who had nominated him, and who quickly

understood the gravity of the crisis that was unfolding: that there were Hazaras who were likely trying, even as Aziz and his G-72 colleague spoke, to turn the protest into an ethnic confrontation. And that if that happened, it could in short order reach a level of intensity that Aziz, despite being a Hazara leader himself, would be powerless to stop. She told him she had an idea, a friend of hers who might be able to help, because he was a person of some influence, a senior adviser to the president. The man she had in mind was a Pashtun, but she said he'd likely see the strikers not as aggrieved Hazaras but as aggrieved students. He was himself an academic, with a Ph.D. from a fancy university in the United States, and not only that, he'd once been a professor at Kabul University, and a chancellor there as well. For Aziz, the prospect of allying himself with a Pashtun at this moment would be a risk; it meant giving the Hazaras trying to further inflame tensions ammunition with which to make Aziz look compromised. His people were in crisis, and he'd be seen as consorting with the enemy.

He'd have to risk it. He asked her to arrange the meeting.

Ashraf Ghani was dressed in tribal clothing when Aziz arrived at his compound. His gray goatee followed his jawline up to a horseshoe of hair around the back of his head, and his forehead gleamed; he looked dignified. When he spoke, it was with a powerful voice, and when he laughed, it was one of those cracking, from-the-diaphragm laughs that's always more powerful than you're prepared for, a laugh that shakes the room. His voice often rose in pitch when answering, so he sounded contemplative, with a little hitch in his breath when he needed a moment to think. But Ashraf Ghani rarely needed to think for long: he had facts and figures he could conjure up so quickly and with such unnatural specificity it seemed he was making them up on the spot. He met with Aziz for just fifteen minutes, but gave the problem his complete attention. Aziz briefed him about the danger to the students, but also explained that there were others—"my people," Aziz said—who were trying to escalate this standoff into something much bigger. Soon, Aziz explained, it wouldn't just be students asking the university for concessions. It would be Hazaras rallying against

Pashtuns. Or students rallying against the very idea of authority. It would be a peeling off of society from government, and it would start to look something like rebellion. The Pashtun seemed to be listening intently.

Just thirty minutes after he left the meeting, Aziz received a call from President Karzai's national security adviser. "Ashraf Ghani just called and spoke with the president," he said. "The president is concerned. He wants to resolve this immediately."

That very afternoon, President Karzai's adviser arrived at the scene of the strike, along with the minister of higher education, to address the students. The minister issued a short statement. "Today, all your demands are accepted," he said. "They will be implemented tomorrow. So we are requesting that you all end your strike and return to your dorms."

A few days later, after the strikers had packed up and gone home, satisfied they'd brought about some justice, a parliamentary commission quietly issued a statement. They reviewed "university documents," they said, and decided that the students' claims were false.

The dismissed faculty members were reinstated.

12

THE ASTRONOMER

Yunos Bakshi arrives at the television studio exactly on time.

The room is less impressive than he expected. When he'd seen it on television, it seemed more modern, red paint and flashing lights and anchors walking around with shiny white teeth and bright white porcelain-doll faces. Instead he finds the room dark and small. And eerily quiet: where is the prebroadcast commotion?

Still, it can't dim his excitement. He's been given a cause for wonder in the midst of an ominous time. A satellite launched forty years ago has just left the solar system, the first ever manmade object to do so. Imagining the machine going out into the unknown quickens his pulse. Like standing on top of a building and looking up even higher above you, there's that one dizzying moment when you feel more connected to what's up there than what you're standing on.

A young man takes him by the elbow and shows him to the anchor desk, helps him get settled, and hands him a pair of headphones. Yunos sits down, puts them on, and hears someone in London, four thousand miles away, speaking as if he were right there in the Kabul studio sitting next to Yunos.

Yunos knows he will be speaking to an audience unreceptive to what he has to say, because in his country, learning is still mostly about memorizing things and yelling them back at a teacher. He knows that these are not the ripest minds for wonderment. But there are exceptions, and that pulls him along. He's due at Marefat tomorrow to teach a class about the stars—Marefat is one of the exceptions. But what he sees on the mean is another superstitious generation coming of age, and he's doing his part to inject curiosity wherever he can: an on-air interview; a trip up to the provinces with his telescope to spread the gospel; translating astronomy textbooks into his country's languages.

It's not easy, of course. Looking up through a big expensive lens feels frivolous when down here people are shooting each other, or doing frenzied attempts to contend with a convulsing economy, as prices keep rising and rising. Not many people have time for the cosmos. That's why today is such a special occasion. the BBC's Farsi-language TV station has identified this contraption leaving the solar system as important and potentially even interesting. And since Yunos has become known around here as perhaps the one person in this country who can talk about such matters—if only in a slightly hysterical, town-crier kind of way—they've called him in to comment.

But there's a problem. They want him to talk about the telescope, but they have no idea where to begin; they don't even know what questions to ask. "So, Mr. Bakshi," a producer says, "do you have any . . . suggestions, for what we should ask you?" Then he qualifies: "Just because, you know, we don't want to repeat anything you've already said."

"It means the first human telescope has crossed the Sun's bundle of magnetic forces," Yunos says, corralling his excitement once the cameras start rolling. "It left the forces around the Sun, the Sun's kingdom, we might call it. It's left the solar system. It's a man-made satellite, and it's now ninety million kilometers away from us."

This idea, how *far* it is, is especially thrilling to him. "It takes more than a year for the messages the telescope sends to reach us here on Earth."

"And I understand," the man in London says, "that one of the instruments Voyager 1 used to communicate doesn't work? So how do we know where it is?" This is a question Yunos had fed him.

"That's right," Yunos says. "It's called a plasma probe antenna, and it broke years ago. So now scientists use the time interval. The time between each signal we receive from the telescope. That tells us how far away the satellite is, and any change in the time between signals tells us that the density of the matter around Voyager has changed. That's how we know Voyager has left the Sun's realm and entered the interstellar medium, where gas is denser. That's how we know it's left the solar system."

The next day, Yunos drives out to the Desert for a series of special astronomy classes at Marefat. He's always found solace in the stars, but they've become an important diversion from what's happening around him in the last months. Now, on the drive out to the school, he's on the phone trying to gather information about a cousin who's missing. It's not clear yet what exactly happened, but it seems that in trying to escape to Australia, this cousin, along with a wife and two kids, boarded a boat carrying other refugees. It's the same cousin who took Yunos in, back when Yunos had finally arrived in Iran sixteen years before, after his own long harrowing escape, having burned through the last of his cash and barely avoided capture on a string of illegal border crossings.

No one has heard from his cousin in weeks, and Yunos understands that this is the time to start accepting the possibility that his cousin and the whole family have drowned.

"This place where the boat went down, it's 1.3 kilometers deep," says a friend on the phone, who has managed to get more information. "It's the deepest part of the Pacific, and it's muddy. The federal police in Australia told me the place where the boat went down, but they said they didn't send the divers. They said it's useless to look for the boat, because it's so hard to see down there. I think they probably won't ever go."

Yunos had been angry when he first heard that his cousin might have bought his way on board. These desperate pathetic Hazaras, it was the constant folly of the migrant to go where his tribe had gone before, regardless of what really awaited him there. These days no Hazaras wanted to go to Pakistan since they kept getting killed there, and in Iran, Hazaras were punished every time anti-immigrant sentiment flared up. No one wanted to come back to Afghanistan. When they couldn't get legal documents to live anywhere better, all these people were giving up everything they had, traveling to Indonesia or Malaysia, and piling into overcrowded trawlers for Australia. They kept sinking. People kept going anyway. His people simply believed, in the absence of all evidence, that it would be better for them.

To Yunos it is just an expensive, elaborate way to die.

He hears all he can bear. He hangs up and is silent for a while.

He decides to change the subject.

"My son asked for pork yesterday!" he says, and laughs. "I said, 'Where did you even *hear* about pork!'" His pride is barely veiled. His son is growing up to be a determined little infidel just like Yunos, pork being forbidden in Islam. To Yunos, each one of his son's heresies is a small victory in his ongoing resistance against the religious police ruling his own home: his wife and his mother. They've joined forces against him, and put forth a pitched offensive to turn the kids into believers.

They have, most recently, made a spirited stance on the matter of circumcision. This, Yunos believes to be a shameful defeat; to him, circumcision is an unnecessarily savage ritual that has only to do with superstition, but to the fascist sisterhood ruling his home a foreskin running loose in the house is a direct insult to God. And so, deciding it was a losing battle and chalking it up to the million domestic compromises a man makes to keep the peace, Yunos relented in the battle over his son's penis.

Which is why, in its immediate aftermath, he allows himself a moment of pride that the boy has, inspiringly, learned about a food forbidden by their religion and demanded it be brought to him. Yunos will surely be blamed for whispering in his son's ear, and the women will say, "What's next, you infidel, will you give the child that alcohol you drink? Will you take him with you and your addicted friends to smoke hash and opium like you do?" But that's a matter to be dealt with later.

On the second floor of the girls' building at Marefat, a few hundred students have crowded into a small room for assemblies. A man from the audiovisual department hands Yunos a microphone. He tests it, and begins:

"This is a picture of the moon," he says, wasting no time. "It's just a rock, right? Such an inept looking thing, it just sits there. But do you know how important it is?"

Yunos has always been astounded by Marefat, ever since he first heard of it. For his own education he had to go to the Soviet Union, and the fact that now almost four thousand of his people were getting such a fine education in their own country, even if it is all the way out here, amazes him.

"If there were no moon," he says, "there would be no life on Earth. Or at least, life would be much different. The moon steadies Earth's rotation." He begins a series of examples that match the slides he's showing. "There are barnacles on the seafloor. They need water to live. But did you know that they also need air? There is a kind of fish that makes a tube in the mud in the ocean during high tide so that smaller fish go in. Then when the tide goes out, the small fish are trapped and become food! Or, look. There are crabs that live and climb on roots under the water, but the roots need air for part of the day to survive. All of those animals depend on the tide coming in and out," he says. "Whole food chains wouldn't exist without this thing: the tide. And there would be no tide without the moon."

The students are attentive, but he can tell what he's saying is distant. He remembers: he's in the Desert, it's likely no one in the room has ever seen the ocean.

He tries a different approach. "Okay, look," he says, pointing to a new animation up on the screen, "so this is how the moon was created. See: two planets crash into each other. And Earth survived, but lots of debris left Earth's gravity when these two planets crashed. Some of the pieces came together and became the moon."

He looks back at the students to gauge their interest. "But here's the mysterious thing," he says, laying it on thick now, as if the moon were a suspect in a whodunit. "Back then, the moon was 241,400 kilometers away. Now, it's 366,000 kilometers away. It's getting farther from us."

He speaks for almost two hours, and afterward, he goes down

to Aziz's office to tell him how it went. He has an afterglow from imparting knowledge and isn't quite ready to stop sharing.

"You know, without the moon," he tells Aziz, "Earth would spin so fast that instead of twenty-four hours in a day, the day would only be four hours long. Imagine that. We'd have to sleep two hours. And then do everything else in two hours."

Aziz has his hands in his pockets, and is smiling politely.

"And also, if the day was only four hours, think about how strong the winds would be, if Earth was moving that fast! It would be too loud; we couldn't speak to each other. It would be a supersonic wind, it would take off the surface of Earth! Trees would all lie down. So you know, without the moon, a creature could only survive if it could figure out how to deal with that."

Aziz listens attentively, head cocked to the side. There is a respect between them, but a sliver of tension they've never quite dispensed with. Aziz sees Yunos as smart and genial, but careless. Yunos doesn't have to worry about being seen as an unbeliever; Aziz always has to. Aziz is under a microscope. Yunos can do whatever he wants, without a community of people looking at him to set an example. Yunos sees Aziz as deserving of admiration, but not quite the leader others see him. More as an entrepreneur: *Aziz must be making money hand over fist,* Yunos thinks. *There are almost four thousand people going to his school, how much does each pay? Why didn't I think of starting my own school?*

But there's something else beneath the surface, a vein of tension neither will bring up to the other. They are similar men, both Hazara, both the same age, the same intense curiosity, the same facility with languages, and the same tendency to swallow up whatever book or article is laying around.

But in the war years, they were enemies. A distance of a few kilometers set the course of their lives, the short space between where each stood when the Soviets invaded, thirty-five years before. Where Aziz had been standing, he first saw the cruelty of the Communists and was flung off to come of age fighting against them, alongside the holy warriors.

Yunos first saw the cruelty of the holy warriors and was flung off to the capital of the Communist world, living and learning beneath statues of Lenin. Now they stand before one another, a man who saw his friends killed by Russians, and a man who joined them.

"There's something called the Goldilocks Zone," Yunos says. "It's a place with the right distance from the sun, so water can exist in liquid form. If you go closer to the Sun the water will evaporate, and if you go farther from the Sun, it will freeze. So Mars is at the far end of the Goldilocks Zone."

Aziz is no longer interested in playing pupil. "It is said now that Mars has water." An assertion, more than a question.

"Yes."

"So we have proof of life there."

"Well, there are other planets that are in that zone. There are stars in the Goldilocks Zone. But they don't spin. So life-forms have to be able to live always in the light. Or, always in the dark. Or maybe right at the border, between night and day."

Aziz smiles again. "So it has to just be perfect conditions for humans to live somewhere?"

"Yes, right, just perfect. The coincidence is amazing."

"But after all of this, doesn't it make you think there is a higher power, called God?"

Yunos smiles, too, now, a huge smile that make his eyelids clench together. "Well, in astronomy, we say we cannot answer directly two questions. The first question is: is there a higher power? I mean, the answer is yes, but we don't say whether it's God or not. We call it a creator. We don't have anything before the Big Bang." He's a little flustered, he's forgotten the second question, so he tries to interest Aziz in something else he knows. "Actually, astronomers believe that eleven dimensions exist, did you know that? Parallel to our universe, there are other creatures in the other dimensions that can never even touch us. Do you know a dinosaur could walk right here, right in front of us, and we wouldn't know it?"

Aziz has still not stopped smiling, but his is a particular kind of smile, mouth closed and the corners of his lips only slightly raised, his head cocked. It's almost condescending, the look of an adult urging on an excited child. "We think about it like this," Yunos keeps going. "There are animals at the bottom of the sea, and they are oblivious to our presence up here, you know? So in the same way, *we* could be like those animals, oblivious to something else."

"Yes, but *we* know about *those* creatures down there," Aziz says with finality, as if he'd just settled a point he'd been trying for hours to make.

Yunos is sure Aziz is toying with him, but doesn't know precisely how, and Aziz doesn't elaborate; the conversation stalls. The two men stare silently at each other for a moment, still smiling, like they've been arguing in code, trying to disguise a fight from people nearby.

"Well," Yunos finally says, "I should get back to the office."

Yunos lost his father to the holy warriors three years before Aziz became one.

"Holy warriors," though, that wasn't the right word. *Arar* is what Yunos and everyone he knew called them. "Evildoers." The Arar were people off in the woods, up in the mountains, foolish and animalistic. A constant nuisance, a scourge made up of delinquents and criminals. Until they became something worse.

Yunos was in sixth grade on the day war came to his home. He was coming back from a rally honoring the Communist revolution, and when he got off the bus, a neighborhood boy came running toward him. The boy was yammering and Yunos had to concentrate to make out what he was trying to say. "There was a rocket! It landed at *your* house!" Yunos felt like someone had pulled a plug and let all the power drain from him. He was still for a moment, before he steadied himself and willed his body toward home. Relatives had already gathered and were closing ranks as neighbors inched closer to his yard, drawn by the spectacle. All the windows were broken, and women were wailing—so many women screaming and crying, he thought he heard his mother but he couldn't be sure, and it occurred to him that the reason he couldn't be sure was that he didn't know whether his family was alive.

He'd never heard a woman in such distress before, let alone three of them, or five, or however many there were filling his house with these awful screams. His mind swam, it seemed like he was in a sea of people, his house so crowded it felt foreign. He went past women reading the holy book, men reading the holy book, up the stairs and into a bedroom, saw his mother catch his eyes and quiet herself, and then she reached out her arms to him. "Don't worry," she said. "Everyone is okay. Everyone else is fine. It's just your father."

He hadn't until then thought much about the ideology of it all. Why some people were fighting against the government and some weren't. He had conformed to the system he was in, and the system was communist. He didn't consider *himself* to be a communist, not really; he considered himself to be behaving. The Soviet Union was helping to pay salaries in his country, he knew government workers got tokens they could exchange for oil, flour, wheat, sugar, tea, everything they needed. He knew he went to a government school. No one in his life, his classmates, his family, had any reason to be anything but thankful for the Soviets. Plus, Afghanistan's worst communist dictator, Hafizullah Amin, the one who tried to get rid of all religion and who killed people without compunction—the Soviets had come to *get rid* of him. Yunos read about the Alpha Group, the heroes of the Soviet Special Forces, who swooped in like delivering angels to rid the country of this butcher. So the Soviets weren't responsible for oppression in Afghanistan; they were the ones trying to prevent it. He watched convoys of Russian troops go by with pride. Big, pale, proud men in their deep bowl-shaped helmets, dropping cans of milk and biscuits for the children. You could go right up close, they didn't mind. His friends did business with them sometimes, you could convince a Soviet soldier to siphon fuel from his tank and sell it to you, and you could turn around and sell it for a nice profit. He watched the show every week on the national TV channel, *Our Big Northern Neighbor*, all about the Soviet Union and the gleam in every citizen's eye.

The Arar, the people the Americans supported in his country, they were animals. They called themselves holy warriors, but that was a joke. What was holy about going up on a mountain above a city and shooting rockets down at civilians? Why would the Americans help kill so many innocent people? People like his dad, who'd done nothing other than going out into his yard to fix the well at the wrong time? Yunos had reached into the coffin that day to touch his father on the leg, and there was nothing there. Beneath the sheet he could feel the skin give way in his hand. It was a cruel thing for his father's shattered body to be the last memory Yunos had of him, and it made him hate the holy warriors, and the foreigners who supported them, for killing in such a careless way. Destroying a body and destroying a family and not even bothering to show up to explain why.

These were forces bigger than him, he understood that much at least, and he couldn't control when violence would erupt or where it would come from. So instead, he controlled the things he could control. He kept the top position in his class. He studied as hard as he could and went to the rallies when the teachers told him to go to the rallies.

After three years as the man of the house he needed a way out. By then the government was low on forces and conscripting just about everyone to fight against the Arar. Soon he would turn eighteen, he'd be picked up and sent to the front lines. The Arar were all grown men, hard, seasoned fighters, bloodthirsty. For kids like Yunos, the notion of fighting them, underequipped and with barely any training, was a chilling, hideous nightmare. His cousin had been conscripted and sent right to the front. His brother had fled the country before they could get to him, and now Yunos had to figure out how to escape or else be sent in himself, chum for the Arar who'd already taken his father, to be dismembered or die in some other gruesome way.

He needed an out. So when the headmaster came into class one day to ask who was interested in a scholarship to study in the Soviet Union, Yunos raised his hand as high as he could.

The first stop was Tashkent, Uzbekistan. It was farther along in its Russification than Afghanistan, and it might as well have been a different world. It was *clean*. It made the country he'd just come from feel dirty and chaotic. Here, there were more high buildings than he could count; the roads were all paved, and all lit at night.

He tried to piece his few Russian letters together to read the signs. He recognized "airport"; he studied the tabloids, and couldn't make anything of them, but he didn't care. He and his new class-mates were there for two weeks, and it was a wonder to just walk the streets: the light in building windows stayed shining; the power never once cut out. Then three nights and two full days on a train, then the center of the Soviet Union: everything even bigger and grander. From the moment he set foot in the Moscow central terminal his indoctrination began. Here, they had trains that went underground, trains that went aboveground, and trains that went days without stop-ping. They had decorations in the station, as if it were the purpose of public transportation not just to convey people between two places but to present them with art. There were frescoes and sculptures of communist leaders, big statues with Soviet armies in various stages of combat. The frowning man with the big round forehead and the goatee was everywhere, though it would be months before Yunos understood this was Lenin, the leader he'd read all about. And here something else he'd never seen before: women smoking cigarettes. They were everywhere he looked.

From Moscow to Belgorod, the White City, where his bewil-derment continued—not because Belgorod was all that much differ-ent from Moscow, but because it seemed identical. He had the bizarre sensation of having traveled for half a day only to end up at the exact place he started. It was something he'd never fully get used to: in the Soviet Union, every city looked exactly the same as every other city. It was an entire country of facsimiles. Where he came from, roads and buildings were like living things. They had their own ideas and purpose and they came into being by some autonomous logic. In the Soviet Union, everything everywhere was where it was because of a plan. He hadn't seen that before: city planning. There was a film, a comedy, that took place in this country, where a man goes to visit his fiancé in St. Petersburg, but he accidentally gets on the wrong train and doesn't even realize it. Not even when he arrives in the city, not when he gets in a taxi, not when he travels through the streets, not when he pulls up to his own house, with his very same ad-dress, on his own street, in his own neighborhood. He doesn't realize that all along he's been in the wrong city. The Soviet Union was some big benevolent cosmic trick.

And it gave him everything he needed. A room in a hostel, a stipend, and an education. An indoctrination, too, but it never felt overt.

Except for the parades, which were bigger and grander than any he'd seen before. His first May Day, a teacher came with flags and flowers for the students to take on the parade and taught them the slogans they were all to chant. The choreography of it all astounded Yunos; he was given a bouquet of red chrysanthemums, told to march with his flowers right up to Red Square, and place them next to the Eternal Flame, a memorial for the martyrs.

It occurred to him that this was a country with a lot of martyrs. Twenty million of them from World War II alone. It was hard to even comprehend that number. More than the entire population of his country. Everything about the Soviet Union was on a grand scale, even the dying. The grandness made his own country seem insignificant.

Except that it was there, in Afghanistan, where people from the Soviet Union were dying at that very moment. He was laying flowers down to memorialize Soviet soldiers, who his own people were at that very moment trying to kill. They were trying to help build things for his people, and his people, in return, were killing and maiming and shooting rockets anywhere a Russian might be close, even in the cities. He put the red chrysanthemums down next to the flame, and stepped back in the procession.

The Soviet Union was a place he knew had its own binds and strictures, but he felt freer. In Afghanistan, his family had been religious, so he'd never been able to ask the size of the universe or how it came to be. Here, no one said to him, "God built it all, don't insult Him by asking."

Here it was the opposite; the very idea of God had been lifted from him. This was a country that considered religion a distraction, a deliberate one even. A grand deception. So he began to read in his spare time. When he read about the stars, the billions and billions of them, it made him feel tiny; he imagined himself as a grain of sand on a long curved beach. But it also made him feel connected to his home. Wasn't everyone looking at the same sky? Wasn't everyone just as tiny no matter where they were? He thought of the ethnic groups, the sects back home, and the religions, how people fought each other for these beliefs and how little what they fought for actually mattered. What a powerful message this would be if someday he could deliver it to them. These disagreements over which people launched rockets at one another, how inconsequential they'd seem when you considered how tiny we all are. How we are so much more similar than we are different.

This is what astronomy did for him. Looking up was so close to looking within, and there was a notion of responsibility there, too: when you shoot and someone dies, no divine hand has guided the bullet. If you launch a rocket, you are responsible for a family's suffering when it lands. It's not God. There's no God who wants to kill people's fathers.

But just as he was finding excitement in astronomy journal articles, there was a malaise settling in around him. The magnificent celebrations were no longer all that magnificent. People stopped knocking on his door to bring him out to parades. Demonstration days became days off.

In the Red Square, he heard arguments.

"Why do we keep sending troops to Afghanistan? Just to die and waste money."

"Look at the Germans. They lost World War II. We beat them. But they have better cars, better cigarettes. Now they are so advanced, but look at the bad conditions we live in here in Russia."

The Soviet Union had reached too far and was overextended. The grand experiment was coming undone. The government didn't have enough money to provide basic services to its own people, yet it was paying for a war in Afghanistan, sending young men to fight and die there.

And then it wasn't. One late winter evening, Yunos was in the television and reading hall, where all the students interested in the news always gathered. The room was their own little Red Square, where arguments were held for argument's own sake. Tonight it was something not at all academic. Tonight the news was showing over and over again images of tanks snaking along the road in Afghanistan toward the Friendship Bridge. Over the Amu River, into Uzbekistan. Smiling Soviet soldiers sitting on top of their tanks, waving red banners.

There in the hostel, the air left the room. This was it, then. The end of the Soviet occupation of Afghanistan. Yunos watched the last Russian tanks leave his country. It was like being left behind on the dusty floor of the Coliseum, a guard closing the gate and leaving the weak people behind to contend, weaponless, with tigers. Yunos lost hope. Everyone in the room lost hope. He was certain of what would happen now: the Arar would take back their country; Yunos and his friends would never see home again. There was terror, and powerlessness, in thinking about their families. Without protection from the Russians, more rockets would rain down from the mountains, until the Arar marched into the cities and tore the whole country apart.

Years of concern followed, of watching from afar as his country unraveled. They were years of worrying nearly every day about his family, until he heard that they were fleeing. The country began to spiral, and within three years of the Soviet withdrawal, his country was engulfed in the civil war he'd known was coming. Those who came together to fight the Soviets lost their shared enemy. Now it was every man for himself.

He did what he could to feel connected to his home in those days, because now that his home was in chaos and his family had fled, he was unmoored. He was a young man in a foreign land and without roots. Worse, he knew he would always be a foreigner. So he got some spare copies of magazines some Hazaras were running out of Pakistan, *The Era of Justice* and *Our Tomorrow*. He read them cover to cover, then read them again, and waited eagerly for the next copies to arrive through a network of Afghans living in the Soviet Union. The most irreverent columns were by the man people called the Teacher, who seemed willing to insult anyone regardless of their authority, and sometimes to insult people *because* of their authority. Yunos would feel his blood boil when he read the Teacher's screeds. He gave no quarter to religious figures, but rather blamed them, as Yunos did, for destroying the country.

Yunos didn't know that this Teacher had been a holy warrior.

What he knew was that the man had a way of arguing Yunos hadn't ever seen, even down at the Red Square where arguing was all people did. On a weekend trip to Moscow, Yunos met a young Hazara man in the market who claimed the Teacher was his uncle. "Teacher Aziz has just started a school," he told Yunos. "It's in Pakistan, for the refugee kids there. They named it for knowledge and wisdom: Marefat." That's when Yunos began to revere this man, this mythical Hazara who, even in exile, had thought about the future of Afghan children. The Teacher's voice became a proxy for his own, since he was so maddeningly removed from what was happening back home. The Teacher's words were all that connected Yunos to his people.

But things were changing in the Soviet Union, too. The president with the big stain on his head had tried to open the empire up, but it didn't go smoothly. People were angry about it, and Yunos sat in that same hall with the same friends in front of that same television, watching tanks once again. But this time there were tanks *here*. They were rolling into Moscow's Red Square, the country's own tanks advancing on the country's own capital, aiming their barrels at the country's own parliament, and Yunos felt an unsettling in his stomach again. He'd learned that tanks rolling cued war. He was watching another war starting, live, like a perverse spectator sport. On television, the man with the perfectly combed salt-and-pepper hair got up on top of one of the tanks and had his moment—Boris Yeltsin, the TV announcer said his name was. Yunos watched it all unfolding, and it seemed like there was something he should be doing to get ready. But what do you do to get ready when the country you're in is turning toward war, and the one you're from already has?

First, there was the matter of translating what the man was saying for his friends, who hadn't taken to the language like Yunos had.

Then, of projecting normalcy for their benefit; they were looking at him to determine the appropriate response, and outright panic felt close, so Yunos tried for calm as best he could. He tried to quiet the terror that manifested as acid rising in his stomach, and for the first time in his life, he actually felt that the only thing to do was pray.

Somehow war was averted. The tanks turned away. But it was the beginning of a different kind of violence. A longer, more drawn-out kind, this disordered march toward capitalism. The new president called it "shock therapy" but that was wrong, there was no therapy in it. Just sadder people who saw the money in their hands buy less and less.

He followed the news from home obsessively, read the Teacher's dispatches from Pakistan, as distraction from the society that began to kneel down all around him. He found reason for hope, at times, when he read about home. A group of young men charging forth from religious schools in the border regions and wanting to restore order. They effected a severe kind of justice, but justice nonetheless, and just maybe, they were capable of ending the violence. Almost as soon as he allowed himself those first hopeful moments thinking about the Knowledge Seekers, he felt foolish. Like a child falling from a tree, grasping even at the small branches he knows won't support him. This new fighting force was that: the thin branches.

All around him money just seemed to disappear. Opportunities vaporized—a command economy lost without its ability to command. Factories in Moscow could no longer just take cotton from one territory, fuel from another, labor from a third, and build things in the middle. Now these were all different territories, each with its own spasms for pride and nationhood. The only thing anyone could do to make money was find small differences in price between two places and move things from one to the other. Yunos and his friends had some experience in this. Back when they'd been able to go to Afghanistan for vacations, they returned with suitcases full of items to sell at a markup. There were enclaves in the Soviet Union where Western items were in demand and, incredibly, they were more plentiful in Afghanistan. Jeans, leather coats, tape players, women's cosmetics. By some peculiarity of international trade, his own backward, violence-ridden country was more flush with upscale Western items than the almighty Soviet Union. So his friends had used their trips home to stock up, and then returned to Russia and sold their cargo. With the civil war, the door to Afghanistan was now closed—if you went back, you might not ever get out. But they applied the same skills where they were.

When a command economy can no longer command, it becomes a nation of arbitrage, on the smallest imaginable scale. The three friends from Afghanistan, stranded in Russia, rented a stall in Pyatigorsk and took turns riding the bus to Moscow to buy whatever was on offer, whatever had just come in from China, Japan, wherever. They didn't discriminate, it didn't matter, as long as it was in bulk. One week it was flashlights, the next it was shoes, then makeup, then hosiery. Six boxes of Walkmans, red, blue, and black: they'd open up the boxes, lay them out on the long table in the market, and sell ten at a time. Always to women. He didn't know why, but it was always females coming to buy his goods ten or twelve at a time and take them farther to the fringes. The only people who figured out how to hustle here were immigrants and women.

He took one of the Walkmans from a shipment and began using it when he worked the stall. Little services for the vendors in the market mushroomed, cafés and record shops, and he began to hear the songs that kept his spirits up while everything he was close to was changing. Ace of Base was his first cassette; after he listened to "Happy Nation" for the first time, he rewound it and listened to it again, and began listening to the one song a dozen times a day, every day. He liked the idea: a happy nation. It lifted his spirits, though he misheard the chorus—"Livin' in a Happy Nation," he thought, was "Lebanon's a happy nation." Which made good sense to him. Of course it was happy! Lebanon had all sorts of different religions and races getting along together. The rest of the song, which he couldn't quite make out, surely explained all the things that made Lebanon a happy place to be. The words settled in with his concept of things, and so he sang along, all day, every day, "Happy Nation / Lebanon's a Happy Nation!" and daydreamed about one day going to Lebanon to see if Ace of Base really knew what they were talking about.

By 1992 the teetering Soviet economy finally collapsed, and there was nothing left for him there, not even hope that it might get better. He wanted to go home, but home was on fire. The Knowledge Seekers were taking more of the country. In 1996, after three days of intense fighting, they would take the capital. By then his family had fled to Iran like so many other Afghan families, and his only option seemed to be trying to reconnect with them there.

It's 1998. Yunos is crouched in a stranger's yard, jittery with fear.

The smuggler told them to wait there, for just a few minutes. Already ten minutes have passed, maybe more. His mind is racing—did the smuggler turn him in?

If that's what happened, what to do now? Sit here and wait in his hiding place, which isn't even really a hiding place, since there's nothing between him and the family whose yard he's in, and nothing stopping the family from coming out into their yard to find four refugees huddled in the corner?

He is hyperalert. He hears noises from the family inside, then he hears wild dogs thumping by, skirting a berm on the other side of the fence. Then he sees a puppy trot by, hardly bigger than a rabbit. It stops, raises its snout to the air, then cocks its head toward them and freezes. It's a harmless-looking creature, but it could give them up in a moment. He turns to the others: "If it starts barking," he whispers, "grab it." He turns to each of them in turn, looks each in the eye. "We have to kill it," he says. "We'll have to strangle it."

Almost twenty years later, when Yunos is a professional interpreter for the United Nations, an American with the World Customs Organization will lead a delegation of Afghans on a trip to Azerbaijan, to show what an impenetrable border looks like. Yunos, by singular coincidence, will be brought along to translate and he will not realize until the presentation begins that the delegation is at this very same border crossing. This place will become, in the intervening years, a model of monitoring goods and people crossing an international border. "There are no less than one hundred and fifty security cameras," the American will say, while Yunos tries to recover and fumbles to translate, "and even a satellite monitoring system. The entire area is under such tight surveillance," the man will say, "not even a fly can cross undetected."

Tires screech outside the yard. He sees a layer of dust rise above the fence, and hears the muffled vibrations of a heavy man huffing up to the gate. Fiddling with the latch, and then swinging the gate open, the smuggler is standing next to an idling taxi. "Get in. Go, go, go!" Yunos wants to hit the man. "What the hell took you so long. They could have come out of that house and found us!" But there's no time, he's being shoved into the taxi, and the taxi is taking off down the gravel while an unclosed car door swings wildly back and forth like a broken wing.

Each successive interval on this journey is equally harrowing: his own little tour of the crumbling Soviet Union. Getting just to this point required bribing a truck driver to take them to the Russian border, bribing a guard to let them across, finding a new smuggler to take them out of the border zone into Azerbaijan. Being in Azerbaijan would have been terrifying even if they haven't been there illegally because Azerbaijani people terrified Yunos; they were always the most aggressive vendors back in Pyatigorsk, always brawling over market stalls. Now, since the Soviet Union had collapsed, they had their very own country, a country full of the people Yunos was most afraid of. And he was in it. Illegally.

Then across Azerbaijan, down around the Caspian Sea, pleading for the hospitality of strangers and paying more bribes to secure it, spending the very last of his money, learning to build small ecosystems of insurance along the way. He manufactures leverage where there is none. Where he is otherwise entirely vulnerable, he comes up with calculated lies to protect himself. That a friend back in Russia is waiting to receive his wristwatch in the post, as proof that Yunos had made it through, and that it is safe to send more, paying, refugees along the same route. "You understand," Yunos explains, "there's more money if you get us across safely." He learns to manipulate his handlers in order to protect himself, to protect the three friends with him, who spoke none of the languages they needed to speak, and to propel himself across these borders as if by sheer force of will.

And after nearly getting chased down by police just inside the Iranian border, Yunos finally arrives in Tehran, to his family, as close to home as he could be.

★   ★   ★

In Iran his cousins took him in. They set aside a couple of spare rooms for him and brought him along to work as a waiter on catering gigs. Iran was okay. In one way, Iranians were a lot like Russians. Two decades into their own revolution, they were eager for information from foreigners, because they themselves only knew what the government wanted them to know.

It didn't seem like anyone especially liked Afghans though; Afghans were considered jobless wards, draining the country's resources without contributing anything to it. But the beauty of it was, no one had to know he was Afghan. He looked Asian like all the Hazaras, of course. But he spoke Russian, so he could pass as a traveler from some other Central Asian republic. Kazakhstan, Kyrgyzstan, Tajikistan.

At a catering gig he met a man who worked for a French oil company, Elf Aquitaine, who was so impressed with Yunos's languages that he offered him a job in his own house. As a servant, really, but a head servant. Yunos was in charge of the house staff, the gardener, the drivers, and he was still allowed to attend parties the family held for the Tehran elite, parties well-attended by the diplomatic community. Mingling at one of the parties, Yunos heard two men speaking in Russian. Ambassadors, he discovered, from Russia and Belarus. Yunos said a few words in Russian, the men were impressed, the Belorusian handed him a business card, and soon he had his second job, translating for the Belorusian embassy in Iran.

When he saw news on the TV at the Belarusian embassy café of planes hitting the World Trade Center and the Pentagon, Yunos couldn't help himself. He was elated.

Not because he still harbored resentment for America, which supported the Evildoers who killed his father. Not because America's biggest rival had taken him in and provided him an education. He was watching with a room full of foreign service officers, all practiced in the divining of political developments in other countries. The attacks had originated in Afghanistan, and so they all knew that, eventually, the Americans would come and drive out the Taliban. It was only a matter of how quickly they'd come. That day, sitting in the café, seeing that first footage, Yunos made plans to return home to Afghanistan. Back to his own country, for the first time in twenty years.

From his journey, Afghanistan to Russia, then across to Iran, Yunos had amassed a portfolio of skills, none more immediately marketable than the languages he spoke. When the United Nations opened up a mission just for Afghanistan that spring—just after the Americans came and the Taliban collapsed—Yunos found that people like him were in high demand. The foreigners needed to talk with the rest of the people, and for that, they needed interpreters. Yunos was now fluent in Russian and English, as well as all the languages of Afghanistan. There was good money in interpreting, though his passions still lay in other fields—he had studied literature in the Soviet Union, and he was by constitution curious. About stars, the universe, the lives of writers.

Like the Teacher. By now Yunos had been reading the Teacher's thoughts for a decade; they'd been the only tie Yunos had to his home. He heard that the Teacher's school had, just like Yunos, moved home to Afghanistan after the Outsiders came. He heard that it was out in the Desert. Yunos was living on the other side of the city—when he came back to Kabul, he'd moved back into the house where his father had died.

But he thought often about how he might get out to see the school, and meet the Teacher—though both were Hazara, they had no family connections, and Yunos had no premise to introduce himself.

He established the Afghan Astronomy Association, and thought it might attract Teacher Aziz's interest. But when he finally met Aziz for the first time, it was happenstance. Yunos got a phone call from a friend. "I'm passing near your office, and I'm with Teacher Aziz. Should I bring him by?"

At that point, neither knew much about the other's past. Yunos didn't know Aziz had been a holy warrior—an Arar—right around the time Yunos lost his father to them. Aziz, for his part, didn't know Yunos had sympathized with the Communists and had lived in the Soviet Union. Those revelations would come later. At that moment, they were both Hazaras who'd had long journeys, who'd found themselves some measure of success, and who were both animated by ideas, by intense curiosity. Both were teaching people things they would not otherwise learn.

Aziz knew Yunos had become consumed with astronomy, and had used his own money to hold classes, translate textbooks, write articles, and travel around the country to set up telescopes and introduce people to the cosmos. That's what Aziz was doing with his school, so that year Aziz invited Yunos to Marefat. Yunos brought a telescope and special protective glasses, so that Marefat students could look at the sun.

A decade later, with the withdrawal under way, their differences were more pertinent. Aziz was under immense pressure; he felt responsible for the very survival of his community, while Yunos looked carefree, a man who need worry only about himself.

Yunos was convinced Aziz raked in cash from his school and was increasingly concerned about his own job. The U.N. presence in the country was shrinking by the day, and friends all around him were getting laid off. Yunos often had to deliver the news. As an interpreter, he was brought on trips to the provinces where the United Nations was shutting down offices, so he could tell people in their own languages that they no longer had jobs.

For a time, before the foreign troops started to leave, the two men represented two-thirds of a Shakespearean drama. They could almost have been brothers, driven in opposite directions by war, aligning with sides fighting against one another. The first two acts: tragedy unfolds, and the audience is taught the theme, that man is no match for destiny.

Except for a time, they were. They were, together, a testament to the power people can have over their own fates. The things they shared—curiosity, an interest in the people around them, a desire for those people to become educated, the life of the mind—overwhelmed the blood debt. Their story reversed the third act—where would-be friends meet their calamitous end by each other's hand—on its head. War takes people and forces them to choose sides; it destroys communities that way. These two didn't let it.

13

EIGHT MONTHS LEFT

Aziz is standing in a crater where his house used to be.

He's looking absently toward Mount Qorigh. In Hazaragi the word means "protected," and for now that's fitting, a last barrier between Marefat and what lies on the other side: two provinces the Taliban controls, where five women and two children are right now in the process of starving to death because the Taliban has stopped food shipments. They are punishing people, they say, who were willing to join the police.

In the crater surrounding Aziz, splintered rebar sticks out like it's reaching for him, support columns that once held the building have been fractured and shards protrude like weapons. It looks like a cruise missile landed in his living room and the whole house got scooped out, a whole building ripped away down to its foundation.

Workmen have built crude retainer walls to hold back the dirt, because in a few months, when the snows come, the dirt will turn to mud and bear down on the rest of the school. The crater is an echo of the World Trade Center's ground zero, in the years after the wound was cleaned out and dressed but before anyone knew what to build in its place. A well-maintained abscess.

The men around Aziz work slowly. It's a dry, hot day. Their faces are sooty; none have all their teeth. They are resigned, weight-of-the-world type men, sinewy and rugged. They look as though they are of the dust, like they emerged from it—dust which is everywhere; which has its own personality; which you can see at night, in the beam of a flashlight, moving through the illuminated cone like it has intent, like it *means* to get in your teeth, eyes, in your electronics, attaching itself to the fibers of your clothing when you hang them out to dry and laying itself down inside the school every single day, so that no one has clean shoes, everyone has a chronic cough, and most people spit, even the girls. Every day, for three hours after the students have left, Shaiq—"priest"—the bighearted janitor, wraps a scarf around his face and moves through the school, hunched over with a hand broom, moving chairs and sweeping beneath them, filling the space with a dark cloud that follows as he moves from room to room like it's loyal to him. The rain holds the dust down, but in the summer it rains almost never, and when it does, it creates rivers of filth running down the middle of the streets. The students weave expertly around these streams without looking, while the small children frown at the puddles and then jump up and down in them, as if standing water were a curious kind of toy.

Aziz swears the depressed-looking workmen are fine. They're just—well, they're workmen. What they're used to doing is insulting each other, telling pornographic stories, handling heavy equipment like it's unimportant. But this is a school; they don't get to do those things.

And there's something else. The workmen know he might not be able to pay them.

Maybe the men who run the construction company will go out of pocket to make payroll; maybe the men will just get nothing. And prices are rising all around them, the economy teetering. At Marefat, little is ever paid on time and nothing is paid up front, because Aziz knows no one can foreclose on 2,700 kids. This is what's on Aziz's mind right now as he stands in his ditch: that it's remarkable the work that can be done on loan.

It was that way back when word first started to spread about Marefat, and they had to build a second floor on top of the first, even though the first was made of baked mud and there were little earthquakes happening all the time then, and no one was sure whether the first floor would support the second.

Back when they built a whole second building because three dozen students had turned to one hundred, then three hundred, then a thousand, it was that way. Then another floor was added to *that* building, then another; and it's that way now that they've become almost three thousand, four if you count the adult learning programs, a little empire risen up from the dust in the Desert, built with the dust in the Desert, built with the sweat of the students and their parents, but mostly, built on loan.

Those were the bullish years, he thinks now. When Marefat really became an institution and the country was still safe, and Aziz pushed the kids. Too much, he thinks. He wanted the school to show kids not just to memorize but to think, and not just to think but to act. It was a democracy the Outsiders were bringing, after all. So he taught the students to go back into their homes and make their families uncomfortable: to ask uncomfortable questions, explain provocative theories from books other than the religious ones. Each student was a depth charge dropped into a household, intended to cause chaos that would resolve in changed, changeable minds. He encouraged the kids to go out and protest things they didn't like if they felt moved to, he helped them plan, and even when the whole school and all its students were nearly crushed under the weight of the Ayatollah's mob, he thought he'd been doing right by them. But he'd made them *known*.

Right now, at this particular moment, it's beginning to seem like that was a serious mistake. He'd made the kids vulnerable. Shouting about things people were not really ready to hear, which most of his life he'd thought was the noble thing to do. As a holy warrior, he had been conditioned to think there was no greater calling then death for a cause, but then he'd surrounded himself with young life, and the rise of Marefat had brought a revelation to him: it was the shallow man's game to tempt fate when instead you could control it. In less than a decade he watched his people go from being porters and servants to being a community that sends girls to university in the United States. Hazara girls. Girls whose parents couldn't read a word.

And all around the school, houses, wedding halls, even malls had risen up. *People* had done this. People had come back from their exiles, and they'd built themselves up in the Hazara part of the city where no one else even wanted to visit and taxi drivers charged extra or just refused if you asked to be taken there. With the Outsiders encouraging progress, their armies protecting it and never far from sight, people began to see that they could do these things on their own. They didn't need powerful men to give them permission. They didn't need the government to do it all for them.

Mostly, they didn't need the clergy.

That was a dangerous realization, though—that people could be pulled away from the clergy. This was a place where many men were powerful precisely because they had a direct line to God. They were men who received money from other countries to talk about God in the way those countries preferred. These men, men like the Ayatollah, had a lot invested in God, and the idea that a regular man was powerless without someone like the Ayatollah to decode Him. These men had reason to fear what Aziz was doing because the practice of faith was being cleaved from the clergy. Marefat students were sometimes religious, but they had learned autonomy in *how* they believed. They learned about Islam, but not just by memorizing passages in Arabic. They knew the history, they knew what was in the holy book, and they knew the parts that had been left out. It was no longer the case that the only way to be a person of God was to listen to the men who were paid the most to talk about Him.

That made the clergy vulnerable. They stood to lose. To lose money from other countries and to lose protection. It is influence over people that made those men valuable to their benefactors. Without that influence, they had little to offer their bosses. Out in the Desert, Aziz was not just challenging their religious views; he was challenging their livelihood. He was challenging their safety.

What irony, then: for more than a decade, Aziz scoffed at these men who relied on foreign countries for protection, when all along, he'd been doing exactly the same thing without acknowledging it. And now his protectors were leaving. He'd tried to prevent it, he'd called up every American he knew and urged them not to leave, but he was a man yelling at the tide, begging it not to go out as it rushed past his knees.

Since the Outsiders came, the change in the community was messy and uneven and it strained some families to the breaking point. There were girls for whom going to Marefat was daily exposure to what was possible in life, and returning home everyday was being yanked back into the past. Small tragedies happened all across the Desert when fathers who never stopped listening to the Ayatollah had children listening to Aziz. Kids were ministered to by two different authorities who were often in direct conflict. And Marefat was accelerating the process of modernization. Already it had been hard for parents to see children with email, mobile phones, and strange new languages coming out of them. Add to that the fact that Marefat students knew—many of them knew very clearly because it was so obvious, and they were not afraid to say it—that they were better educated than their parents. They knew more of the world, and for every parent who was inspired to see his child given an opportunity he himself never had, there was one confounded by a daughter who opposed the Ayatollah, who said sophisticated things about religion, and who no longer respected her father's authority just because he was her father.

During the hunger strike, Aziz saw what he helped set in motion. He also saw that people were not adjusting their behavior appropriately now that the Outsiders were on their way out.

So now he has decided his job is to try to apply the brakes, but it seems it may be too late. The students from his school, especially the young women, always the young women, have taken on their own momentum, and they keep hurtling forward.

Today two of those girls, both from the first class to go all the way through Marefat from the first grade to graduation, have come back to visit. A few years before, Razea had been an unserious girl, smart but joking always, always in the middle of a fit of laughter she wanted to spread. She was one of those kids for whom laughter comes as an urge you try and fail to resist; she laughed like a fit of sneezes. She was clever but not mischievous, she made fun of her classmates, boys and girls alike, but always with obvious affection.

That was 2009 and 2010, when the Desert felt like it was just finishing up a revolution and everyone still thought the Outsiders would be there forever. It had been a hopeful time, especially for a particular kind of girl, the kind with big ambitions, who'd seen her mother's generation stunted and meant to grab hold of the chance her own had been given.

But now, when I see Razea for the first time in three years, she has become a serious person. She is thinned out and hunched over, as if adulthood for her was something you recede into, a shedding off of the extraneous bits. She is barely twenty but she walks with a stoop, and when she comes into Aziz's office, she doesn't smile. She doesn't look me in the eye. I have the feeling that she has moved on from the time in her life when she could look at me as a friend, a teacher, a partner in crime, and entered the period in which she has to regard me as an unrelated male. Later, when she finally smiles again, it will change her whole face up.

She'd formed an alliance with a group of other girls who had graduated from Marefat and went on to the same college abroad. They are all on summer holiday from that university now, working at the same internship for the same ministry here. Back home for the first time since leaving for college, they're all having the same problems with their families. So they have all pledged to do exactly what Aziz wanted to do when he started the school: to change their community from within, beginning in their own homes.

Aziz invited them to do a radio show, and it's going well. The girls are in the studio, all with heads covered and feet bare, and Aziz is kind and encouraging, inviting each to speak about her experience abroad, making each of them comfortable, making kind jokes so that none are nervous. When they finish the show, they move down to Aziz's office to continue their reunion, off air, and Aziz begins to speak to them in a way that they're completely unprepared for.

"It's time for you to get married and have kids," he says.

There is a stunned silence, like they've just seen something violent happen in front of them. They begin to object, but he doesn't let them. He interrupts: "You need to realize that by not marrying, you are facing new restrictions, and new dangers." He tells them that right now, in this place, they have to marry for protection.

Two of the girls repeat the word "protection" while putting it in air quotes. It's the best they can do because Aziz is the absolute last person they expected to hear this from. Finally, one of the girls musters a response. "Maybe marrying gives protection against some things, but a lot of times the husband is the one you need protection from."

"I say, marry for *perfection*, not protection," another adds. Aziz winces.

"You need the protection of families," he says. "If you don't have that, you have nothing and you are vulnerable. If you go to protest, to speak up, you'll be alone."

They're confused now. The man who told them to stand up is telling them to sit down, be quiet, find a man and be servile. He is telling them precisely the opposite of what they thought his instructions had been when they left his school. "If you do not marry, in this community," he says, "you will have institutional pressure. You cannot live here single. It's impossible."

"Nothing is impossible, Aziz," one of the girl's says, using his first name, like he's lost his right to an honorific. "*Impossible* is impossible."

He doesn't want to respond to this comment, so he just waits a moment for it to dissipate.

"If you are bringing changes, you need to apply a certain amount of pressure. You can't fight on all fronts." He tries a different approach. "Could your mother survive without her husband?"

"With education, yes!"

"No!" He is forceful; the girls are taken aback. "Even *with* education! Because our culture, our structure, doesn't exist that way."

Another pause. The girls are disoriented. Is this a joke? They anticipated this fight, but this is the last person they expected to have it with. Why is he saying these things to them?

They don't yet know that Aziz is worried, and that as part of his preparation for next year, he is walking the school back. That he is, for the first time in his life, worried that he's been too provocative. The project of progress has become secondary to protecting the progress that's been made already. And to the task of protecting people. Which means these girls left a school that taught them they could do anything a man could do and more, and came back to an institution in retreat. They are finding, in Aziz, a man no longer much different from their own parents, and in Marefat, a place which no longer seems so different from their own homes.

"Having a husband," Razea now says, "is the first protection *and* the first source of violence against women."

Aziz knows she's right. There's nothing he could say that would both refute this and be true. So he reverts, weakly, to a point he already made. "If you don't have support of family, you're vulnerable."

Then he has an inspiration. He'd been able to understand the hunger strikers by going back to his own years as a young man, violent-minded and inconsiderate of risk. Perhaps the way to convey his directive to these girls is to do it from their level. Not to deny them their right, but to make them defer it. "Look at myself," he says. "I was really serious about changing the way people felt about religion, I had a dream of changing the way people thought about religion. I was really furious when I saw someone being made to kiss the hand of the clergy. Now I see all around me how people have changed. The family is not against you girls having rights, they may or may not admit that. I was against people sacrificing for clergies, and you can also be that way about this. But be *wise*. Don't pay huge prices."

Then he pauses but keeps his head cocked so the girls don't interrupt. He looks at me. "Don't go home today and talk about the sanctity of Judaism. Don't say Jeff Stern is a Jew, he's an infidel that's here and we're spending time with him." They laugh; the mood lightens.

"But ten years from now," he says, "that will happen. My family, ten, twelve years ago, they also believed shaking hands with an infidel would make you dirty. Now my mother, my father, my wife, now at least once a week will shake an infidel's hand!" They all laugh some more.

"The Ayatollah Khatami once went to France and shook hands with a lady. It caused huge problems when that happened, but he did it. And people changed."

This seems to go over better with the girls. Aziz is, for the moment, satisfied.

For the moment, it doesn't matter that he's not so confident that what he's just said about the future is true.

A few years ago, right when attendance at Marefat had begun to outpace construction of classroom space, the school was desperate for a new building.

A Hazara businessman saw what Hazaras were doing for themselves out in the Desert, and he offered to help. Aziz asked him to provide some steel at a discounted rate and a deferred payment, so they could build a new building and accommodate the growing student body, even if they couldn't quite pay for it yet. The businessman said that was a fine idea, he'd be happy to help, and Marefat began digging for the foundation.

They dug one meter across, twelve meters down, carving around the house Aziz and his family lived in, between the two other Marefat buildings. The hole had to be deep, because the new building was to have rooms below ground level. That's best in a Desert, because it's natural climate control: rooms underground stay cooler in the summer and hold heat longer in the winter. Aziz was dreaming of plays and assemblies and movie nights, even in the height of both seasons.

When Marefat had done its part, and the ditch was dug, Aziz called the businessman to tell him they were ready for the steel, when could they expect it? But the businessman said he'd had a change of heart. There'd been a shift in the market, he said. A shock to the steel supply, something about prices. "At the rate I've given you it will take you twenty years to pay me back!" And he retracted his offer.

So there was no steel to build, but the foundation had been dug, and it now sat empty. Aziz, who prided himself on being accessible to anyone at any time, had effectively installed a moat around his home. The ditch had been dug so dangerously close that as more dirt fell away, it began to look like a house built atop a hill, and the winter rains were coming.

It was slow at first, chunks of the foundation breaking off and slipping into the ditch. Then winter came in full force and the snow weighed everything down and the moisture in the air loosened everything up, and one night, when everyone was asleep, the house groaned, the floor rumbled beneath them, and a sound like a long unfolding explosion came from the kitchen. Aziz's mother ran toward the back of the house and screamed: the kitchen had sheared right off the side of the house and slipped into the ditch.

After that the ditch kept growing and changing shape; every few weeks it took another gulp at the house. When it took his parents' bedroom, they had no choice but to leave. The board rented them an apartment next to the old school building.

So the school fell victim to Aziz's own ambition. The empty ditch was no longer totally empty because it had been filled by Aziz's own house, and that's how it stayed. He abandoned the idea.

Until this year, when he had another vision: an amphitheater for the students.

Or, not an amphitheater, someone said that had bad connotations, of gladiators and violence. Actually, he hasn't thought of what to call it yet, but it will be a big half dome where he dreams of students assembling to put on plays and watch American movies that the school already knows to censor since of course there's a lot of kissing in American movies. It was the perfect solution. It was cheaper than the building. It had to be deep on one side—that would be the side they'd already dug. It had to be shallow on another, which was good, because it wouldn't threaten any more buildings, and because the ground sloped naturally. Aziz was beginning to fit his ambitions to the environment.

Christa D'Souza told Aziz she liked the idea and would raise some money for the project, and that was encouragement enough: Before she'd secured a single pound, construction began, Aziz paying the builders with the promise of money coming from England.

First, the ditch had to be cleaned out and expanded.

Aziz loves this new project even more than the original one. He stops and stares at it whenever he walks by. He finds excuses to go there when he misses it, and he misses it if he hasn't seen it for two consecutive hours. He will be walking by and in midconversation he will stop talking, put his hands in his pockets, and just watch. Or he will lower himself in to the ditch and hold a plumb line, give instructions to the foreman, announcing what's being done wrong. He gives engineering advice to the engineer. The engineer sighs. He is resigned to being micromanaged by a man who knows so little about engineering that his last foray into the discipline cost him a house.

There is not unanimous agreement that this auditorium is a good idea. Aziz is building an extravagant thing when there's only enough money promised for a portion of it; the school is in debt before the first bag of cement is cut open. The future is uncertain, and it seems imprudent to sink so much money into a place so soon before the Outsiders are all gone. The Taliban is holding provinces all around them, just over the mountains, in every direction, and all over the Desert people are making plans to leave. Why put money into the land when Marefat may need to pack up and leave tomorrow? There's no money to pay for it, and soon there will be no one to protect it.

This is precisely why Aziz wants it.

He knows the students believe he is possessed of some higher source of information they themselves can't access. Aziz has been to America, Aziz knows some Outsiders, there are pictures on the Internet of Aziz with foreign generals. The kids ask him, "What will happen when the Outsiders leave?" as if he's known all along and just forgot to tell them. But he doesn't know. What he knows is that the school can't leave, because there's no place for it to go. "What country?" he says. "Pakistan used to be a good place for us, ten years back or twelve years back, now Pakistan is a hell itself. Everyday you can see that the Hazaras, the Shiites, they are targeted. We cannot go to Iran because in Iran there are lots of restrictions and lots of problems. Every day they are kicking refugees out. We are stuck here."

Even if there was someplace to go, Marefat is no longer something that can be moved. It's become a web of connections between an institution and a community, a community that has changed because of a school, and a school that means little without the people in the houses around it. It can't be moved, any more than a whole slum can be picked up from one country and laid back down in another. They're stuck where they are, and if the storm comes, they'll either survive it, or it will crush them here.

He doesn't know what happens next. Will there be another massacre like Afshar? Will the Taliban or one of the others, the Haqqani Network or the Army of Jhangvi or some other unholy mob march into the Desert and destroy the Hazaras?

The only thing he knows for sure is that if they come, there's nothing he'll be able to do about it. It will be too late to protect his people.

When he first resigned himself to the fact that the Outsiders were leaving, he would sit up all night with his two youngest splayed out on the carpet next to him, thinking: what to do? The children at Marefat could spend their days looking toward Mount Protected, thinking of the dark forces assembling on the other side. If they did that, they would suffer today, and it wouldn't stop them from suffering tomorrow. But if he couldn't make them safe, maybe he could still make them *feel* safe. Maybe he could allow them this last look at progress in case it ends tomorrow. Maybe, if he couldn't control what happens tomorrow, he could smother the fear they feel today, for at least a little while.

"For me, Jeff, building these types of buildings, at a time when people are worried, it is just a counterbalance, a psychological wall. To let people, most of the people, even my students, when they look at me, most of the time they think, 'If there was really something bad happening, he would not have dug this ground, and would not be busy with these kind of constructions. It means that he is hopeful, and there is nothing to worry about!' "

Anyway, the Hazaras have disarmed. What good is it to think about what's coming, if you can't do anything about it when it arrives?

14

THE TROUBLEMAKER

Ta Manna stands on the roof of her house, gauging the wind direction.

Which is important, because the weapon she designed for today's operation has to get all the way from here, Pakistan, to India, which is—she doesn't know how far India is, but it's pretty far.

Ta Manna is six years old, and this is her first terrorist attack, so it has to go well, because maybe she's not an expert, but her plan is foolproof and soon everyone will be proud of her. What with all this taking matters into her own hands and showing initiative.

Her planning has been flawless, like on TV. She convinced Behrang to save his pennies for a month and she saved hers. That part was easy, all the cousins get an allowance of one cent a day but she gets two because for obvious reasons she is her grandmother's favorite and therefore deserving of special treatment.

And today, the day of the attack, the day India will finally pay for—she's actually not sure what India needs to pay for, but India apparently owes someone something, according to the news her uncles watch—they bought as many of those tiny firecrackers kids throw around on holidays as they could afford.

Which, it turned out, was not as many as she had imagined. But still enough to show India that We Will Eat Grass to Build a Bomb!

That's also what the news says sometimes. Which on second thought is sort of confusing because grass is disgusting to eat, for a human being, but anyway now India will pay . . . what it owes.

Up on the roof, she covers her hands with rags so they don't leave fingerprints on their weapon. That's a thing spies and assassins do, she's pretty sure, also because of the TV. And together she and Behrang assemble their foolproof weapon: the fewer-than-expected firecrackers taped to a toy helicopter, with a fuse cut from a ball of string she found in her grandmother's cupboard. Now it's time to say a prayer, but she can't really remember any prayers at the moment, and she doesn't want Behrang to know that she hasn't memorized her prayers yet, so she doesn't ask him to say the prayers either. She points the toy toward India and begins a countdown, and then Behrang asks, "How do you know that way is India?"

She hasn't thought of that. That was God's job and also the wind's job. So she's just silent because maybe Behrang will think she's not saying anything because it's such a dumb question and not because actually she doesn't know where India is. Another thought: how will she know whether it hit its target? But that turns out not to be a problem because when she lights the fuse the flame races right up the string and the helicopter has barely lifted off when the firecrackers ignite and turn the cousins black with ash and burnt paper.

Their mission has failed, but they fall on each other laughing.

There is a dream she starts having in fourth grade: she is home, but at the same time she is in a strange land. Like a room she recognizes has been picked up and placed in someone else's house. The walls are thin like paper.

It's China, she decides.

She is with her cousins, and they're all eating tomatoes. It's a bright day, the sun is strong through the translucent paper walls, and she is thinking how much she hates tomatoes, when something traveling at two thousand kilometers per hour hits a mountain and explodes so loud and strong that the mountain becomes a million pieces of fire.

After this, still in the dream, she comes to, it is maybe five minutes later, and she looks for Behrang. She finds him unconscious, his face black with soot, and she tries to find the others, but it is completely dark. The sky has turned black, the sun is gone, the only light comes from flames where the mountain used to be, and where things are still burning. Corpses, maybe. There is no one else around, they have all died, or vanished. This is her own lonely horror, nobody left in the world to explain it to her but Behrang, and Behrang can't speak. There is such force in the dreamed violence that her mind keeps on rattling long after the explosion was over, and it all fuses together as one long trauma that she suffers alone, with Behrang in her arms, trying to wake him.

Then she wakes for real, and she's confused. The dream was disorienting and horrible, but it has meaning, she is certain, and she must find it.

She is young but her mind is already powerful. She'd be a gifted child in another place, but there are huge things happening in the world around her, too much for anyone to protect her from or explain to her, so she sees and hears more than she understands. In the countries nearby there are no vacation spots or weekend destinations; there is only war. Violence in the county to one side, war in the country to the other, conflict between the one she's in and the ones all around. She is a child standing on a crack as the earth breaks apart and she can see what's happening, but she doesn't know why, or what's below.

From the doorjamb, she often watched the television over her uncle's shoulder. That's how she saw nuclear weapons on the news, deconstructing a mountainside. She saw all the violence, but she didn't understand it. She was protected from its direct effects, but she and Behrang picked up its signals, felt its vibrations. They absorbed violence like a toxin before they were old enough to understand that's what it was. It was too much, and she was too young, and it metastasized in her mind. In her life, soon, she began to see killing with her own eyes, but the notion of death had already invaded her dreams.

Ta Manna is in second grade, Behrang is in third, when they go to the new school that teaches them for the first time that they are different. They no longer go to school in "Hazara Town," the place with so many people just like them that they never thought about who they actually were.

They had to bring their refugee birth certificates to register for the school, and their teachers started in: in Ta Manna's class, the teacher said, "You have extra homework," and when Ta Manna stood to protest, her teacher said "You are Hazara, know your place, sit back down."

A classmate leaned over and said, "Why did you admit you were a Hazara? That means you have nothing, not a history, not a faith, nothing."

After school, she found Behrang; his day had been the same. "I don't understand," he said. "One of the teachers made fun of me. Why would he do that?"

"Don't worry—we'll have our revenge," she said. But in truth, she didn't understand, either. It seemed she'd done something wrong, but she had no idea what. When they got home, they told Ta Manna's father what had happened, and asked him what it meant. He sighed, and he sat the children down.

"We are Hazaras," he said. "We have—it's the structure of our faces." Ta Manna saw he was struggling. "We don't have good faces."

Ta Manna and Behrang were silent.

"But we have good minds. We have bad features," her father said, trying for clarity, "our nose is like *this*," and he pushed his nose down, "and our eyes are like *this*," and he stretched his eyes out to tiny slits.

It's all too much to take. She runs to the mirror and looks at herself and tries to understand. *So I have a bad shape,* she thinks. *Why are my eyes like this? Why is my nose down like this? Why is my history bad?* What she understands from her father's words is that she is ugly. She is an ugly person, and she belongs to an ugly people, with an ugly history. So she closes her eyes and wishes as hard as she can that she could go back and be born in another house. A Baloch house, a Pathan house, whatever, anything else but a Hazara house.

There is just one small saving grace: she and Behrang experience this jolt at the same time, and like two objects touching when something is superheated, they become fused. They have tormented each other most of their lives, but now they realize it is time for a thaw in relations. Ta Manna offers Behrang a truce.

"From now on," she says, "*we're* going to make fun of all *them*, okay? Teachers, students. *Everyone*." They decided at the same moment that it was time to settle their differences with each other and, together, strike back. Together, they took on classmates and teachers and administrators. And as Ta Manna grew into a fierce young thing, Behrang became the one person to whom she would show kindness, and prove to herself she was still capable of it. *I will fight to protect myself always*, she thought, *but I will also protect him.*

Everyone else was an enemy.

She led, Behrang followed, and once he caught on, they were unstoppable. They broke every rule they could, they terrorized other students, they took no prisoners, and they had no reservations. They snitched on classmates when classmates cheated and made up crimes for classmates they didn't like. To get back at teachers they cheated on tests, and when they were caught, and were made to stay and clean the school, they laughed the whole time, turning the empty halls into their own playground. They received beatings, their hands held in ice water and then their raw knuckles rapped with sticks, but they were having too much fun with each other, and it felt *good*: school for them was one long act of retribution. Everyone was a target. The school couldn't figure out how to make them stop.

Behrang told his classmates he had figured out a trick to change their Facebook Timeline so they could play with their pasts; all he needed was the password. Then he posted embarrassing admissions of love and outlandish sexual predilections. Ta Manna, meanwhile, had found the spot on a shin where if you kick just right you can leave someone's leg throbbing for hours, and she went around kicking the boys that weren't Hazara. She told the teachers that girls were pinching her, and the teachers had to sort out webs of accusations before anyone got in trouble. Anytime Ta Manna was marched off to the principal's office, she would just start bawling.

Behrang began to use another weapon: though he was shy and a little vain, he was growing into a handsome young man, and the girls began to whisper about him. Ta Manna saw he was popular even before he knew he was, and decided that it presented a strategic advantage. They picked out the girls that had picked on Ta Manna, and he would lead them on, making eyes at them across the classroom, sending them affectionate notes. Once he got her alone, he read off all the insults Ta Manna had prepared for him.

The principal took his time recognizing that the two kids terrorizing his school were cousins, and that punishing them together wasn't punishment at all. The only deterrence would be keeping them separated, so the principal assigned teachers to chase Behrang and Ta Manna down the halls every time they were seen together. And when that didn't stop their reign of terror and the hapless principal took to calling their home to complain about the two disruptive Hazaras, Ta Manna would step forward. "Look at our grades, Dad. So what can you say?"

They stayed up all night whispering to each other, all the way to morning, giggling about the their plots, planning new ones for the future.

First, it was a murder.

For her, that was the beginning, when things began to change in Pakistan. By then she had switched back to a Hazara school, so she was back among her people, but the whole notion of this country being a safe haven was cracking apart.

It began when a Hazara politician was shot with a gun that didn't make any sound. After Yusufi's murder, there were flyers that appeared out of nowhere, hideous messages to Hazaras. Her parents didn't talk about them, but she caught her teacher reading one at school.

"Until we drive all Hazaras out of this land we will not remain silent," it said. "If we cannot kick them out, we will kill them, we will keep killing them. We will make an environment such that they cannot bury their dead, because there won't be enough room in the ground."

A day went by without incident, then another, but she couldn't shake the feeling that something else was going to happen. *Maybe they're waiting for the situation to calm, and that's when they'll strike again.*

Then there was a bus on its way out of Quetta, full of people on their way across the border, traveling to jobs and holy sites. The bus was stopped, there was shouting—"God is great"—and gunmen climbed on board and separated the Hazaras from all the others. They were men from the Army of Jhangvi, terrorists bent on destroying Shias. They dragged the Hazaras outside and sat them down along the road, covered their heads, and then told the bus to get back on its way. They had no quarrel with anyone else.

Before the Hazaras were allowed to say anything, the men from Army of Jhangvi lowered their Kalashnikovs and began shooting. Their guns went left to right, right to left, until all the Hazaras were slumped over. Then the men from the Army of Jhangvi walked up to them and kicked the bodies over into a ditch.

Hazara Town fell into shock. Schools closed for three days. Ta Manna didn't see a single person on the street. *I don't even see a single cat outside.*

They had no one to blame, and no one to be angry at. An enemy that never showed itself was killing Hazaras. The Army of Jhangvi crept up, attacked, and disappeared, an invisible enemy that could be anywhere, at any time. The government wouldn't do anything, she knew. The only Hazara leader anyone had listened to was Yusufi, and he'd been murdered.

Then there was an explosion at the marketplace where all the Hazaras shopped.

Three days later, another one, this time a shopkeeper's truck, which made it seem like not just Hazaras but people doing business with Hazaras might be targets. Everyone stopped coming to the Hazara market, and for a week there were no fruits or vegetables in Hazara Town.

The school opened, not because it was safe but because no one had any idea whether it ever would be, and it couldn't stay closed forever. Ta Manna was happy to go back, but her teachers were terrified. "I can't send you home," one teacher said, "because on the way there might be fighting. And I cannot keep you here, because if they attack the school, I can't protect everyone."

That's how the adults thought. She was embarrassed for them. They kneeled before the threat. They were cowards. They'd sit there and do nothing until all of them were killed, and they'd die without even a little revenge.

She was braver than that. She'd make her adults braver, too. She'd push them to fight back. Her own father was even afraid to go to the bazaar, so the first thing was to get him there.

She and Behrang teamed up: "Bring us to the market to buy books," she said. "If you don't bring us I'm never talking to you again."

"We're going to be killed if we go," her father said.

"Look how many people have been killed," she said, "maybe we *should* be killed." He saw her anger; he relented.

So they went, and she browsed slowly through the store, taking her time, letting her father soak up this bravery she'd given him. He teased her as they left with her bag full of books. "You spend so much money," he said, "even if I work my whole life I don't know whether I'll ever"—and then the sky cracked so loud it sounded like it had happened inside her head and in an instant she realized that even with all the violence happening around her she didn't until this moment known what it felt like. There was smoke, and then silence. They'd been spared, only by an absurd chance. Bodies had opened themselves up all around her. Ta Manna stood and stared; she felt Behrang beside her, but she couldn't take her eyes off a young man whose head had opened and whose brain had spilled out onto the ground behind him, a white smear on the pavement. He was wearing a school uniform; books lay by his side. Another boy lay next to him, legs blown in both directions, like a sick kind of child's toy, a length of gleaming pearl-colored bone sticking out and his eyes locked on hers. There was blood everywhere—she couldn't understand how so much of it had been produced in such a short period of time. She didn't move. Behrang didn't move. She didn't feel like she was actually *there*. She'd left her body and had no control over it; things moved around in front of her eyes but she was unable to interact with them. Ten minutes passed, thirty minutes passed without her even moving, and then her father returned—she hadn't known he'd left—he'd been at the hospital he was saying, where he'd gone to help someone with something, and then he was looking at her with what she understood to be panic, and only then did she see that her aunt was lying on the ground, not moving. Ta Manna's thoughts moved in a loop: the broken leg, the brain out of the head, the school books, the blood, the eyes staring—all night, the images moved through her mind, a spinning mobile of hanging snapshots that wouldn't stop even when she closed her eyes.

After the images began to fade, the thing that stuck with her was how unbearably innocent those boys had been. They seemed more innocent than her. They had just been on their way to class, and then their bodies had been ripped open so that everyone could see the hidden parts of them. It was an invasion of their privacy, as if the bomb had been designed not just to kill but to shame, to take the boys apart in embarrassing ways.

She decided to keep the books her father bought her that day, always in their own pile in her room, as a reminder of what she'd seen. Because she felt shame, too, and guilt—hadn't it been her idea to go to the bookstore? Hadn't she survived, and Behrang, too, and her aunt—who, it turned out, had only fainted—for no reason that made any kind of sense? So she used the books to atone, making sure she'd never forget about the violence. She could suffer a little less now if she knew she still would later.

She learned the boy's name, the one with his brain out on the pavement. She learned that he was supposed to graduate from university that very day, and she thought, *I can work hard my whole life and study and in the end I'll just be like this, dead, with my brain on the street.* She was angry, without anyone to be angry at, so she decided it would be Pashtuns. She would not discriminate, just as the killers had not. She hated all of them. And she began coming up with plans. She'd join the Taliban, she'd join the Army of Jhangvi. *After my college, my university, however long it takes, I will join them, and then after some time, once I've gained their trust, I will destroy them from the inside.*

The Army of Jhangvi next sent out a warning that they were going to shoot a rocket at a hospital Hazaras used; the next day they did, but they missed. Then they sent a letter to Ta Manna's principal and school was closed for another three days.

In English class, a teacher broke down. "Last night I had a dream," he said. "I had six golden bracelets on my wrist. That is a shame for me, that I am a man and there were golden bracelets on my hand. Something wrong is going to happen." Then he said to the kids, "We all need to start carrying guns. I myself am carrying a gun now. If they arrest you for it, I will come to set you free from the jail. You have to protect yourself."

A student next to Ta Manna shifted in his chair, and then reached into his backpack. Something heavy clinked down on his desk. "Sir," he said, "this is a gun."

Ta Manna was envious. She was fourteen, but she felt more than old enough to follow the teacher's instructions.

The killing accelerated; there was no escaping it anywhere. It was in the market, at home, at school. She had to have a gun, too. Her family had one, she knew that. She asked her grandmother to give it to her. "Are you mad, child? Are you joking?"

So she woke up early and searched for it. She had a good idea where it was, a container on top of a bookshelf with a padlock on it. It was the only container in the house that locked. She dragged a stool over and was reaching up when her grandmother walked in.

"What are you doing up there?"

"Nothing. I'm searching for my pen."

"Oh, yeah? And what would your pen be doing up there?"

After that, things happened quickly. The family knew Ta Manna needed to leave. She didn't have the instinct to move away from violence. She sucked it all in and then went looking for more. She was barely a teenager and she'd seen far too much. Everyone could see the way trauma had turned in her: when she looked out the door, the world she saw was a place full of things for her to attack. She was cruel to Pashtuns, mean to her neighbors, she plotted to beat a man for being the wrong race, she wanted to carry a gun, she was an adolescent vigilante. Anyway the school was saying she couldn't continue because the government school was only for citizens. They were refugees, and they'd gotten away with it until eighth grade. But for high school it wouldn't work. There was always private school, but her father said those were for the children of important people. So what was a place of refuge if people who looked like you were being slaughtered in the streets and you couldn't even study?

An uncle in Afghanistan called. He was living in a dry slum in the west of the capital, but he said there was a school nearby where thousands of their people were becoming powerful. Kids studied hard there, he said, and then laughed and yelled between classes and were getting good scholarships to good places like England. He told her that they themselves had a cousin studying in the United States.

So it was decided. She would go to her country for the first time in her life. Behrang wanted to get out, too, but his family had bigger things in mind. They were trying to get asylum in Australia, so they decided to stay, because if their papers came through they'd be off to a country with lots of jobs and clean cities, good universities, and no one blowing up Hazaras. Ta Manna begged him to come with her, but he mocked her. "So you're going to escape," he said. "You're going to abandon us all alone here?"

"*You're* the one escaping from here! You're trying to go to the other side of the ocean; I'm just going to the other side of the soil. I'm going to another backward country, and you're going to a first-world country. Tell me which one of us is escaping?"

He sighed and laughed. "Just say good-bye to me, okay? The way you'd say it if we were never going to meet each other again."

So she did. And then secretly, she prayed as hard as she could that his petition to Australia would be rejected. That way, he wouldn't be able to leave.

When she arrived with her father, her uncle took her aside and sat her down. "Sacrifice yourself for this school," he said, "because you cannot find a place like it anywhere in the world."

What she first saw was the old building, uneven and the color of dust. It looked like the earth had rumbled and coughed up some rooms. But the morning lineup impressed her, all those people with bad features like her all full of energy, all following the rules. Everyone was so *proper*. She'd never been so proper her entire life. And the boys and girls she saw weren't wearing black uniforms like students at other schools, but pastel blue. She thought, *This makes sense. Black is the color of darkness. School is brightness.* When she went to the finance department to pay tuition, the girls building was so strong and solid it made her feel her school in Pakistan had been fragile, all brittle glass windows that seemed to break once a day and could barely withstand a loud noise. Here the windows were small and the walls were thick and sturdy. It felt substantive and strong, and there was one floor on top of the next all the way up she didn't even know how high. When they paid the fee, the man handed her a stack of books nearly up to her chin.

Inside the classroom that first day, everyone was friendly. No one was yelling insults. No one was planning attacks. Everyone had energy.

She got home and sat her uncle down: "I'm so thankful to you that you've brought me here to Marefat," and then she went online to send Behrang a message. She wanted to tell him how amazing this place was, and how he should come and then that last good-bye they had wouldn't have been like he said, never seeing each other again.

She felt something strange in those first few days at Marefat, which at first she couldn't identify, but which she then understood as pride. She was proud to be a part of this school, and she'd never actually been proud to be part of anything before. One day Ashraf Ghani visited because he had worked with the headmaster to solve some kind of crisis, and she thought, *Even famous people come here, even if they're not Hazara.*

She messaged Behrang about everything. "You have to come here. Look, we have a radio station, music class, everything is here. You come from the mountain, okay. I used to live there, but come to *your* country, come and live in the city, come and meet Marefat."

"I want to," he wrote back. His family was still trying to get to Australia. He was torn about it, but he promised her that she'd convinced him, he wanted to come.

There were hiccups, of course. On the second day, in Pashto class her teacher began teasing her about her accent. But that was okay.

I love it here more than my other school. If we don't face difficulty, we cannot reach anywhere. But her life in this country was different. The streets were muddy and uneven. In Pakistan, at least everything had been paved; here almost nothing was, she was always tripping and falling, and within a month she'd ripped a pair of shoes to shreds. *This isn't how people were supposed to live, in mud like this. This is how animals live.* And the family she was living with had old minds. The boys were free, but when she got home one minute late, there was an interrogation. "Where were you? Where did you go?" The girls in her family here were always doing housework. She had never done housework. She was the oldest child, and the only daughter, so her father had always said, "You should not do everything for me. You should read, you should study." Her grandmother, too. Whenever an uncle or an older cousin would ask why Ta Manna wasn't cooking or cleaning, her grandmother would say, "She's too young for that kind of work." When there were family gatherings, she stood by the doorjamb and listen to what they were talking about. "She should be doing housework." The pressure kept mounting on her father until he exploded at her. "You don't know how to be like a girl! Why can't you just act like a girl!"

"I don't *like* the things that the girls do! I don't *want* to be like a girl!"

She began to understand that here, in her homeland, life was hard for girls. Her first week in school she saw a cousin in the halls and reached out to take his hands, and the girls next to her gasped. "What are you doing!?"

"Why, what have I done?"

Mostly, though, she missed Behrang. With this backward, old-minded family surrounding her, she missed having a contemporary who thought the same way she did. She didn't let him know she missed him, though. Instead she acted angry with him, to see if she could get a reaction. But there was something strange: he hadn't sent her a message for three days. She went on the computer and left an angry message for him.

"Why aren't you replying to my messages? You're too proud. Stop ignoring me." No reply.

A day passes.

She checks when she gets home from school. Still there is no message.

On the second day, she checks again. No message.

On the third day, a message in her inbox. "Calm down," Behrang says, "you're crazy. I have a lot of work, okay? I can't be on the computer all the time."

Back in Quetta, Behrang closes his computer a little after 6:00 p.m. He puts on a new white outfit and calls his smallest brother over. "I'm going to go and get you an ice cream, okay?" He leaves on the back of a motorcycle with another cousin driving, and a third riding separately, heading toward the middle of Hazara Town, stopping at an intersection on Four Ways Road.

Behind them, a young man pedals a bicycle toward the same intersection, and is stopped at a checkpoint. The young man is trying to get to the middle of Hazara Town, but he can't get any farther, and is about to be caught. He screams his prayer right there and detonates the bomb attached to his body.

Just like the time Ta Manna and Behrang were nearly hit by the bombing, Behrang's back is to the explosion.

This time the bomb is bigger, and Behrang is just too close to it. The motorcycle is blown over, the expanding gas carries the two boys through the air with the shrapnel. The other cousin moves through the carnage and finds the two boys next to the overturned motorcycle, both of them still breathing. But a piece of shrapnel had hit Behrang in the back and carved him out, another has punctured his skull. There's not really any hope. He lifts Behrang up and begins carrying him toward the hospital, but Behrang's back has been peeled open and what's inside is torn up, his spine severed, his ribs crushed. A piece of metal is lodged in his head. He dies as they carry him. His cousin on the front of the motorcycle survived, because Behrang's body blocked the worst of the shrapnel. Over the next week, he would occasionally wake up in his hospital bed, say Behrang's name, and slip back into unconsciousness.

★ ★ ★

Ta Manna knew it was a joke. Her uncles here did that kind of thing often—they had stupid, dark humor. Still, she went online just to make sure. There was a video showing the victims of a bombing that evening in Quetta, and a thought flitted into her mind before she could suppress it—*He always wanted to have his photo published!*—just as the video scrolled through images. Then she saw Behrang's face.

There was no mistaking it. It didn't make sense, it wasn't real, she was looking at a picture of him but in the picture he had no life in him, his color had changed—and then the video moved on to another victim, and Ta Manna felt a hand on her head. "I know how you feel," her father said, whispering. "But your grandmother still doesn't know. You can't tell her. You have to be patient."

She didn't say anything. She hated to be hugged; her father knew his hand on her head was the most physical affection she could countenance. After a moment, he pulled away. "Ta Manna, if you tell her, I will punish you." And he left the room.

She got up and wandered the house, unsure what to do. Everyone was asleep. She felt the need to talk intensely—she was carrying something huge and poisonous all alone. No one could explain about a thing like this except her grandmother, who couldn't find out, or Behrang, and Behrang was—not anymore. She went to a cousin's room, and he cursed her for waking him up. She told him what she'd seen on the computer, how their cousin had died, and he cursed her again because she woke him for such a weak joke. When she insisted, he said, "You're computer is probably ruined."

"No! A *human* is ruined!" He rolled over, and his eyes met hers.

"Who?" Now there was weight in his voice.

"Behrang," she said, and he fell back and began to wail. The news was a disease spreading through the house, and now she was worried her grandmother would hear the commotion. She rushed to the sink and filled a bucket with water to revive him, but when she helped him up to his feet, his knees buckled.

In that moment she understood that when you are helpless, and when those who are supposed to protect you are helpless, too, you can salve yourself by seeking out small things you can control. The earthquake you can't escape, but the aftershocks you can be ready for.

In treating the grief of others, she found she could make use of her own. Her cousin kept weeping, crying into the blanket as Ta Manna stood over him, and finally he began to move. He crawled to his feet and then went down the stairs. He left the house, and she let him go. She gave him some time. And then as the lace curtains over the windows began to glow with morning light, she pulled her coat on and went out after him.

She knew where he'd be. She went to the graveyard, and she found him there, heaving, having exhausted his tears.

"What can you do?" she said. "If you cry, can you bring him back? So stop crying."

She helped him up and together, they went to Marefat, arriving just as the sun began to show. Stray dogs lumbered down the dirt path on either side of them, heading home to wherever they hid in the day. Ta Manna found her place in the perfect rows of pale blue and white bodies, and the school day began.

15

SEVEN MONTHS LEFT

On the day the British ambassador comes to visit, Aziz is especially happy to see me. "Ah, he has arrived! *Kaffir tarib,*" he says, "'the worst infidel,'" and he gives me a long, hard hug and a big kiss on the cheek. Shaiq is excited too. He grabs my hand and doesn't let go until he's assembled in his mind everything he wants to say, and then it all explodes out of him all at once: "Hello thank you I am fine how are you you are welcome!" Shaiq is happy because Shaiq is almost always happy, but also because Aziz is happy. Aziz is happy because today is a day he gets to show off for the ambassador, and having an infidel on hand is the best defense against bullshit. Important Outsiders can't be too cute if another Outsider is there, watching.

Aziz holds my hand as he completes his circuit through the girls' building—boys are allowed into the big new building, but the idea is, when they're here, they're here as guests of the girls. It affords the girls some power.

He pokes his head into classes, he checks that all is in order, he returns to the dirt path in front of the school, where an anvil-jawed British security officer stands awkwardly. He's part of the advance team, securing the scene for the ambassador's arrival. Aziz goes and stands next to him, trying to make himself available for casual conversation, but there doesn't seem to be anything to say. The security man is trying very diligently to be unassuming, but he might as well be another species. He is very apparently wearing a flak jacket, which makes his torso huger and even more square, and over it he wears a cargo vest with two extended magazine clips, to go with the two already on the weapon. One clip engaged, the other fastened to the side. As he stands, he fingers the brass of the half-exposed round in the chamber. He seems to realize it's a menacing gesture and he quickly lowers the weapon, shifting it behind him, holding it behind his thigh with one hand, like he's trying to hide it. He's trying for discretion, but the gesture has the reverse effect, a dozen boys who are just then moving between classes are immediately drawn to the weapon which has just been relocated to their eye level. Within ninety seconds there are a dozen of them standing behind him, transfixed. From the front, the weapon is no longer visible, so the boys just look like they're drawn in by his backside, as if he had some Pied Piper–like trance emanating from his buttocks.

"I don't know if you know," he says, breaking the silence with Aziz, "but one of my—uh, colleagues is on your roof."

Aziz gives a half nod. "We're used to such kinds of gestures." This part of the city presents itself as threatening to Outsiders. The Desert has none of the comfortable things Outsiders are used to hiding behind in this country. HESCO containers, razor wire, and sand bags—heavy things to duck under when snipers start shooting at you. Here, half-finished buildings rise up on all sides. In the last decade the area around Marefat has gone from the vast empty expanse Michael Metrinko saw to one of the most densely populated parts of the city. A person tasked with security and trained to neutralize threats sees danger everywhere. Where the man now stands, there are potential sniper nests all around him. It doesn't matter that there are very few people out in the Desert who would have any reason to wish foreigners harm; Marefat is far out in the slums, in unfamiliar territory, far from help, isolated between narrow twisting alleys that can trap a large vehicle and feel like shooting galleries for people inclined to think in a particular kind of way.

Aziz is polite. He knows the Brit is uncomfortable, he knows that this is a man who is trained to identify threats and that he's probably trying very hard not to make Aziz feel like one. He tries to maintain idle conversation as they wait for the ambassador to arrive.

But something strange is happening: the Brit keeps going silent, midsentence. His eyes roll up to a point somewhere on the horizon. He seems vacant for a moment, and then his attention returns to Aziz, as if nothing happened.

Aziz tries not to be distracted, but it's like trying to talk to a man who keeps having tiny seizures, and he's is unsure how to handle it. He decides to just keep on talking as if nothing was happening, and it takes several mini-seizures before Aziz finally understands that the man is having two conversations at once, speaking to Aziz while also listening through the dongle in his ear to his colleagues updating him on their respective positions.

"We're going to have an amphitheater here," Aziz says.

"Yes, mate."

"We have a music program."

"What, uh—instruments do you teach?" It doesn't really sound like a question.

"Piano is the best. Once you learn piano, it's easy to learn every other instrument."

Then another small seizure, this one longer, then his attention returns to Planet Earth and he looks Aziz directly in the eye. "Excuse me," he says, as if he hasn't been standing next to Aziz for ten minutes, "but those two vehicles, are they yours?" He points to two dirty old Corollas, both empty. They've been spotted by the sniper on the roof, who, being either bored or antsy, has started imaging threats and relaying them over the radio.

"Yes, yes," Aziz says.

"Okay, fine."

It's not fine, that's clear, so Aziz yells toward the school and two skinny boys go bounding off toward the car to move them farther from the school. The threat is neutralized.

Finally, a convoy of black SUVs comes lumbering down the dirt road, all of them screeching to a halt in front of the school, kicking up dust and vomiting military-looking people with weapons at their chests, who take up positions all around Aziz like he's some kind of

fugitive they've finally cornered after years on the run. The ambassador and his aide share a greeting with Aziz, the ambassador's eye catches the sign above the girls' building for a moment, and then Aziz is off without any more niceties. He takes them into classrooms, interrupting students, on to the computer lab, then a girls' class, then they're on the third floor and Aziz is a little short of breath. "Students, this is Sir Rich-Ard," he says, "This is the first visit of the ambassador to this—part of the city."

"It's a pleasure to see you learning English," the ambassador says, not quite ready to speak. Another silence. "I've been to India before."

More classes, then the art room. Aziz takes him to the library, where a table is set up for a discussion with a select group of students. Ta Manna has made the cut, and she sits in silence, watching the ambassador closely.

Aziz prompts the ambassador to speak again; he has not been briefed for this either. "From our point of view," he begins, "a little bit about why Britain is in Afghanistan. We're here because—in 1992 we closed our embassy. We decided that Afghanistan would be happy without us. Sadly that proved an entirely mistaken conclusion. Your country went through a decade of great disturbance, violence, and misery, and we're now very determined to do what we can to stop that from happening again, and to ensure that what we see as great achievements in your society, in your economy, in your government over the last ten or twelve years, that that progress is sustained, and that you can look forward in your generation to a very different life from what your parents had to suffer in the period before 2001."

A student raises his hand and asks the ambassador, "After next year will security still be the same? When international armies leave Afghanistan, what will happen? As you know with the presence of international community, Afghanistan developed a lot. But after they leave Afghanistan, what will happen? Will these progresses continue or will they be stopped?"

The ambassador makes his polite smile and says, "I think that while I understand the reasons for your concern, many of my own staff, as I said at the beginning, have exactly the same preoccupations, but we believe that objectively there are good reasons for being more

hopeful than many of you are." He gives some reasons, then says that "we and the Americans and others are happy to retain some presence here." But, he adds, "your president is of two minds."

This is salt in the wound. For the Marefat students it may be the most frustrating, terrifying, demoralizing thing of all: that their own president, speaking on *their* behalf, is pushing the foreigners out.

"My own view is there would be benefit in a continued presence of international forces," and then: "But that's a choice for your government." And then, finally, he strikes another nerve. The ambassador says, "I think in any case that the problem of the Taliban will only be fully resolved by negotiation."

This also most of the students find terrifying. For these Hazara kids, especially girls, who've been able to go to school their entire lives, the idea of negotiations with the Taliban is chilling. But it's worse, because there is a conspiracy theory making the rounds, which, as far as the students are concerned, the ambassador has just confirmed: that the foreigners are supporting the Taliban. When the Taliban opened an office in Qatar, with the approval of the international community, and then raised their own flag, panic shot through Marefat. The Taliban was coming back to power; that's what the students took from it. Not just that. The foreigners were going to help them.

A sixteen-year-old girl raises her hand to ask about this Taliban office in Qatar, but her question quickly unravels into an unnerved accusation, in which the ambassador is cast as personally responsible for a tragedy she's sure is about to befall her. Aziz is expressionless. The ambassador responds politely. "On the question of women's rights," he says, "and the question of whether they're going to be rolled back . . . if there's a deal with the Taliban, will you pay the price . . . ?" He pauses, allows himself a breath. "In part, we think the changes of the last ten or twelve years are irreversible. No one can take from your minds the knowledge and understanding that's there. I think the use of mobile phones to improve interconnections between people, and particularly between women, will not—I don't think you're going to find a reversion to the period before."

The students listen impatiently. They're just warming up and ready to extract more information from this man. Each time the am-

bassador finishes answering a question a dozen hands go up. But Aziz wants him over for lunch, and he knows the ambassador will try to wiggle out of it, so he ends the discussion, and the students stand up reluctantly as the ambassador exits.

Out in the alley, a new security man is being overtaken by another crowd of boys, drawn like magnets to the assault rifle strapped across his chest. He keeps a gloved hand on it like it's an untrained pet, as the mass of tiny people whose language he doesn't speak press toward him. One of the boys slips through the crowd to the middle of the circle, reaches a finger out, and touches the butt of the rifle. "Don't touch that," the man says, "it might go 'bang.'"

Aziz walks the ambassador to the rented house, and they settle into the living room, the Brits doing their best to look comfortable sitting on the floor in their suits. There is more silence, and then the ambassador tries to make conversation. "So are you approved by the Ministry of Education?"

They eat a little, the ambassador trying to find the polite way to take his leave, but Aziz applies some guilt. "But you arrived here late," he says, "so you must stay late." The ambassador smiles and politely deflects. "I'm sorry—we have a meeting back in the city," and Aziz smiles, too, and the ambassador is gone.

After lunch, walking back to the school, he stops for a moment to commune with his ditch. "The tarp is too low," he says to one of the workman. "It's not protecting anything."

16

THE TROUBLEMAKER

She is a changed girl now. She used to be enthusiastic about school; now she is detached. Behrang is dead. As if to honor him, she again devotes herself to causing trouble. She finds new sidekicks at Marefat, Jamila and Adila, and leads them on her own campaign of terror. She spreads rumors about the heavyset head of the English program, who, she tells everyone, almost failed the international English test, so how was he qualified to teach? She says she knows it because their ancestors came from the same village. She skips class and giggles with her friends under the ledge behind the bathrooms, where stray cats pick bits of scraps from trash and the threesome plan their next rumor campaign. She sprints through the halls while everyone else is in class, sliding on the dust past the teachers whenever she can, fishing for the angriest responses. "I'll skin you alive!" was the one to beat.

The other girls are thrilled; they've never seen anything like it. Ta Manna verges on reckless, and she knows that's what her appeal is to them, what holds them in her thrall. She is breaking down walls for them. They had been shy, demure girls, and then she came along, barking at authority because it hadn't done anything for her and asking what it had done for them. What's the point in doing what it says? Our parents are uneducated, she says. The people who led the Hazaras took for themselves and left their own people vulnerable. The

Outsiders are leaving and the Taliban is coming back and the people who are supposed to handle things like that are either ignorant or blind or afraid or all three. Why listen to them? Why not shake a boy's hand? Why not go out after school, have lunch somewhere away from campus and spread rumors about Marefat? Why not tell Jamila's parents a small lie, that they are staying at school late to do homework, and instead go cause mischief for a few hours in the afternoon—go to Ta Manna's grandfather's house to wrestle on the foam the family uses to stuff pillows, and tease Ta Manna's small cousins?

Jamila and Adila had lived behind a wall of fear, afraid of some kind of damnation if they did the things they weren't supposed to do. Then Ta Manna came along, casting off fission and marching them right across all the borders they weren't supposed to cross, showing them that nothing happened. For Ta Manna, it felt like being a leader. Mostly, it felt like a purpose.

Teachers gathered and said that this new girl from Pakistan had cast a spell over the other two. That Ta Manna had recruited them to her side and turned them against authority.

It was true, they were partial replacements for Behrang; it was a process of coping no one else could understand. She couldn't entirely understand it herself. Ta Manna knew what Teacher Aziz was trying to do: create a place where girls could nudge the walls that confined them. But he wanted to do it too slowly. *Well, Teacher Aziz may have his opinions, but why are a man's ideas about how a girl should make progress better than a girl's? Is it him or is it us who have to live in this prison of a country? Why should we be content behind prison bars that moved out an inch at a time? Is it he who gets humiliated just for trying to shake a boy's hand, or is it me?*

But there was something Ta Manna didn't realize. When she came along and showed her new friends what it looked like when you stopped caring what people thought, she was showing them an illusion. This was not the world they actually lived in.

Adila could handle it, she was world-wise already. She could see being around Ta Manna as being lost in a story, an adventure she knew was not really her own. But Jamila was desperate for it to be real.

When she left Ta Manna every day, she went home to a place that hadn't changed in a generation. She told Ta Manna: "My father took a second wife." He didn't treat the woman well, and she in turn lorded over Jamila like a warden. Jamila, just by being the man's off-spring was grazing against the woman's wounds. Jamila felt punished for being alive. The second wife was uneducated, and in a household with another wife, she was also redundant. She had no purpose other than to marshal over the family's store of virtue, so Jamila became her mannequin.

Every day Ta Manna showed Jamila what it was like to run through the Desert's alleys without caring who saw, and every day Jamila went home to a woman trying to turn the girl into her own monument to honor.

The first time Jamila slit her wrists, Ta Manna was furious.

How foolish, she thought. She'd lost Behrang, and before that, she'd seen a boy with his brain spread out on the street. How wasteful for someone to give up life, on purpose. "If you do that again," Ta Manna said, "I'll do it, too."

The threat worked for a few weeks, then Jamila tried again. Ta Manna kept her promise. She cut deep enough to leave marks she could show Jamila.

But the third time, Jamila was serious. She put a deep striation diagonally across her vein so it wouldn't close, then did two more; Ta Manna got a call with Jamila screaming on the other end of the line and thought her friend was being attacked. When she sorted out what had happened and told her father she had to run to Jamila's house to save her, her father grabbed her by the arm.

"You can't go," he said. "I'm sorry. This is a matter for their family, you can't interfere in their business."

Jamila survived, but the marks were so deep they became blue scars and it was inevitable someone at Marefat would take notice. When they did, Ta Manna was summoned to the principal's office. *They think I convinced her to try to kill herself? I did the opposite!* Ta Manna believed she should be praised for being the only one trying to help the girl. But then she turned it around in her mind. *Of course they think that. Of course they have it completely backward.* Proof, then, of what she's always thought, that people with authority are clueless and she's better off ignoring what they say. Just like it's always been, she's better off taking matters into her own hands.

She decides to plan Jamila's escape.

The first idea is for Jamila to slip away when she's traveling abroad, and her family will have to come home without her. A decent plan, because the family has the means to travel once or twice a year and are due for a trip.

Ta Manna decides that's too long and too passive. They need a plan she has more control over. So she comes up with a better idea: Jamila will run away and they will move her to her own apartment in the city.

They can't be seen working together, so the first step is to stage a fight. Everyone has to think Jamila and Ta Manna fell out, and that Jamila is furious with Ta Manna, rather than under her guidance. So on the day before the biology midterm, Jamila sneers at Ta Manna in class. "I've broken your chalkboard."

"Okay," Ta Manna says, with great, patronizing calm. "Well, you're still my friend, don't worry. If I can help you, you just let me know."

Jamila yells at Ta Manna loud enough that the whole class can hear, "I don't *want* you as my friend!" And then does a passable job of bursting into tears and storming out, leaving the class in a stunned silence and Ta Manna biting her lip to keep from laughing.

The plan fails. Renting an apartment for a girl by herself proves too much even for Ta Manna. Jamila's salvation comes, eventually, in her country's damnation. Or at least, in the way her family sees its damnation. With the bombings picking up in frequency, her father decides to move the family away. To Dubai, then—done with this country. Of course, Jamila will still be stuck with the same family, but Ta Manna imagines Dubai as a place with fewer walls and boys who aren't as stupid as they are here. Maybe in a different environment, the family will ease up.

Meanwhile, Ta Manna's relatives from Pakistan have come to stay so they can give Behrang a proper memorial in his home country, and she is surrounded by people thinking about his death. His little brother, five years old, is still coming up with extravagant reasons for why he hasn't seen Behrang in half a year. "Don't worry, Mom," he says. "Behrang is on the pilgrimage! He comes home to visit sometimes, but he just keeps doing it when we're gone!" Only five years old, and the boy has an instinct to comfort his mother.

Or maybe he's just resolved not to face the truth. And maybe Ta Manna has, too. Maybe she's just looked away. Pushed her cousin to a place in her mind where she didn't really have to process it, and could distract herself with anger.

Her grandmother brought a big photo of Behrang and insists on putting it up in the living room. Ta Manna can't look away anymore; she has to look at him all the time. Perhaps it's not a coincidence that her dreams are now about Hazaras dying. Sometimes she dreams of the Afshar massacre, where all these Hazaras died a few miles from where she lives now. Sometimes she dreams of just Behrang. When he visits, he's just escaped from his grave, and he has his coffin next to him. He's somehow holding it up to her with one hand, like a child showing off a drawing, looking for approval.

"I don't want to go to that world," he tells her, each time. "Not yet."

Aziz tried to talk to her once, about all her anger. "Why are you talking so much about revenge?"

"Sir, the fire that has burned inside me, no one can put it down," she said. She tells him all about the bomb attack she and Behrang saw together in Pakistan, and about the two boys, their mangled bodies beneath their school uniforms. "Sir, it was really—I was only thirteen years old when I saw that situation. But that affects you. Sir, what can we say? Should we say, 'We will take the hand of the enemy to help them,' so they can just kill other people? That's injustice, sir, to our own people."

"It's not injustice. Mostly, forgiveness is justice."

"Sir, we cannot be that simple, like the Prophet Mohammad, peace be upon him, that we can forgive everybody."

"He did not forgive everybody. But *you* can."

"Maybe somebody can, but I cannot." She thinks again of the bombing. "Because, you know? The brain out of the skull. It was—"

"I've seen lots of those cases in my life." He is firm now. "It doesn't mean you should live in the trauma of the bad times. You should come out of the bad times."

"How, sir? There is no way. Everything again turns us to that thing—"

"Just imagine this. Imagine that there are no words such as 're-venge.' They don't exist. And then revenge will leave your mind. Just expel it. And insert a new word, like 'forgiveness,' and it helps. Don't hate any person."

Ta Manna is quiet. She's convinced for the time being at least that Aziz means well, and that he may even be right, but she does not think that what he's saying is realistic. Finally, she sighs, and speaks again, this time, in a defeated tone.

"But it is like a needle that pinches your heart every second. Everything makes the fire more and more. So there is no water to make it cool, to finish the fire." Now it's Aziz's turn to be at a loss. The master at speaking to rooms full of elders finds himself out-matched by an eighth-grade girl's emotions.

All he can manage is, "You're just taking it too seriously."

She is, in that moment, beyond convincing.

Even in her grief she's indomitable. In her exasperation, too. When she makes plans out of anger, she cannot be convinced they are foolhardy. She says she's going to beat up the Pashto teacher who makes fun of her accent, she says she's going to become a terrorist so she can kill terrorists from the inside, she says she's going to be a doc-tor. She is constantly evolving, and she is astoundingly observant. She has an impressive command of language, human behavior, even politics. She is confident in her understanding of the world, which is so often correct that when it isn't you almost overlook it; she dreams of a nuclear bomb dropped in China, and she could almost convince you that the way it happened in her dream is the correct version of history. She is convincing even when she is definitely wrong.

Even when she confuses facts, she has a wider worldview than most children you've met in the West, and than her own parents. She speaks even in English like a student at a liberal arts college; it doesn't quite compute that she's only in eighth grade. You don't know why you don't doubt her when she speaks, or when she lets you in on her plans, even when they sound absurd. There is such conviction in this girl that it's hard to imagine anything getting in her way. Of all the women who could be forced down if the worst happens—if democracy fails, if the Taliban takes over or if civil war turns women's progress into a distant, secondary concern—this girl will stay standing. Perhaps it's as simple as the fact that she's resisted for so long. No one has managed to get her to pick up a cloth yet, to clean the kitchen table, or be helpful in any remotely domestic chore. That's somehow encouraging: it sustains this faith that she'll survive, and not just survive, but emerge on the other side of whatever happens next, leading a revolution.

Maybe this whole notion is borne from naïveté. Maybe we just need to believe she's going to make it.

17

SIX MONTHS LEFT

On the last day of June, a storm moved in from the west.

The rain lasted no more than five minutes and was gone as quickly as it had come, the sun back out and punishing. But those five minutes brought the city back into focus. The people believe it's because the water keeps the dust from rising, but it must be something more, it's as if the rain scrubs the air on its way down. It's a different city after rain, color comes back, like the world was hidden behind a filthy window that's finally been cleaned. The squatter houses up on the mountains step forward, the mountains themselves get their texture back. If you look up at them long enough, you realize there is motion—there's community up there. People you didn't at first notice but you now see walking back and forth. The homes are built into such steep rock face that the lives look lived in two dimensions; it's like watching characters move around on a screen in an old video game. From down below, it looks like people walk past each other, but they're not walking past each other—one is twenty feet above the other.

And there's something that empties you out about people up there on the hills, their lives on display but removed. Maybe it's that they're people who are close enough to you, and exposed enough, that it's almost intimate, but at the same time, they are people you will never know. You see them perform the trivial tasks of daily life—rinsing a carpet, carrying water—but you will never meet them. They will have kids, get sick, fall and break bones, meet friends they didn't think they'd ever see again, live entire lives you will come close to but never touch.

Down on the streets in the Desert, men sleep under pushcarts to escape the sun. There's no siesta here, so it's just lost time. During these dry-hot, dusty days you wake up thirsty, but now it's the holy month of Ramadan (Ramazan, as it's called here), so when you wake up you can't drink, or eat, not until the end of the day when the sun sets and the mullahs come over the loudspeakers to tell the country it's okay. The holy month moves each year, creeping earlier and earlier, and this year it falls right at the height of summer. Fasting and skipping water during daylight hours is especially hard when daylight lasts so long, and when it's so relentlessly hot and dry.

Aziz projects optimism. "During Ramazan," he says, "I am working or producing three times more. Because part of my brain is not busy with eating or planning the meals."

Aziz never plans meals.

For a time, at the very beginning of the holy month, everybody is excited. Families wake up in the middle of the night to eat and drink before the sun rises, and these midnight meals are celebratory, as are the *iftars*, the break-the-fast feasts, every sundown. But by the fifth or sixth day of Ramadan, the novelty has worn off, things are slow and languorous, and the whole city moves to a pause.

It's the same at the school: in the beginning of the holy month, there's still energy. The bell still rings, a cloud of dust still rises with a stampede of children emptying into the halls. There is a trend among the boys now: bald heads. Some of them say it's because there's a bad batch of shampoo for sale out in the Desert with something toxic that makes their hair fall out. Others say it's on purpose, because they want to look like the foreign soldiers.

Whatever the reason, it has the effect of making the halls look like an upturned crate of potatoes tumbling toward the door whenever the bell rings. And as the commotion continues downstairs, up in the finance office, Aziz is bargaining with builders over the price of work they've already completed. There is lot of yelling, some laughing. It's impossible to tell how a meeting is going because yelling and laughing are present in equal measure. Inside the office, the negotiations take the form of a game Aziz has grown adept at, but which the builders have, too: Aziz will say, "Give us a break, we're just a school." The builders will say, "We already have," and recount all the accommodations they've made. Then the builders will ask for their money, Aziz will appeal to their sense of charity, and the process will repeat, the same points made by each side, through at least two refills of tea. There are three main bargaining points Aziz deploys during these negotiations, and he won't give up until he's cycled through all three.

Charity is the first, though it's dulled with overuse.

The second is still potent: the fact that his dreams for Marefat's growth are boundless. He reminds the builders that there is a new building to be built, the ceiling of the auditorium they haven't even spoken about yet, and someday, maybe, Marefat University, plus the flicker of an idea for campuses in other parts of the country. The prospect of future work is infinite, if they'll only consider making this one last concession, lowering their rates just a little more, allowing payment to be delayed one final time. Because— and here's the third point in Aziz's negotiating combo—"We don't have cash."

He still occasionally finds success with this one. He wins himself lower prices by telling the builders he can't actually afford the work he hired them to do, and probably shouldn't have asked them to do in the first place. Aziz is opening the holy month with a little bit of extortion.

It's only after several rounds of negotiations that the real, unspoken, but ever-present reason for his continued success begins to emerge. Marefat may be cash-poor, but it is flush in collateral. The one thing no one can deny is that Marefat has 2,700 kids, plus a few hundred on the wait list, plus a few hundred in the adult learning program, plus a board of directors stacked with people who provide value of varying sorts, discounted steel, wood, occasionally coal. In nearly every class, in almost every gaggle of girls clapping in the halls and giggling, is evidence that this crazy beast Aziz has built is working.

It's why, ever since the disaster with the businessman happened and the ground swallowed Aziz's house, he has insisted on having meetings with builders *at* the school, where all the evidence of success surrounds the people he is negotiating with. It's why he can build so many things without ever really being able to afford any of them. And it's why he whispers later, "After these years, we owe $55,000, and still continue to owe more!"

The meeting ends with all parties apparently satisfied. They say their good-byes with warmth, even as Aziz has managed to further delay payment.

As the city settles into Ramadan, classes end temporarily. Not to give the students a break for the heat or to make the fasting easier on them. Because it's time for midterms.

It's exceptionally bad luck for Ta Manna that her first Marefat midterms are during Ramadan. She'd become accustomed to, and succeeded at, school in Pakistan where she had five or six classes at a time, and therefore five or six exams; at Marefat, she was pummeled with the seventeen different subjects the Afghan education system prescribes and, correspondingly, seventeen subjects she had to master for her exams: biology, chemistry, physics, algebra, geometry, religious studies, Dari literature, Pashto literature, English, history, geography, Arabic, sport, ethics, Quran, arts, civic education. She is entirely overwhelmed trying to study for all of them while fasting. Her exams don't go well.

Aziz sits down in the media department. With the students off cramming, he's taking advantage of the quiet time to make some progress on a new project: building an archive of old videos the school has of its special events. Today he's writing English subtitles for them. It has the feeling of building a time capsule to make sure a legacy is left behind. Aziz wants to make sure it's a legacy that doesn't need a translator.

Today on the to-do list is a video of a poem sung during a

celebration of Grandfather Mazari, the Hazara patriarch who had become something of a saint for them. Aziz is adamant that the translation be exactly right, which is a problem because he finds English to be less poetic than Persian. Direct translations yield clumsy, clinical poems that never satisfy him. So the video plays, is scrolled back, plays again, is scrolled back again, as Aziz searches for the right words. On the screen a man sings on a stage, women weep in the audience, then it all happens in reverse, then plays again, until finally, a half hour later, he's managed to get a single verse he doesn't mind.

> *When I die, from the dust of my decaying body*
> *Let my throat become a flute*
> *That a mischievous boy plays*
> *Disturbing the rest of the deep sleepers.*

Afterward, Aziz and his oldest son, Abuzar, retire to the living room in the rented house. Any other month it'd be lunchtime, but Aziz is fasting. Abuzar is not. At least, not every day, and Aziz is unbothered by his son's lapse. He encourages his children not to fast if they don't want to; he doesn't want their faith to enslave them, "because it should not be a thing that grabs your collar and forces you." It should be a thing where you say, "I'm just in love with God, and he doesn't care for me to suffer, he doesn't care, he doesn't want to disturb people."

When they were first building the school, there were complaints from all corners because the plans did not include a place to pray. Aziz never even considered changing the plans to include one. *This is a school,* was his thinking, *not a mosque.* There have been other small resistances. He didn't put *Bismillah al Rahman al Rahim,* "in the name of God, most gracious, most compassionate," a phrase that's supposed to begin every important venture, in the beginning of his memoir, and people were shocked. When they asked him, "How could you dare skip the blessing?" he said, "Look in the book, and see for yourself if you find God there." Anyway, as far as he's concerned, if you want to get technical, God is everywhere. "In the Quran it says if you were sleeping on your back, or side, and even *think* of God, then you are looking in God's direction, you love God, and that is a blessing."

As flies flit around the room and Aziz settles into his rest, one of his nephews bounces around on the carpet. The child is of the age when his head seems cartoonishly large for his body, so his walking is marionettelike, little limbs yanking spastically to keep up with the mass of a head floating across the room. He stumbles around and collapses into my side, then looks up at me. Then he rolls to the middle of the carpet, and begins targeting flies with a series of grunting kung fu jump-kicks. Outside, the rest of the Royesh children race tricycles back and forth across the concrete courtyard, crashing into each other, toppling, skinning knees.

"Tell me," Aziz says, "when you see these kids, does it make you miss your childhood? You know, I have an envy. I didn't really have a childhood. I guess before the Communist coup I had a childhood, somehow. But I had to leave. When I had kids myself, I think I deprived them of a childhood, too. All Abuzar had for fun was to follow me around to speeches and practice writing."

Abuzar is sitting across the room, but he doesn't say anything. "When I brought him a toy, it was maybe a toy pen or a notebook. But these kids," he gestures at the boy still attacking flies unselfconsciously, "I leave to be as free as they want to be, as naughty as they want."

The thought of children moves him to nostalgia, and he closes his eyes for a moment. I can see him moving back to that time, when Abuzar was small and the family was in exile.

"Back then, I would tell stories," he says. "I wanted to tell them about the Taliban, but in a softer way. I would tell them, episode by episode, about a 'cruel wind' that was dominating the jungle. And through that, I also taught them English." Abuzar was four and Farida was six when Aziz began reading them *Alice's Adventures in Wonderland* in English, translating some of it but keeping the rest just out of reach so they had to learn the language to find out what happened next. Even though he was constantly worried about assassins from Iran, and even though it was lonely in a country not his own, still he is nostalgic for it, because it was simpler. Simpler at least than now, after all that's happened since. Since he built a school, since America came to Afghanistan, since he brought the school home and built it up because he believed the Taliban was gone forever, since, instead, the Taliban came roaring back, since the Americans began to leave. Now, things are complicated. And now, there are many more people he has to worry about.

"If the zero option happens, Jeff, that's the end of Afghanistan. I take that as the end of the country. That's something I cannot persuade myself even to think about." His tone changes, from sad to something more like pleading. "Why would America do that? There is no reason to throw all our achievements on the ground and just go!" He is almost disdainful. "Afghanistan is not an expensive project! It's not Vietnam. It's not Iraq! This is a place where more than ninety percent of the people *want* the international community here. Most people here think international people are a gift of God. Now we have a middle class, thousands of university students, millions of women going to school. They are all supporting the presence of the international community. What's the reason to leave the country? Just because of Karzai? Just because one or two of our members of parliament are lying to themselves, calling for jihad while eating from a bowl given to them by the international community? Driving in cars given to them by the international community? No others besides them have lost with the international community here. Except the Taliban lost a monopoly on power they did not deserve. Other than that, no one is a loser."

He is frightened but also frustrated, partially because he blames America leaving on something as simple as miscommunication between his president and the American one. "In your country you're supposed to make a direct point like a machine. But here we are not accustomed to this with-us-or-against-us kind of language. Here it is 'hopefully.' It is 'if God wills.'" What's most frightening to Aziz is that the Americans may be serious about the zero option, and President Karzai simply doesn't realize it.

"You know it's a dream I have to meet my American friends here without any fear of security. To have natural attitudes with them, just to take them and roam around my school." He sighs. "I guess we're

a country of dreams. Of wishes. Or envies. We're a country of envies."
His eyes close for a moment; he is resisting the need to sleep. "Now,
when I talk to students, especially kids, especially girls—especially
girls, I wish there was time for them to run around and play and talk
without fear. It's their right. You have hundreds of kids, they long for
free moments just to walk in a park and play with their friends." An
idea seems to flicker in his mind; he's distracted for a moment. He
mentions a graduate from Marefat, who left excited to make something of herself, but who came back to Aziz looking like college had
constricted her. "I really like to see her running, dancing, singing.
She should be free. But when she goes out on the street, she has to
protect herself. When she goes to Kabul University, she has to be
conservative." He sinks down onto his elbow, shimmying into a re-
clining position. "There are just a few times a year when kids are
singing at Marefat. But as human beings, the kids need to have joy.
With their friends. They should not be like me, all the time thinking
of the zero option, thinking that it's really something true. They
should be just as other kids." His eyes are becoming moist; they take
on a glaze, moist from fatigue, and from emotion.

"If we're not toppled and the country is not destroyed," he finally says, "then I'm sure that in three or four years to come, I am
sure we will have the environment for some of these needs to be
filled. There are lots and lots of good possibilities here if the zero option doesn't come true."

He closes his eyes for a beat, and opens them again. "If it comes
true it will be the end of . . . it's the end of *logic*. It's the end of everything. It is time for us to face the music."

It seems, then, that the conversation has become too much for
him. He shifts his body again and relaxes into the carpet.

"A good way of passing the time during Ramazan is just to
sleep," he says. "Let's rest, my Jeff." He lays his heads down on the
patterned square pillows, the kind Ta Manna's family sold, fashioned
out of plywood with a thin layer of fabric that does nothing to mask
how uncomfortable it is to sleep on wood. But neither the wooden
pillow nor his children and nieces and nephews yelling each other's
names outside and crashing tricycles into one another bothers him.

It all seems to soothe him. He opens his eyes one last time. "Here in this small house," he says, "the kids playing is just the music of our sleep."

He smiles, and within minutes, he is snoring softly.

Ashraf Ghani summoned Aziz for an iftar at his home. Since the two men formed an alliance to end the hunger strike, Ghani has been pulling Aziz into an inner circle, starting with a group of intellectuals he assembles for Friday discussions. The discussions are ostensibly to help prepare for a lecture series, but really, Aziz assumed, they were gathered as an exploratory committee for a Ghani's political ambitions. For Aziz, it felt like perhaps the opportunity he'd been waiting for.

This evening, when Aziz arrives, Ghani has just showered and is resting, having returned that day from a trip to Lebanon to visit his wife's family. He still seems tired from the journey, but he rouses himself quickly to greet Aziz. He wants to tell Aziz in person, he says, that he has made up his mind: he will run for president. He wants Aziz to be among the first to know. Because he wants Aziz to help.

It is exciting and flattering all at once, though Aziz knows immediately that helping Ashraf Ghani would make a lot of his own community unhappy and risk losing their respect entirely. Supporting Ghani means being seen as shilling for a Pashtun, and many of his people will call him a traitor. They'll have extra cause because the Kochis, the nomadic subgroup of Pashtuns to which Ghani belongs, have a special animus with Hazaras. Two hundred years ago, when the Iron Amir was trying to subjugate Hazaras, he gave the Kochis deeds to land the Hazaras lived on. These days, when the Kochis' annual migration takes them through Hazara land, the clashes are especially violent. The Kochis are armed. Many Hazaras have lost homes and even family members to the conflict, and many consider Kochis to still be agents of bigger powers trying to suppress Hazaras. Aziz helping a Kochi take power would be seen as helping to subjugate his own people. To some, he will look dangerously naïve; others will wonder how much he's getting paid to turn on his brothers and sisters.

Aziz has his own news to share with the Pashtun. Marefat School, he says, is officially inviting Ghani to become a board member. They have seats on the board reserved for non–Hazaras, and as long as he was reaching out to other tribes, he might as well reach out to the most controversial one possible. So the two men make an exchange of commitments, and along with it, an agreement: neither Aziz's help with Ghani's campaign nor Ghani's seat on the Marefat board will be made public. It could hurt Ghani to be seen as too cozy with the Hazara institution, just as it could hurt Aziz to be seen as too cozy with a Kochi. It will be a silent agreement. But the link between the two men is set.

Then, as if in demonstration of what his new political connections would entitle him to, Marefat gets a favor from a well-placed friend: electricity. For the very first time, Marefat is connected to city power, because a member of the G-72 who works for the Ministry of Water and Energy has called in a favor and bumped the school to the front of the line. The first night that Aziz works on his computer without having to worry about the battery dying is surreal, like he's been suddenly given an inexhaustible fortune. He keeps forgetting he doesn't need to check the battery meter, a reflex drilled into him from so many nights trying to cram as much emailing as possible into the ninety minutes before the battery died. So he spends the first night with city power sending out messages, chatting with faraway friends, and habituating to life without a worry he's always had.

18

THE DRIVER

Asef was in first grade on the day the war began for him. It was 1992. Aziz was a holy warrior in another part of the city. Yunos was in Pyatigorsk, watching the Soviet Union break apart. Najiba was in the remote highlands of Afghanistan, sneaking time with her father's books and avoiding his beatings. Nasir was a young boy. Ta Manna had not yet been born.

Asef was on his way to the Burnt School—that's what they always called it, which seems strange now, like someone from history had known all along what was going to happen. That day, there was a curious thing, a man up on the roof, standing in a place no one had ever stood before, yelling. "Leave! Go home *now*! The Pashtuns and the Hazaras are going to fight!" At first it seemed strange. The man didn't look afraid—from down below it looked to Asef like he was pleased with himself. Then there was noise and Asef understood it was time to run, so he started running, but he made it only two blocks before the earth tipped and things began to tumble. People ran out of houses and stores. The streets filled with more and more things moving faster and faster, shooting around him, at him, he couldn't tell, but the walls next to him were coughing tufts of dust like they'd all become sick at the exact same time, and he covered his ears and tried to run faster. He saw Hazara shopkeepers screaming that their

stores were being looted, and it seemed like everything was backward, it was morning time and everyone was emptying out of their
offices and homes like it was the end of a day, not the beginning. He
couldn't make sense of it, but he understood right away that whatever it was that was happening, he wouldn't be going to school anymore.

The fighting didn't stop that day. It left, but it came back, coming closer and closer and staying longer and longer each time, and it
drove Asef's father out of his mind.

One day Asef watched him go outside and start digging a well
in the yard. Like he was trying to bury the concerns for what was
happening outside by exerting himself on a senseless domestic chore.
Asef watched him dig and dig all day, every day, moving big stones
around while Asef and his siblings huddled by the window to watch
their crazy father. It took a week before Asef understood that it wasn't
a well at all. It was a secret underground room that his father wanted
everyone to *pretend* was a well. It was a secret hiding place.

His father gathered the children around and explained to them
how they were to use it: they were to think of the popping that echoed
off the hills as a call just for them, announcing that it was time to
climb down the ladder into their secret place. Then they were to sit
down there in the dirt and wait for the all-clear. It was less a room
than a cave, a small orifice in the earth that swallowed them up and
squeezed them together; they sat on dirt in a space less than the height
of a man and really only wide enough for two sitting people, though
all five had to find a way to fit. Asef learned that the blindness down
there was just a temporary thing: if he was patient, sight would come
back, his siblings would reappear. He learned to wait whenever he
felt panic coming on. When the popping was fast or loud, his father
would pull a stone down over the opening, and then there was nothing for their eyes to adjust to, no light at all.

They spent longer and longer in the dark. Whole days, sometimes overnight. With the lid on, air was cut off, so it wasn't just hard
to see, it was actually hard to breathe. Going down into the bunker
was suffocating slowly and alone, dying in a place no one could see
you, and you could see no one.

To distract themselves they made up a gambling game with toasted wheat stems, a miniature sword fight in which the winners took the loser's weapon, which was also the loser's food. Which meant the stakes were high, because they never had enough food, just the tasteless soup with wheat flour his mother prepared in order to make supplies last longer, and the fried salted wheat they fought with.

Fighting passed the time, but it was also a way of communing. When you couldn't see your sister, and you couldn't talk because you weren't supposed to make any noise, the only way to converse was by touch. Asef assured his siblings he was still there through the tiny vibrations in a brittle piece of wheat. There wasn't space to lie down, so when they got tired of sitting knees to chest, they had to find a way of cooperating without seeing or hearing one another, and whenever someone lay down, he was lying on a raft of his siblings' tangled limbs.

Their endurance grew. Over two years they habituated to time in the dark with one another, and Asef learned to be comfortable in small lightless spaces. Still, even when he began to feel he could endure anything, sometimes it just became too long. They would become restless. They'd fidget and fight until the space began to close in on them, and they'd erupt from the bunker before his father gave the all-clear. Those times, his father didn't argue. When Asef had children of his own he would understand his father's predicament, that protecting his children meant imprisoning them, and when they broke free, he didn't have the heart to lock them back up, even if he knew it was the only way to keep them safe.

Sometimes they came out too soon.

They were eating lunch in their house aboveground that one day, giddy with the thrill of doing something they shouldn't be doing and getting away with it, and then the next moment they weren't getting away with it anymore. The house was shaking like it was angry, and there was a crack so loud he thought he could see it, then smoke, and his family disappeared in front of him. Asef understood it first as a divine punishment for coming out too early, because it's hard to see something that opens your world up with such tremendous force as just an accident, a poorly ranged mortar meant for someone else, though later he'd understand that's what it was. They gathered and held each other for a moment, and then moved outside and saw it was the neighbor's house that had taken a direct hit; saw the father stumbling out into the street with a child on his back, bloodied and limp. Asef watched. The moment the father and the unconscious boy made it outside, ripples of gunfire broke overhead, the man stumbled and fell, got up and hoisted the limp boy back onto his back, then stumbled and fell again. Asef watched the father stop and bow his head, then turn, and begin crawling back toward his house, the dying son left out in the street like an offering.

Asef would find out that the man had another son back in the house, a boy who'd been upright and walking but bleeding, and there had been no way to get that child to help either as long as the fighting kept up. Both children died. But it was the image of the boy in the street that lodged in Asef's mind. He couldn't file it away because he couldn't resolve what he thought about it: a father crawling away from the bullets, leaving a son to die alone. It was either the most cowardly thing a man could do, or else it was the bravest. He couldn't decide, so it was always there, and it was what war became to him: a thing that takes men and reduces them, makes them too fearful even to save their own children. War forces men to see clearly how little power they have, and then to make impossible decisions. It's why Asef resolved always to run from it or hide under the ground, or at least duck down until it had exhausted itself for a while.

When word of the Knowledge Seekers first circulated the family waited expectantly, and the first weeks after they arrived saw some stability. The economy righted, the World Food Programme started giving coupons for bread, more than enough, and paying the bakery Asef had started working at to make extra bread for the needy.

It was calm for a while, but then the Knowledge Seekers came unhinged. Violence returned, but a different kind than before. It was no longer rockets that might arrive at random; now it was the kind of violence that came looking for you. Asef started hearing screams in the night, rumors of neighbors robbed or beaten or worse, and his father decided that this new government was going to steal from them or kill them if they didn't get out.

They fled with all the others trying to make a go of it next door in Pakistan. They did what all their friends did there. They wove carpets, the only way anyone could think of to make any money. The whole family gathered around a loom for twenty hours every day, and it didn't take long for Asef to begin to miss his home. His father did, too; Asef could see that exile wore the man down. Asef missed their house, the neighborhood he grew up in, people who said hello to you when you passed. What he missed most was familiarity. Here, they were strangers. That's what it felt like living away from home: that the people didn't know you, but the place didn't either. Its angles and alleys pulled away from you like it didn't really want to let you in. The city resisted him.

Then one day Asef saw pictures of his home on TV and hushed his siblings. He didn't understand the language the newscasters in Pakistan spoke, but the images were clear enough: smoke coming off hillsides, blurry images of planes, so high and tiny against the sky they were like insects crawling across a pane of glass. Tall, dark-bearded men in disorder—Knowledge Seekers, he could tell, being driven out. On TV he saw the son of Ahad Karzai, the old Afghan parliamentarian who'd been assassinated a few years before. Asef didn't understand the language Karzai's son was speaking either, but he knew what it was: English. That was enough for him to piece it all together. The English-speaking world was coming to Afghanistan and the Knowledge Seekers were fleeing.

His family came back with the wave of returning Afghans, and it was back in the Desert where he ran into an old friend returning from a different part of Pakistan lugging a pile of books down the street. "I was studying there," this friend said. "There was a small school, only about thirty of us. They decided to move the whole thing here now that the Knowledge Seekers are gone, but Mr. Aziz said we all needed to carry part of the school ourselves."

"Who is Mr. Aziz?"

"He's the teacher, the main one. He's the head of the school. The U.N. people told him he couldn't bring so much back with him, so he split it all up and gave different parts of the school to the families to bring back."

"To bring back where?"

"I'm bringing it to the room where the new school will be. Other kids have chairs. Some of them brought desks."

A school broken down, disassembled, moved piecemeal across the border and into the country to be reassembled. Asef reached in and drew his hands through the pile of books, picked up one about their mother tongue.

"Where is the school going to be?"

Soon he and his brother were taking a placement exam at Marefat, both qualifying for the second grade. Asef was twenty years old, but he wasn't embarrassed. It didn't matter that the last time he'd gone to school was thirteen years before, and he hadn't been inside a classroom since that man stood on top of his school yelling at them to go back home. It didn't matter that all he'd ever done in school then was try to memorize things and repeat them back to the teacher, never knowing what any of it meant. Now he was actually learning.

Even after he left the school because the family needed money—just two years of Marefat, reaching only the third grade—that confidence stayed with him. He'd been listened to. A poor Hazara, a twenty-year-old second grader, and still teachers paid attention to his ideas. That was power. Back at the bakery, as men came in speaking of their little enterprises, he listened closely. People were making money off the way the country was changing. Everything was growing, people kept streaming back in to the capital from their various exiles, and they wanted houses, restaurants to eat in, stores to shop at.

And they wanted cars.

The plan he came up with was simple. He'd convince his mother to let go of the family savings for a foolproof investment. He and his boss would fly west to a city near Iran, where you could buy cars just arriving from across the border. They'd each buy one, bring them back to Kabul, and sell them at a premium. Just like that—just by

understanding the difference in a vehicle's price between two cities—
Asef would make his family a few hundred dollars.

He couldn't drive, and neither could his boss, but his boss had a
few friends willing to come along for the trip and drive back for them.
All was in order. But they'd failed to anticipate one thing: it took
three weeks to arrive in Herat, pick out the vehicles, drive them back,
and begin looking for buyers. In three weeks, with all the other people bringing cars to sell in Kabul, the price collapsed. Asef returned
with a big piece of steel he couldn't sell unless he took a loss.

So it sat there, losing value, taunting Asef, costing his family
money just to keep it parked in a lot, until finally he decided that if
it was just going to sit there, he might as well learn to drive it.

Going out in the van the first time felt like wearing a big boxy
costume; he had that sense that everyone was staring. He was sure
everyone knew he was doing something he wasn't supposed to be
doing. He got more comfortable; he felt a rush. He decided to try
and pick up passengers. When the first ones boarded, it felt like he'd
pulled off a con. When he dropped them off, he almost laughed out
loud.

But when he went to turn around and do the route in reverse,
he froze.

He'd dropped the first passenger off in a crowded market and
was sure if he tried to turn around he'd hit someone, or something.
He let the van begin to move, he wasn't sure what he was doing, but
had the vague notion that maybe things would work themselves out,
that if he kept going past the square he'd find empty space eventually. But the van was picking up speed and the space in front of him
wasn't emptying, it was filling with people, and he wished he'd never
left the house. People moved faster and faster on either side of him
like they had some new urgency, and out of the corner of his eye he
saw two police vectoring toward his path. He was sure they were
going to notice him, to see panic on his face—then they did, one
started hurrying toward him with his hand out as Asef went barreling forward.

"Stop, sir!"

Just as the policeman positioned himself in front of the car, Asef decided to guess at the brake, and slammed his foot down hoping the van would stop; instead it roared like a prodded animal and leapt forward—the policeman's torso popped against the hood and twisted off the corner of the car. Asef switched his foot to the other pedal and felt his body go cold—he'd killed a policeman!

The policeman popped up with rage on his face. Asef was too startled to know what to say, so he lifted his foot and opened his mouth to begin an apology, but the car had started rolling again, so he had to make another guess, the man was now skipping backward still in front of the car and still yelling at Asef, and again Asef guessed wrong, again the van popped the policeman, and again the policeman went twirling gracelessly off the hood.

This time he righted himself, swung around, opened the door, held Asef by the shirt with one hand, reached back with the other, and slapped him across the face. "I'll take you to prison, six months you'll go, how dare you!" He was fumbling with his words. He dragged Asef out of the car and began slapping him, and Asef was too relieved that the man was alive to very much mind the beating.

Once he'd exhausted himself, the man told Asef to get back in his car, because they were driving to the police station.

They rode in silence toward the traffic department.

Asef had another idea. Nothing to lose now, he figured. "If you let me go without any more problems, there could be something in it for you."

The policeman was silent. Asef went cold again, maybe this isn't how you're supposed to offer a bribe? He had no idea.

Then, after a pause: "Well, you hurt my back seriously. I'm going to have to see a doctor; maybe I won't be able to work again—$100 in afghanis at least."

Asef offered a lower figure, the policeman stayed higher, and finally the policeman said, "Fifteen hundred afghanis, but your car stays here until you pay."

So Asef went to the bakery owner and asked to borrow $60. The owner, his protective instincts stirred, didn't hesitate. And on the way back to the police station, Asef came up with another idea. *This man is taking a bribe,* he thought. *He'll want to take the money as quickly as possible. Is he really going to count it right there in front of all the other police?* Asef took out the roll of bills, pulled $10 from it, and put it aside.

"Now take your van," the policeman said, when Asef arrived with a handful of cash, "and get out of my face."

In the span of a day, he'd broken the rules, got caught, bribed his way out of trouble, and secured a bonus he'd essentially stolen from his boss. He'd gotten away with all of it. He finally understood how you got by in this new version of his country the foreigners had brought. There was so much money coming and so many bribes being paid that everyone was touched by it. Even the ones who didn't know they were—who didn't know why police paid attention to some crimes and ignored others; how a company could win a contract to build a school or fix a road and never actually do anything. Bribes were everywhere, influencing everything, even when it was invisible. It was a transparent coating that had seeped into every crack and fissure and changed how the whole machine moved. Asef hadn't known it existed until now, and now he decided better to be the one paying the bribe than the one bumped to the back of the line because somebody else was. Asef decided he liked being a businessman.

At the bakery he was always the lowest. Everyone who worked there was his superior. In the van, no one was. He had total control. Once he figured out which routes made the most money and had some regular passengers, he saved enough to tear down the gate to his house and build a bigger one, so he could finally bring the car home.

One night another driver he'd befriended had a job he couldn't do, and he asked Asef to cover for him. "Some teachers from that school out in the Desert need a ride to university." Asef agreed right away. There was nobody Asef admired more than Marefat teachers. They were a council of elders to him, possessed of unfathomable knowledge, and for some reason also the desire to share it. They were celebrities, but beneficent ones. When he picked them up Asef recognized a skinny, kind-looking man who had been a teacher when Asef was a student. He smiled often, but a pained smile, the kind someone gives when tormented by anxiety he doesn't want to show, but does a bad job hiding. Hafiz, Teacher Aziz's younger brother. As caring a teacher as there was at Marefat, but the one who always looked the most frazzled.

Asef felt gratitude toward Hafiz. He wanted to express it but decided not to bother him. He dropped the teachers off for the class at the university and then drove home, wishing he'd said something. "Thank you," or "You were a good teacher," or "I remember you," or even just "Let me know if there's anything I can do." Something. He'd had a chance to reconnect with Marefat, and he'd let it pass. He went to bed anxious about the missed chance.

Two days later, he received a call from Hafiz. "Our main driver just sold his car and is leaving for Helmand. We need a new driver," he said. "Do you have time early in the morning, and then in the afternoon, when school gets out?"

"Yes, I can be available then."

"Every day?"

"I think so."

"For the students who come to the school from far away, and for the teachers, too. You could still do your own driving sometimes, but you'd have to be available for us whenever we needed you. Are you interested?"

Asef said that he was.

"Good, good. How much should we pay you?"

Asef declined to answer; making such a demand would be out of turn. Not to people as esteemed as Marefat teachers. "Sir, it's up to you, you pay me as you wish."

"Well, we paid Jafar nine thousand afghanis a month. Is that fair for you?"

"Yes, of course, that is fine with me."

"Okay, thank you, Asef," he said. Then there was a pause, and Hafiz added, "By the way, it was nice to see you again, after a few years." And he hung up.

The last year before the Outsiders left Asef began losing passengers. It wasn't gradual. Suddenly there were so few people looking for rides and so many people offering them that he made the circuit up and back through the Desert empty as often as not.

The men working at the ministries all had their own cars, nice ones too, with heating and working windows and those snorkels that stick up out of the engine like a single, peering eye. When they had time off, they picked up passengers, too. So did the shopkeepers. On their way into work, on their way home. Everyone needed money. Asef was suddenly competing with half the city, for half the passengers, since fewer and fewer people were willing to pay extra for the nimble little vans. They took the big crowded buses that lurched along slowly to their destination. Or else they walked.

It's the Outsiders leaving, he's sure of it, and what a man in his profession notices is that things start to get *still*. Around him, fewer things are moving. At first it was a relief: less traffic. Then it became unsettling, how an empty road is at first a luxury, but then what takes you over is the notion that everyone knows something you don't. There are fewer people going from one place to another, fewer people moving across the city; people are settling into place. He sees it across the city. From people selling fruit on the street to the men with big businesses, no one is immune, and it's upsetting, not least because he's going broke.

He sees concern on the faces of the people on the news. Their eyes have changed; they look how he remembers people looking on TV during war. He sees them talking like men talked back then, like they might reach across the table and start fighting, line up their armies right here in the city and shoot at each other like they shot at each other twenty years ago. He is seeing changes that could swallow the school up.

It reminds him of the day a few years ago when Aziz went on TV and had an argument with the nomad, Hashmat Ghani. Most people were proud of Aziz then, but Asef was frightened. How clear it was what that man on TV felt about Hazaras. It was something deep and untreatable. How clear that if someone like that nomad were ever in power, it'd be disaster. The man had stood up right there on the TV and just about grabbed Aziz by the throat, yelled at him like Aziz was no more than some stubborn animal. *You ungrateful Hazaras! You should be happy for what you have and stop asking for more!* He thought the man might hit Aziz, or spit on him.

So now, how strange it is that the nomad's brother has begun inviting Aziz to his house just about every week. Aziz surely knows something Asef doesn't, but Asef doesn't ask. It's not his place.

Instead, he squats next to his van parked inside Ashraf Ghani's compound when Aziz goes into the house, and he tries to imagine what it is they could be talking about. What could they possibly have in common?

But as he sits and thinks it through, it worries him less. He turns it into something hopeful. If these two men from rival tribes that keep killing each other can sit down and talk like friends, it is a correction of everything he's seen. He thinks of his childhood again, people fighting and firing rockets at each other so carelessly that they landed on the neighbor's house and killed their boys, and drove him for days underground into their tiny hidden bunker. It's as if those people who fought over his head were meeting together to try and fix things. Asef lets the thought of Aziz and the nomad fill his mind, and it pushes out the strained faces of men yelling at each other on TV.

Maybe there is something more to it. Aziz sees the other things, things out of the picture, which the rest of us can't see.

back their usurped territory, and the usurpers will not find refuge anywhere in this land."

"God willing," it says, "the invaders will soon have no choice other than leaving." And for the Hazaras, he leaves only one option: "Repent and remember your God, come back to the arms of the nation," he says. "Wash off the black stain of slavery from your forehead. Get out from under the skirt of the invaders, don't ask for their presence in Afghanistan any longer. Your wishes will not come true, and you will be left out in the middle of nowhere, like the slaves the Soviets left behind. But your fate will be worse than theirs. You will be enemies of the nation, and you will face such a dreadful outcome that we will make you a lesson for future generations."

The holiday had barely even begun and the specter of massacre found its way into every corner of the Desert. For Aziz, more alarming even than the open threat to his people is the fact that no one else has said or done anything about it. No one in the government responded. Not one person in civil society. A powerful man is talking about killing Hazaras and the response has been silence.

It's not often that Aziz travels with his family, but this is a special occasion. The G-72 member hosting today's celebration has asked all the members to bring their families, because what better occasion to include wives, husbands, and children than Eid, a holiday without sectarian connotations, whose very name just means "holiday?" So Aziz and his family are on their way to one of the Microrayons—"small districts" named in Russian, built by Russians, to squeeze people from different provinces into the same tight space. The idea was that by rubbing up against each other the friction might buff away their distinctions, and everyone would eventually forget they had different heritage, different mother tongues, that they practiced religion a little differently. The Microrayons—which were supposed to sanitize people of variance so that what would emerge was a good monochrome communist workforce, harmonious and conflict-free—are now among the city's more desirable homes.

"We're trying to bring back the old culture from before the wars," a G-72 leader says, once he's ushered Aziz and his family in-

19

FIVE MONTHS LEFT

The holy month ends, the holiday begins. The capital overflows in the days just before, engorged with people coming in from the provinces to stock up on food, new clothes, and gifts for the kids. It's a celebration for everyone, and everyone, having deprived themselves for thirty days, and therefore with thirty days' worth of health and holiness on the ledger, feels a little gluttony is pardonable. Three days, then, of visiting families and eating sweets in new clothes, and for far more than will admit it, even a little forbidden drink. Off-brand vodka from Central Asian neighbors, home brew that can steal your sight, or if you're lucky, the Johnnie Walker Red Label you can sometimes find for a hundred dollars on Chicken Street.

But the holiday takes a dark turn.

From his hiding place, the terrorist leader Gulbuddin Hekmatyar sends an open letter to media outlets in Kabul. It begins as a holiday greeting, but moves swiftly into a declaration of war against Hazaras.

"The Hazaras have joined with the American Special Forces and together they have committed the most horrible atrocities that have shocked the world," the letter reads. "The day will come soon when the oppressed people of Afghanistan will stand up and fight to take side. "Pashtuns, Tajiks, Hazaras, all together, and their families as well." It's harder to fight if everyone's kids are given a steady dose of everyone else's kids, so the idea is a kind of inoculation. "Before the war," he says, "I knew my neighbors, the whole family. And I even called my neighbor's mom Aunty. But since the war, these values are all dead."

The list of attendees is impressive. A minister in the president's cabinet is there, two former governors, many people who have lived and worked in other countries and learned other languages, techno-crats of various status. As the guests settle in, Aziz's son Abuzar nods toward a G-72 member and his kid, who are drinking amber-colored liquid. "Is that whiskey?" Abuzar asks, and smiles. It is tea, of course, but not in the kind of loop-handled glasses tea is usually served in. "Those guys just came from Germany," Abuzar says, "maybe it's whiskey."

The mood in the room stays light. When a woman arrives after most of the seats have been taken, a large man with big talonlike eyebrows and long traditional robes unfurls himself from his chair and says to her, loud enough for everyone to hear, "I'm from Kanda-har, we're famous for how we treat women! So we're going to treat you well. Take this seat!" Later, she introduces herself as "an adviser on domestic issues . . . for my husband." Everyone laughs, and the man from Kandahar raises one of his massive eyebrows. "Well," he says, "I'm an adviser to the president. In the true sense of the word, which is that the president doesn't listen to anything I say!" Again, the room fills with laughter, and the man from Kandahar has succeeded not just in establishing himself as the afternoon's comic relief but also in leaving an impression on Abuzar.

"I like him," Abuzar says quietly. "I like Pashtuns. Some of them are so chivalrous and gentle." Abuzar is right at the age when bright young men pick up and put down philosophies like clothing. He has, after all, just finished his freshman year at an American lib-eral arts college, so he's passed through the obligatory socialist phase, which didn't last too long, because he also kind of liked nice things. His bible for the year was *The Bottom Billion*, about the poorest people on the planet, until Aziz stole his copy. For the moment, his philosophy is contrarianism, praising his people's biggest ethnic rival.

Now he looks around and says, "Do you think it's exploitative to have the families of politicians participate in politics?"

Aziz doesn't quite know what life is like for his son at "The Thufts," which is what he insists the name of his son's college back in America is. There are changes in his son he can't account for. Abuzar seems to be turning into something different, but slowly, one pixel at a time, so there is no way to tell exactly how the picture is changing until it's irreversible, and Abuzar is already unrecognizable to his father. Not that the changes are all bad, or even mostly so. Abuzar laughs now. Aziz has never seen his son laugh so much; he'd always been such a serious child. *My fault*, Aziz thinks, *bringing the kids up in exile, making the boy spend his formative years with threats and seriousness all around.*

But Aziz found that acknowledging fault doesn't make it any easier to witness its effects. He is, frankly, a little afraid of his son. Abuzar disobeys. He uses technology Aziz hasn't heard of. The way he dresses is unfamiliar: T-shirts and Ray-Bans, hair gel and contact lenses. He carries a couple of fancy mobile phones; he sent videos of the family's break-the-fast feast to friends, but when Aziz asked to see them, they'd somehow disappeared. He makes his father hyperaware of a generation gap between them. Aziz knows there's some poetic justice here, because he himself has pushed so many students past what their parents were comfortable with. It was Aziz's mission to agitate at a rate perfectly throttled not to alienate the community, but to make them a little unsteady, so that they could be shoved forward in increments. Send the kids home with books full of unsettling ideas, with ways of arguing about which leaders they should support, and about the limits of religion—all blades for cutting little wounds that heal back stronger. Now it's happened to his own son, and Aziz empathizes with the parents whose households he's turned upside down. Like them, he now feels mostly powerlessness. Like them, he does not get to decide whether to accept the changes happening to this new generation. He's being forced to submit to them.

"You and your parents are very different," Aziz will say later, up on the roof of Marefat. "But still you are connected like *this*," and he makes his hands into a knot of interlocking fingers. "But here in Afghanistan it's not . . . most of the parents, they accept something, they submit to it, but it doesn't mean they are really consciously approving. That's why any time a fanatical person comes and shows strong support for tradition, all the old people just *run* to that. That's what happened during the attack on school. We have to be aware of this," he says. "We know that kids and their families are connected just sixty-five or seventy percent. They have transformed themselves, but they can still be pulled apart."

Aziz's youngest daughter, Roya, has been still and quiet for most of the celebration, but she now becomes impatient. She's been holding onto the armrests of her chair as if she's waiting for it to take off, her tiny feet sticking straight out in front of her. Now she begins to stir, squirming in the chair, and finally, once the adults begin talking in earnest, she tries to climb down. The chair's upholstery catches her dress and Abuzar has to lower her down so that she doesn't fall right out of her clothes. She turns around, her back to the room, leans on the chair with her elbows, rests her chin in her hands with a sigh, and begins to converse earnestly with herself. Quietly, though—she's learned to do the things that small children do without getting in the way of the adults discussing important things nearby.

A young man sings a verse from the Quran in an arresting, pained way, as if it requires physical strain to pull words from the holy book. Although some members check their phones while the young man is singing, when he's done, they all, except for Abuzar, bring their hands to their faces to complete the prayer. The host asks several people to speak, finally it's Aziz's turn, and he stands up. Hands clasped together, he begins to tell the group what this holiday has been like for Hazaras.

Aziz tells the group about the terrorist threat, and explains that what's worse than a fanatical terrorist grasping for the spotlight by making an example out of Hazaras, is the fact that no one has done anything about it.

The men and women in the room don't make a sound. The

people who checked their phones during the recitation from the holy book are still while Aziz is speaking.

"If these direct threats can come to us, and the government doesn't do anything about it, and *you* don't do anything about it, we'll never trust each other. It's just an atmosphere of hatred and violence. And people hide behind some false reason." Aziz pauses for effect, and then continues, the man with the fifth-grade education giving a history lesson to a room full of graduates from elite universities all over the world. "There was a conversation between a philosopher named Habermas and a friend," he tells them. "The friend was trying to say that when the Holocaust happened, it wasn't the German people's fault. The friend said to Habermas, 'It was the Nazis, not all the Germans, who committed these crimes.'"

Aziz is again quiet for effect—it's during this kind of oratory that his talent for expression is most valuable. "Habermas says, 'Yes, my friend, you're right. It was not the German people. But tell me: Where were the German people, what were they doing, when the Holocaust happened?'"

Driving back as dusk settles over the capital, Asef has the sunroof open and Aziz's daughter Sameen wraps a white shawl over her mother's hair. There's an odor coming off the river, which is almost entirely dry, as if we're driving though a port where the smell of fish affixes itself to everything.

Asef navigates the traffic expertly, making way for the police and army vehicles zooming by with their video game siren sequences. *Just the authorities, the people who are supposed to protect us, using their privilege to get to their next holiday party.*

Asef has heard about the letter, but he doesn't know what Aziz is doing about it or what the purpose of this meeting was about. And Asef won't ask. It would be for him a breach to burden Teacher Aziz with his own concerns, so he is silent. But he's frightened. The terrorist leader's letter got him thinking. Everyone else has a strong leader they can rally behind, but Hazaras don't. Some follow Aziz, some follow the Ayatollah, some like the old warlords. When the fighting starts, they'll scatter, and they'll be decimated. Asef knows the contours of the city almost by feel, and he knows that this time, when people start fighting, it will be worse. Every seam of the city is filled with people. Most came like he did, flushed with hope about what new world the Outsiders would bring. Then they had families, and then their relatives came back from abroad to join them, and then those relatives had families, too.

In the wars before, when fighters fought over people's heads, people died, but mortars found empty land as often as they found homes. Now, there is no empty land. Now, wherever there is shooting there will be dying. He keeps this to himself, as he always does.

Aziz and I walk with his brothers from an Eid meal at Ta Manna's house, where she'd hosted us so she could serve Pakistani food for the holiday. Now Aziz is heading home, where he will have guests shortly. Everyone sweats in their new holiday clothes, until the wind picks up off Mount Protected. So much dust fills the air that the sky goes overcast and the festive energy of a summer storm sets in. No rain comes, the wind just moves the dust with growing ferocity, flicks it up into eyes, moves it vertically and horizontally, whorls of it carry trash down the street and mix with hair and teeth. Aziz's eyes go bloodshot.

Before his guests arrive, he wants to talk more about the terrorist leader's threat. "People are thinking about the massacres from the past. Hazaras are vulnerable. The attitude is that now that Hazaras have been doing civic education, they're studying at university, they're not learning fighting anymore." This is on him. At least partially: he wanted Hazaras to forget fighting. "Everyone else has their armies," he says. "But look how vulnerable we are now. If the international community is pulled out tomorrow, the ground remains for these bad actors. Hazaras are the most vulnerable—who do they have? General Dostum is a powerful leader in the north. Tajiks have strong hands in the north, too. There are weapons in Panjshir, in Shamali. But Hazaras have no one. These days, we are detached from Iran completely. These two days of Eid, I learned that all literate or educated people from university, all are worried about what will happen."

When his guests begin to arrive, Aziz switches moods. Everything is light. The first to come is a master's student in chemistry with a penchant for limericks; Aziz fought alongside his father in the time of jihad. Aziz makes the young man say a limerick, laughs, closes his eyes, then makes him say another. A dozen young Hazara technocrats arrive, filing into the room and exchanging pleasantries and jokes. Aziz welcomes them and addresses one of the young men with a greeting he learned from me: "How's your wife and my kids?" Everyone laughs charitably. Even the young men with their prayer beads out aren't too pious for a joke about the capital crime of a woman's infidelity. The mood lightened, they talk courteously, and it's half an hour before one of the young men is bold enough to bring up the threat.

Aziz dutifully changes his tone, and still sustains humor, but he's tearing up, too—the dust is beginning to swirl again outside, and it's followed the young men into the room. One of Aziz's eyes is swollen almost closed, the other a cracked surface of livid, risen veins, but the young men are across the room and too far away to see it. What they see is a man sitting on his knees, dressed carelessly in traditional pajama-like pants and an undershirt that needs washing, telling stories about his jihad days and weaving each one through with humor; his purpose right now is to take a violent thing and reduce its power. The guests laugh, go quiet and somber, laugh again. Outside the air grows so thick with dust that it looks like night, and the wind picks up, whipping trash through the air so women in the streets stop, kneel down, bow their heads, and put their hands over their children's eyes. The sky threatens. No rain comes.

Aziz tells more jokes, he even makes fun of Massoud, the commander who killed thousands of Hazaras, but who the United States supported because he also fought the Taliban. Massoud is Afghanistan's "national hero"; the airport is named after him. There is a national holiday for him. His picture is on billboards all over the capital, even though he was one of the only commanders to use planes to bomb it. He also led the Afshar massacre. He is a sore spot, but though Aziz dodged bombs from Massoud's planes and saw civilians die from them, he doesn't find humor about Massoud inappropriate. Or he doesn't care if it is. Nothing is off limits, and when we all rise to leave, he sees that my socks are mismatched. He yells, for the benefit of all the young men gathered, "Look, a typical ab-sentminded Jew!"

Then he grabs me, gives me a wet kiss on the forehead, and whispers into my ear, "Travel safe, my infidel dear, we will have to talk soon," and lets me out into the swirling dust.

At that very moment, a few miles away, a flash flood takes the city so suddenly that cars wash away, sewers overflow across roads, and un-paved streets became swamps. The city's rivers, usually dry, fill up and disgorge themselves onto the roadways, crowding out streets already too narrow to oblige the holiday traffic. All around the city, children stop and cry as their new clothes are splashed with street filth flying off the tires of passing cars. Thirteen people die from the storm.

And still, in the Desert near the school, it doesn't rain at all. The wind comes down off Mount Protected and blows the moisture away from the school, so all they get at Marefat is more dust from the di-rection of other provinces, as if the whole country was trying to bury them. Then, finally, in the middle of the night, after every one has gone to sleep, for just five minutes, it rains. By the morning it's all dried, and few of the students knew it came at all.

20

—————

THE STUDENT

Her confidence was creating problems. When she heard of women being abused in the homes of friends and neighbors, she interfered on their behalf. She had education they didn't have, and she felt it elevated her enough to tell men what people outside their little closed community thought about people's rights. When she tried to help a cousin whose husband had become cruel and abusive, she was blown back by the husband's wrath, and then her family piled on.

Her brother-in-law yelled at her in front of her children. "Who do you think you are, Najiba, the human rights commissioner? This is a matter for their family to deal with, not you."

In the quiet moments, she sees that her new confidence is attached to a creeping resentment. What she could have *done* with all that lost time. Who she could have been, if she'd been allowed to study when she was a child. If she hadn't been banned from tutors by a cruel father and foolish brothers who enforced his commands, who stood like thoughtless guards between her and the books. She mourns the lost chance.

Even now, when family come to tell her about a politician speaking nearby, she hates them for waiting until she was a mother of five to take her seriously. It's worse when she listens to the stories of her classmates. When they speak of their lives, it fills her with envy.

Tahira's father had always pushed her to study, and all the time apologized that he couldn't afford tutors. Fatima's husband hired extra help in the house so Fatima didn't have to worry about her children or making proper meals. Najiba was weighted down by their stories. Every moment in class was a moment her children were without a mother, especially her young son, who had a nose for trouble. Her mind was still on mothering, and mothering was still something that couldn't be reconciled with learning. They were two different languages mixing in her mind. The mothers in her class only confirmed this: they were studying because they no longer had to worry about their children's well-being. She doubted herself. Was she being irresponsible? Was going to school foolish when you are a grown woman with five kids to care for? Was it one big selfish indulgence? At home, all the neighborhood women knew that Najiba was going to school, and they laughed at her. "Come, let's see Najiba, the first grader with five children! Oh, Najiba! Do you want to be the president? Or just a government minister?"

"No, I don't want to be any person of the government, I just want to be able to solve my own problems." She managed their ridicule, but resistance came from everywhere.

The troops started to leave, and the economy began to flutter. Prices rose; the currency fluctuated. Her husband's work at the clinic had always been inconsistent, but with foreign forces leaving, the NGOs started winding down and local companies doing work for them had to downsize as well. Her husband lost the job he had, and he couldn't find another. By Eid he hadn't worked in more than a month. Money got tighter. With Najiba away at school and her husband out looking for jobs, the children were often alone.

She asked Benazir for help, but Benazir was starting her senior year and had her own future to worry about—college, hopefully. She couldn't do that and be burdened with the care of four younger siblings. One summer afternoon, Najiba came home from school and found her son asleep. She asked Benazir, "Is he okay?"

"I don't think he's eaten."

"Did you offer him anything?" Najiba shook him, but he wouldn't stir. She shook him harder; finally he opened his eyes, but he looked ashen, damp with sweat, and so lethargic he seemed almost paralyzed. She helped him up and brought him to the pump in the courtyard. She doused him, made him drink, rubbed water onto the back of his neck. She brought him back inside and gave him food, but he couldn't hold it down. He threw up everything she gave him, but she kept feeding him and held a cold compress against his head. Finally he calmed, but not until the middle of the night, far too late for him to do his homework. Or for Najiba to do her own.

The next day when she came back from school, it was her younger daughter who was sick. The same affliction, barely moving, unable to hold food down, this time with a headache as well. It felt like a punishment from the heavens, or a warning maybe. If she continued to abdicate her responsibility to her children, they'd be taken from her.

She tried to push this anxiety aside for another month, to convince herself it was coincidence, not a message. She tried to dismiss her own thoughts as superstitious. She tried to be a mother at home and a student at school. But the guilt rose up and spilled over the dam she'd built against it. When she was in class her eyes were on the teacher but her mind was at home, in the kitchen, where her kids were eating junk food, fries and soda, and getting sick from it because she wasn't there to turn whatever wheat or okra they could afford into a decent meal. Then the teacher would drop the chalk and Najiba would realize ten minutes had passed and she hadn't retained anything. When exams came, she struggled. In political science she got three out of ten. Math was worse. When she saw her scores, she was ashamed, and what she needed to do became clear. She'd been in school three years, she was in eighth grade, she was catching up to her daughter, but now, it was time to quit.

Before she left, a student writing for the school magazine asked her to comment on her experience for the next issue, and she answered honestly:

Because of the problem I have taking care of my son at home, the continuation of my lessons has become very difficult for me.

Once I was a victim of the wars and being a girl in my family and I lost the opportunity to get education. This time, the affection of motherhood demands that I give up my right to education. I don't want my son's future to be bad. Because then, even if I blame myself, it will be useless, and too late. On the other hand, it is very hard for me to take myself away from my lessons. I don't want to live in the world of ignorance. I'm tired of ignorance. I want my life to no longer be filled with illiteracy.

21

THE MECHANIC

Nasir sees the president on the news kicking the U.S. special forces out of the province next door. His heart sinks. *What is he thinking?* It's one of the most dangerous provinces in the whole country, and there are also thousands of Hazaras living there. If all the U.S. troops leave, who fights the Taliban? Surely Karzai knows what would happen if Hazaras there were undefended. Which either means he doesn't care about Hazaras there—or maybe he's trying to anger the Outsiders on purpose?

Things are going to start spiraling out of control, he can sense it. He's angry. When war starts, the influential people who are responsible for it will find a way to survive. The commanders and politicians and the businessmen will fight or they will leave the country, and the people who will suffer will be the ones who had nothing to do with making the problems. He sits his wife down and tells her, "We must prepare for the troops to leave. We must be ready for anything to happen. We need a plan for you to take the kids and go back to the village, while I stay and look after things."

"What things will you have to look after?"

"I'll need to stay and just make sure our house is wrapped up."

"Our house is small, how much time could that possibly take? If it's not safe here, come back to the village with us."

He hadn't expected her to question him. At first he doesn't know why in his plan he envisions himself staying behind. Why is he thinking this way?

"Because if the troops leave and there's civil war, I'll have to fight. No matter where I am, I'll have to. Even If I go back to the village with you, I can't be neutral; I'll have to fight there, too. I know Kabul better now, so it's better I fight here."

He knows she doesn't believe him. He doesn't believe himself. She looks at him like she knows something, and then he sees it, too: the reason he keeps imagining himself staying here after he sends his family to safety. "Because I love the school," he finally says. "I need to stay and defend the school."

Teacher's Day comes. It's a happy diversion for most people at Marefat, but Nasir is always three tasks behind, so whenever he gets pulled away to attend ceremonies, he's anxious. Generators need oil, printers need to be unjammed. He sees the school as one big machine that might break down without his full attention.

Especially today, because the ceremony has been hijacked by a television station. A producer caught wind of the big to-do Marefat puts on for important anniversaries and holidays, and he decided to film a Teacher's Day special at the school. They brought their own TV crew, an overcaffeinated anchor and two chubby kids who trade shifts as playful-funny emcees. The effect is a sitcom. The three of them bounce around the stage and try to fuse their performance with what Marefat students have already planned, but the TV crew keeps pausing the proceedings because the emcees are stumbling over their lines. The students are respectful for most of it, but an hour in, they get impatient and start to laugh when the anchor or the emcee kids have to say a line twice. This only makes the emcees more nervous, which makes them stumble again, which makes the students laugh more, and the cycle continues.

The students have come up with a clever conceit for the day: each department serves as a platform for a presidential candidate. The students celebrate the math and science teachers by making stump

speeches for advancing research; the language department by celebrating a policy of international cooperation.

The athletic department is honored by a student who challenges
a gym teacher to an arm-wrestling contest; they sit on either side of
a table on the stage and go at it to raucous applause. There is a skit in
which one student acts as a tribal warlord—playing with prayer beads
and spitting tobacco—who doesn't allow girls to go to school. A student pretending to be a teacher—wearing Western clothes, full suit
and tie—is escorted in by the warlord's guard, who's armed with a
miniature plastic Kalashnikov. The teacher tries to convince the
warlord to let girls study. The warlord is angry at the teacher for im-
posing his values, so the teacher tries a more nuanced approach. He
reminds the warlord how he once used ear medication for eyes, and
how when his own daughter fell sick recently there were no women
to care for her, because he'd forbidden women from studying. If there
were more women studying, there would be more women doctors,
and if there were more women doctors, perhaps his daughter would
be better, didn't he think? Finally, after much back and forth, the
warlord is convinced; he changes his mind and even donates the finest land in his fictional province for a woman's hospital.

After the skit, the welfare platform is introduced, honoring the
janitors. The student running this campaign takes the microphone
and says, "We're the populist ticket, we fight for the masses!" and in-
vites the janitors and cleaning ladies up on stage. Nasir looks uncomfortable on display in front of everyone; he stands up on the stage
swaying awkwardly, but after his name is announced, he has to keep
putting a thumb to his eye, because he's started to cry.

This year, Nasir brought his oldest son to Marefat, to start first
grade. Walking up to school that day was different from any of the
thousands of times he'd made the trip before. Different especially
from that first day ten years before, he thought, when he was just a
scrawny frame filled to the brim with childish rage, desperate for
work, without money even to rent a room. *Now, I'm the father of a
Marefat student.*

22

FOUR MONTHS LEFT

Marefat, people admitted to one another over tea and across market stalls while sorting through vegetables, was vulnerable.

When the Outsiders first came to Afghanistan, and Marefat followed them in, the school was so far from anything, and anyone who might mean it harm had to cross the long open Desert to do so.

Then as the Desert grew more populated, Marefat was easy to protect because it was so hard to find. It was a row of classrooms the color of earth, crouching quietly beneath buildings that rose all around it. For the men Aziz argued with on television and in his newspaper columns, coming out to Marefat meant traveling an hour through dust and congestion and pollution and throngs of Hazaras. It meant navigating a network of side streets that had emerged as the slum had—not with any logic, but as the reaching, curling tendrils of an organism expanding at random. The school was protected because it was small, hidden, and really, really far.

But the school had risen up. It became two stories, then two buildings, the second growing floor by floor until it rose above all the other construction around it. Many people knew the school just by accident. From the wedding hall that sprang up next door, blasting harmonium every night through an amp dialed to max and drawing crowds—different people every night, thousands every week—down Marefat's dirt alley. The skeleton of a new mosque rose across from Marefat, as if in confrontation. Aziz had nightmares of clerics blasting religion across the street at students learning physics. Tensions rose, and just as everyone felt the money being sucked from the country with the Outsiders, Aziz had to keep raising tuition. No one had just one kid to pay for, either. Aziz hadn't anticipated a scenario in which hundreds of people wanted to pay for their kids to go to school, but suddenly, all at the same time, became unable to.

So he did what he always did. He rolled up his sleeves and tried to solve problems, one family at a time.

He took meetings in the day and night. He helped parents find jobs.

He made an announcement at morning assembly: "A friend of mine has a construction project, he needs a few good workers. Tell your fathers in case they're looking for work."

Four hundred men came forward.

People who had jobs with the foreigners were losing them or expected to lose them soon. The departure was having all sorts of strange effects. At lunch, the teachers looked at each other after trying the bread from a new supplier. The baker was cutting the flour with some cheaper powder to make it last. You could actually *taste* the changes happening. And then a man who lived next door to Marefat walked into Aziz's office with his scarf in his hand and said all the wells had gone dry, could his family please use the school's? So now water had begun to run out; even the earth was giving up.

Asef likes driving at night most, when it's calm, the dust settled, and the people on the road too tired to be aggressive.

Second best is early morning, when it's still dark and cool and he can make extra cash on his way to pick up Marefat's richer kids. Most live outside the Desert in Karte Seh—"Area Three," it means in Russian, one of the names that stuck around even after the Russians left. His van has enough room for ten people if they squeeze, unless there's a woman, because a woman gets the whole backseat even if she's alone.

The city rises early. Asef is on the road just after 4:00 a.m., and there are people out even now. But they are calm and quiet at this hour, each engrossed in his own predawn ritual. Butchers on the side of the street tug on the skin of the day's slaughter; detached heads of animals are lined up neatly in front of the market stalls, all facing out, as if they like to watch the city wake up, too.

He sees no women on the street this early, except the young girls in pale blue and white; Marefat students drawn through the Desert's nooks and alleys to their special morning English classes, all moving in the opposite direction as him. He's never learned a word of English.

But lately mornings are not so nice. The weather is turning. The early dark is no longer just relief from the heat; the air has a kick to it now. The van has no heating, so he draws his scarf from the top of his head down to his neck and tightens it against the cold. And there are so few people looking for rides. He used to have to sit and wait while men piled in and rearranged themselves, strangers sitting thigh to thigh behind him, their cargo humped up onto their laps. He'd carry so much weight he wouldn't get higher than second gear all through the Desert. Now his drives to Area Three are mostly empty.

Today he has some luck. Two passengers by 4:30 A.M. They're talkative, so he's content. His radio works but he hardly ever turns it on; he prefers what real people say when they don't know they're being listened to.

He moves quickly down the Road of the Martyr Mazari, at this hour still free of the boys who move their motorcycles into traffic to impress one another, and the half-blind old men who let others do the work of avoiding collisions. Still without the bicycles full of families, four or five on old rickety frames, the littlest with their legs flung forward over the handlebars.

Mostly those who emerge this early are the few still looking for rides and the municipal workers in their nearly incandescent orange suits, who stand with brooms and shovels, swinging at the dust that advanced overnight. He passes other drivers on the side of the road, whipping rags at their cars to scare off last night's coating.

At quarter to five he picks up a third passenger.

This one says something strange.

"There's a battle going on," he says. "Up by Burnt Bridge. We shouldn't go there."

From here, Burnt Bridge is the only way to get out to Area Three.

"We can still go," the other passenger says, "if they've closed the road there, we'll just turn back."

Asef agrees. They keep going. But before he gets to Burnt Bridge he sees a crowd of people and a policeman flags him down. His passengers get out to see what's going on. There's commotion at a mosque, a dozen or more policemen, and Asef sees flashlights arcing through the dark in the mosque's courtyard. Blades of light move haphazardly, briefly illuminating other men, the stairs to the mosque, and then, just for an instant, they wash over two lumps on the ground and Asef knows immediately that they are bodies.

His first thought is about the students. Not their safety, but that they are going to be late for school, because he'll be late picking them up. He worries that they'll get in trouble and it will have been his fault. He should call someone at the school to apologize for them.

The policeman waves him on, and his passengers climb back in the car.

"Suicide bombers," one says. "Someone in the crowd said it was two suicide bombers."

Marefat's head of security and discipline, Mr. Mirzaei, is on his morning trip to the public bathhouse when his phone rings. His number is on every student's ID badge, all 4,000 of them, so he's always accessible to each of them and to their parents.

"We're near Burnt Bridge." He recognizes the voice of a frantic parent. "We heard shooting and then the police stopped us, and now people are talking about suicide bombers in the Desert. What's going on? Should the kids come to school?"

He tells the parent to stand by, he'll call him back. He hangs up and dials a contact in Afghanistan's intelligence service.

"Wait," the officer says, "I'll call the District Thirteen branch and see if they know anything."

Mirzaei is not surprised at first. As the Knowledge Seekers and other insurgents have stepped up the frequency of suicide bombings in the city, most of Mirzaei's friends took comfort in the fact that there had never been such a bombing in the Desert. Mirzaei didn't. He noticed attacks getting closer and closer. One just recently in the western part of the capital, another even closer on a bus transporting army officers. He saw the attacks as marching mortar rounds that hadn't hit the Desert yet but were zeroing in. Since he has the safety of 2,700 children to worry about, he considers it part of his job to never let anything surprise him. As far as he's concerned, it was only a matter of time before they hit the Desert.

The Desert, after all, had been getting more and more crowded in the twelve years since the Outsiders came. It was full of soft targets: civilians were packed in, living in close proximity to one another with no security. He heard of a few Hazara government officials who'd moved in now, too. And hadn't the terrorist leader Golbuddin Hekmatyar threatened Hazaras just last month? Whatever was happening over by Burnt Bridge was likely Hekmatyar making good on his threat. So Mirzaei focuses on sounding calm, even though he knows immediately the situation could be very real and very serious. This was the task he assigned himself every day—showing calm for the benefit of the students, and he thought he did a good job of it.

The students did not—they called him "Mr. Bruce Lee" behind his back, because they found him spastic and excitable—but they liked him for caring.

His contact in the intelligence department called back.

"I can't tell you much. I can't give out details of our intelligence, what the motive of the attack was, or how many people were there, but I can tell you there were two bombers over by Burnt Bridge. It's safe now, so tell parents that they can take their children to school. Tell them it's secure."

So he does. For two hours the day proceeds almost as normal, save for the whispering he hears as he makes his rounds through the halls. It doesn't take long before everyone in the student body knows. By the second break, the suicide bombers in the Desert are all anyone is talking about.

Mirzaei overhears a troubling rumor that he dismisses at first, but which becomes more alarming as the day goes on. A teacher claims to have a government source who said there had been not two attackers, but four. That meant two were still unaccounted for. As

Mirzaei makes his rounds the rest of the morning, the rumors draw into focus: the new attackers are somewhere in the Desert. And, this teacher was saying, police believe the bombers have three potential targets, but, maddeningly, wouldn't say what they were.

Of course, that meant Marefat. If you were trying to cause mass casualties in the Desert, you might pick a wedding hall, or maybe a mosque—but mosques weren't crowded here, not at this time of year. And a wedding hall had little symbolic value. Not like a school for people known to be sympathetic to the Outsiders.

The rumors were all consistent in that, chillingly, the bombers were hiding out with a prominent member of the Unity Party. The same party Mirzaei had fought for. The party Aziz had fought for. The party for whom Aziz had first started holding classes, long before Marefat started in a refugee camp in Pakistan.

This part made no sense. Why would anyone from Unity Party harbor suicide bombers in The Desert? The Unity Party had been mostly Hazara. He decided it was a piece of information that only had sticking power because it was so bizarre and so oddly specific. He dismissed it, and went about his day.

Then he heard it again, dismissed it again, heard it a third time, and finally decided the information was too precise and too consistent to ignore.

His first instinct was to check the information with the intelligence officer. But now he was anxious, his thinking confused. By the time Mirzaei had finally decided to take the information seriously, hours had passed. The intelligence department would ask when he'd learned this information and why he waited so long to tell them. It would look suspicious. They would want to know where the information came from, and that would mean giving up the names of teachers. The teachers would feel exposed, and worse, it would confirm for them that the threat was real. He changed his mind again. For now, they'd have to just not know. Whatever was happening, he'd have to handle it in the dark.

Mirzaei, moving at a fast waddle, entered Aziz's office and told him, walkie-talkie chirping in hand, that this morning's bodies may not have been the last of it. "Sir, I have fresh news about the security situation."

Aziz knew immediately that there was nothing he could do. If suicide bombers wanted his school, they would have it.

The board had talked of building walls with razor wire around Marefat, turning it into a citadel, but how could they pay for that? Even if they could, it would mean sacrificing the one security advantage they had, which was that the school was hard to find. It would announce to everyone around that there was something valuable here, or else something controversial—something that needed to be secured. Could they build a fortress strong enough to justify the attention it would draw?

But mostly, they'd decided against it because it would remind the students every minute of every day that there were people who wanted to hurt them. It would lock them up, when the purpose of the school was to do the opposite. So right now, the only backstop Aziz has against an attack was the man standing in front of him, a man out of breath, overweight, and sweating through his second shirt of the day.

Aziz did a quick accounting. What did he have to protect the students? Aside from Mr. Bruce Lee, who, Aziz could tell, was now too keyed up to think straight, he didn't have much. The best he could do was try to prevent panic. Which meant, in that moment, the best thing to do was to laugh in Mirzaei's face.

"Come on, that can't happen here!" Aziz said. "I mean, if they wanted to attack a school, they could go downtown! A private university there would be a much easier target. Here in the Desert, all the way out here, it's difficult for them to get here, it's so far for them!" Mirzaei's expression didn't change. "Look," Aziz said, "don't be too shocked by this, okay? I don't believe in these kinds of things."

A calculated lie, because at that moment Aziz was visualizing exactly what the attack on the school would look like. He imagined the morning lineup, the rows of students looking up at him with all their attention, an explosion right in the middle of the courtyard, their tiny bodies flying apart. *This will keep me awake tonight.* "I don't believe it," he said again, "but I suppose it doesn't mean we should do *nothing*. So let's do this: why don't you send some extra students from the discipline council up on the roof to keep an eye out, starting tomorrow. And Mr. Mirzaei," he added, before dismissing him, "let's not tell anyone anything else. Nothing more to teachers or to students, not even to the students you send to the roof. Tell them to be on high alert, just in case they see anything suspicious, a strange person hanging around, things like that, but don't tell them anything else." He knew they'd figure it out on their own, but no need to worry them now. Just get extra eyes up there.

And that was it. That was all they could do. The next day, the students went up, the girls in their pale blue dresses and headscarves, the boys in their red ties and boxy suits, walking back and forth on Marefat's roof, following Mr. Bruce Lee's orders to be "extra vigilant" against a threat he refused to explain.

Aziz had no illusions about what would happen. The students were smart, they'd piece it together. Everyone in the Desert heard about what had happened the day before and the few who lived outside the Desert had seen the commotion with their own eyes on the way in. Today there were extra students on the roof. Rumors would start, and eventually everyone would know that there was some kind of threat against the school. Aziz couldn't stop that knowledge from getting out. But he also knew that even if they understood the precise nature of the threat, there would still be nothing to do about it. If he could leave a little doubt in their minds, delay that knowledge by a day, even an hour, he'd be giving them just a little more time with a little less worry. If he could keep it as a rumor instead of a certainty, he felt he'd be doing right by them.

He also knew that most of the time these things didn't resolve neatly. Every once in a while, there'd be a happy story of a bomb defused, an attacker detained before reaching his target. But usually, one of two things happened: the attackers hit what they wanted to hit, or they didn't even try, and no one had a satisfactory reason why no attack ever happened. It just didn't. And people were left to wonder whether maybe it still would.

Two more times that day, Mr. Bruce Lee came to give Aziz updates about the two attackers roaming the Desert, and to ask what should be done.

Both times, his instructions remained the same: nothing.

★ ★ ★

For a day, it was quiet. Then a student woke in the night to screams from a neighbor's house, and ran up to the roof with his parents to find out what was going on. The neighbors yelled across the rooftop that they'd been robbed, and the student cupped his hands and yelled and screamed, a big communal siren to alert everyone that there was trouble. When he went back downstairs with his parents, they found that their own home had been robbed, too.

The day after that, a teacher returned home from Marefat and found her parents tied to chairs, her house relieved of all the jewelry that had been collected for a wedding.

No one could remember robberies ever happening in the Desert, just as there'd never been suicide bombers. Now in the span of three days there had been both, and two attackers were still out in the Desert somewhere.

What worried Aziz most about the robberies was that both families said the police weren't at all interested in helping. He'd been worried police and soldiers were going to lose their commitment, and that their own parochial interests would rise up and snuff out everything else. Family and tribe are important, that's where loyalty always flows, but concepts like "rule of law" would be little more than abstractions when they weren't paid for anymore. The army and police were set up by the Outsiders; their salaries were almost entirely underwritten by the Outsiders. What reason would there be to stay loyal to an organization when its guarantor was leaving? The men in uniform were already starting to look out for themselves. Aziz thought this might happen, just not so soon. But for now, that was the worst of it: robberies, with no serious effort to find the guilty parties.

In the meantime, there were still bombers hiding in the Desert preparing to hit Marefat.

Aziz escapes for the few moments of solace he allows himself in times like these, up on the roof of the girls' building where he can see the whole campus and a few miles beyond, and where everyone knows not to bother him. The only people still at school at this hour are a handful of teachers working late.

Aziz stands with his arms crossed, looking down at the stalled auditorium project, four stories below. He ran out of money again after the framing had been installed for the basement level, and he had no idea when the next donation might come, so the builders finally walked off. It's just a ditch again, this time with naked rebar sticking up like the ribs of a giant upturned carcass. It feels less like the beginning of something special, more like an open grave. The place where a big idea turned over and died.

Just a few months ago he would stand next to the construction, drawn to it like a magnet, sometimes stare at it, often hopping down into the muck to hold a plumb line or offer his engineering advice. Every time he left his office he found himself next to the excavation, watching the men work. Now he walks by without looking at it; it's a fraught thing he tries to ignore, a relationship that ended in a mess. A big open pit, useless except to collect water and break a child's leg if she slips walking by. It is a monument to his ambition and a rejection of his whole approach to progress: that if your idea is good and you're pushy and you smile at people who tell you no, if you basically just ignore them and keep trying anyway, eventually resistance wilts away. That reasonable people will always, eventually, recognize a good idea. Now kids walk by and throw pebbles and candy wrappers in, watch them go down, and then march off toward home. Mourners at the graveside, doing their part, bit by bit, to bury it.

Aziz hasn't lost all hope, but up here, where he can see everything and no one can see him, where no one else can hear what he has to say, he allows that he is scared. This morning a classful of students come to his office because their teacher hadn't shown up. One of them said to Aziz, "We're ready now. Tell us what will happen with the withdrawal." The suicide bombers in the Desert had washed away any pretext that things would proceed normally and it was time to get the straight story. Thirty-seven girls, looking at him, waiting for him to answer. He couldn't. He deflected, made a half-hearted attempt to turn their question into a teachable moment.

"Well, what do *you* all think will happen?"

And now, up on the roof he's ashamed. "This is not something good. Because even though we are not going to turn the students into partisans, we should be using these opportunities to develop their sense of citizenship, and this is the time for that. But I can't do that. Because I'm starting to feel abandoned."

Metrinko is gone. General Allen, who made such a show of support for the school at the change of command ceremony, was gone right after it. All his allies are gone; there's no one to ask for support. It used to be that when he called the U.S. embassy, someone would call him back. People there are strangers to him now, as he is to them. He's unsure whom to call if there's trouble, and what to do at school; his teaching philosophy all twisted up and conflicted now. He's always taught his students to be clear-eyed and critical, because if you don't like what's happening around you, you can change it. But if you can't actually change things, what good is trying? It's just taking on risk.

A few months ago, he told college students not to demand their rights. Then he told girls to keep quiet and get married. What was he becoming? And now it seems like even if they all did what he told them, it wouldn't matter. *So what do you do? Teach them to be realistic? Teach them a fiction so at least they don't worry? Keep teaching them to fight for their rights out of principle, even if it will only get them hurt?*

"Now we have to take ourselves two or three feet back. Just to remain alive. Just to remain safe. For the time being we should shut our voice, shut our mouth, not use any provoking remarks. When the pressure is coming from different sides, you feel yourself unsafe or unprotected, you feel it more with your subconscious. When you feel that the whole environment is unsafe, you should not pose yourself to risk another's reaction. You should be calm."

It's almost dark now, and the muezzins begin the call to prayer, first one, then another, then several as if they've woken each other up and are singing to one another, some low and mournful, some high and ecstatic-sounding. He listens for awhile, then his cell phone rings: he's been summoned to a meeting with Ashraf Ghani. More and more he's drawn away to work with Ashraf Ghani, more and more of his time is spent driving out of the Desert, away from the school. He thinks this work is the right thing to do, that the Kochi is the best hope for his country and his people and the school. His connection to this powerful man does not make him feel less alone, though. It does not make him feel less vulnerable—it makes him feel more so. He is trying to help a man from a rival ethnic group come to power; he hears from other Hazaras that he is betraying them. Helping Ashraf Ghani is thinning Aziz's roster of allies. He feels the isolation acutely. This is all a gamble. We climb down off the roof.

"For me," he says, "whenever I walk around, I see hundreds of kids looking at me, and they ask me, 'Will we be okay tomorrow?'" He shakes his head. "We will remain here in Afghanistan, we *have* to remain here. So what should we do with this bad and nasty situation here? Should we go low, cut programs? We have been doing that, gradually, gradually reducing our initiatives, just for the sake of—existing. Of not antagonizing people. Maybe it's natural, the ups and downs of growth in a community, like a wave."

Night has fallen and the school power is off, so he descends in complete darkness, his feet navigating by memory. "But maybe if you cannot control the ups and downs of the waves, then you are just hitting on the rocks." He stutters here; ocean metaphors don't come naturally to a man who's lived his life in a landlocked country.

"You should go carefully to shore, to not be beaten on the rocks, so that someday, maybe, you can return back to sea."

With that, he climbs into Asef's van, and sets off to meet with the Pashtun.

Today is September 11.

A symbolic date, of course; Mr. Bruce Lee is on high alert every September 11, and things are especially tense on this one. The new crime wave has everyone off balance. Mostly it's the bombers. He waited and waited for them to strike. Every day he listened for a scream, an explosion, a gunshot, footsteps that sounded heavy or strange—any indication that the attack was happening. He was hypervigilant, and every day that passed, the coil wound tighter. Days passed, nothing happened. A week passed. Then Mr. Bruce Lee woke up understanding why with total clarity: the attack hadn't happened because the bombers were waiting for a symbolic date. They were waiting for September 11. For today.

The school day goes by normally, except for him, every sense is heightened. His anticipation is physiological: he sweats through his shirt earlier, he walks faster and with more purpose. He's worried all day but knows he does a good job hiding it.

By the end of the day, the attack has not begun. He returns home and tries to unwind. He turns on the television and moves through the house, listening to the news in the background as he goes about his domestic tasks.

It's during a commercial that he hears the first pistol report. A small handgun, but there are more immediately, then the staccato crack of a machine gun on full automatic over by the school. Then another series of cracks, and now he can make out at least four different guns firing. Four or five rounds at a time, then silence, then four or five more rounds, and then he's ripping through the drawers to get his own pistol and he's out the door at a full sprint with weapon in hand moving as fast as he can in the dark toward the school. Even before he has fully registered what's happening he knows that there is no way he can protect the school. He's alone and has only a small-caliber handgun with a single magazine; in the last forty-five seconds he's heard a hundred rounds or more. He has the fleeting thought that this is way more than just two bombers, so the rumors had not been right after all—this sounds like an entire platoon. Gunfire comes from every direction; they must have taken up positions all around the school. In the unfinished mosque, in the wedding hall, maybe even in the neighbors' houses. Overhead he sees blood-colored streaks crossing the sky and disappearing midflight—*Tracer rounds, so we're being fired at from far away, too*—then he hears the heavy *clack-clack-clack-clack* of the old Russian PK rifles, which are usually mounted on armored vehicles—*Is there an armored vehicle attacking us? Is the National Army attacking the school?* It's clear to him that he is absurdly outnumbered and outgunned. He will be killed quickly. Still he keeps running toward the school, and he has his first clear thought: *This isn't useless: I can occupy three or four of them with a few well-placed shots, and maybe that's enough. By the time they see it's just me, help will have arrived.* He knows as soon as the thought crosses his mind that it is fantasy. He is running to his death.

He arrives, wheezing, in the alley behind the girls' building. The whole sky is lit with fire, and people are yelling all around him. From where he stands, he can't see anyone aiming at the school. And now that he is standing still for the first time, a second clear thought occurs to him—*It does not make sense to attack the school at night*. If you wanted to hurt students, why would you attack a school when students were sure to be home?

He tries to catch his breath and calls his contact in intelligence. "Listen," he said, "there's heavy fighting all over the Desert near the school. We need help!"

"It's a celebration!"

Mr. Bruce Lee is sure he's heard wrong. "It's what?"

"The soccer championship! We beat India! You didn't know?"

He'd never seen people shooting at the sky to celebrate. He hadn't even known his country's team was playing. Even if he'd known, it wouldn't have occurred to him that this was how people would cheer. That when Afghanistan won, beating a country almost four times its size, a few people would shoot at the sky in their elation, and that it would catch on, and that all over the city the sky would light up with gunfire.

Four people died that night in the Desert and many more were injured by bullets coming back down. But for Mr. Bruce Lee, it was a relief, a thousand times better than what he thought was happening.

Still, the bombers waited.

When the shooting started, Ta Manna chased her father up the stairs and out the door onto the roof, where he began firing the family's Kalashnikov. She yelled and begged and screamed for her own try with the gun, and finally he gave it to her. She turned the barrel up, pulled the trigger once, the gun kicked like a child adjusting itself in her arms and made such a roar that her head rang for two days.

"This," thought the aspiring double agent, "will put a damper on my plan to join the Taliban."

23

THREE MONTHS LEFT

Everyone tries for normalcy. Aziz and his family are settling into their new house. The lease ran out on the rental before the new one was complete, so they've been living in an unfinished house, without doors on the bathrooms or glass on the windows. The builders worked outside-in, so the walls were finished first. The house is set far back from the street, with one gate to get onto the property, another to get into the yard. Aziz's father insisted on it. He's shaken by the shrinking economy and by all the attacks happening. The space between them is shrinking, the city hums with violence. All while Aziz is venturing even further into the public eye, forming a controversial alliance with a rival tribe. The family needs to protect itself, and its patriarch wants them walled in. Aziz doesn't like having high walls keeping the students away. He doesn't object, though, out of respect. He just won't talk about it.

Anyway, there are other domestic concerns. It's been a week of embarrassing bathroom encounters and nighttime raids by flies, until the glass is finally installed on the windows and doors are put in. The kids run around the house turning the lights on and off, then go down into the basement and play tag around a cauldron over an open gas flame. Aziz's wife is only mildly annoyed by the swarm around her and has positioned herself between the pot and the action, blocking the kids from danger with her own body.

These days, she's making a point of brightening up when she sees me. She is a small, sturdy woman, but she has always been a ghost in Aziz's house. The little indentations she leaves on their lives are everywhere—in the orderly arrangement of shoes on the doormat where a moment ago a chaotic pile blocked entry; in the food that appears whenever Aziz gets home, whether he's alone or leading ten guests, at five thirty in the evening or at midnight. But she is seen only in fleeting glimpses, a wisp of fabric curling behind a doorframe. I lean on Aziz often about this. Why must his wife always hide? I ask less because I think Aziz needs some kind of enlightening I can provide, than because Aziz delights in making other people uncomfortable and I like to return fire. "Isn't it hypocritical," I say, "that for someone as eager as he is to make other men grant their wives and daughters autonomy, his own wife must hide when unrelated men are present?" He laughs. "It's her! She is herself uncomfortable. She can't speak your language and doesn't know what to say to you!"

When the important men who do speak her language gather with Aziz, she's too intimidated to come out. Of course it's a presumption of mine that she'd even want to, but Aziz insists he'd be happy with her chiming in on matters of politics if she felt like it. She's in the accelerated learning program at Marefat, so one day she might, but she's moving glacially through elementary school, because—here, Aziz laughs—she's not very studious! She hardly ever does her homework, she doesn't listen to the teacher, she's something of a problem student. I can't be sure, but when Aziz says this, I think I see a glimmer of pride. Like he thinks she's used school to grow a rebellious side.

Where before I understood her to be a timid woman, vaguely supportive of her husband's crusade but unsure exactly what it meant, now when I see her, she stands up straight, quickens her pace, and gives as strong a handshake as Aziz ever has. Seven years into my friendship with him, I am, for the very first time, starting to know her. She is soft-spoken, but she is a brave, bright woman. She has a bit of the armor Aziz has, the ability to stay uninjured by what happens around her because she sees it all as a little ridiculous. She stirs the pot. Nearby, the children shriek and cackle.

Her youngest, Roya-e Zendagi, "dream of life," has changed, too. She's always seemed so tiny and fragile you could knock her over just by looking in her direction, but now she has moments of boldness. She detaches from her mother's hip, marches herself right up to me and offers her hand. I take it, her whole fist between my one finger and thumb, and for a moment, she is unintimidated. Then her hand retracts and she runs back to bury herself in the fabric of her mother's clothing.

The music from the new wedding hall next door picks up. The wedding hall construction boom has somehow escaped the effects of the downturn and remains, by all appearances, everyone's idea of a can't-miss investment. A new venue opens every week, and this one has an event every night. It's especially loud because the weekend is beginning, which means a constant assault of harmonium from speakers the size of full-grown men. The whole street shudders. Aziz's brothers shake their heads. They each have a floor of the house, with their wives and children; none of them can stand the throbbing music, the saccharine master of ceremonies saying the same thing about tonight's couple he did about the one last night, and the one the night before that.

Aziz gets up and closes the curtain, as if that might help him to ignore it. His mood is plaintive. Having just moved, he is thinking about all his old homes. How many *things* they own. A truck's worth, the detritus a family of nine collects over a lifetime.

He thinks of how few belongings they had when they were in exile, when they were hiding in Pakistan. It was a frightening time, but for him it was also a thrilling one, and he had assumed all the while that it had been for his family, too. After years of marriage, it was the first time he and his wife had lived together. Surely she enjoyed that as much as he did. Surely it was a relief for her, after the civil war years, in which she stayed behind in the highlands, while he was at the front. At least in Pakistan they were all together.

But now he thinks back to Pakistan and he's ashamed. He'd convinced himself that that time was a gift to his wife. Of course it wasn't. It was just another kind of prison. His wife was away from home for the first time. Her first time living outside the valley where she'd grown up was as a refugee, in a land whose language she could hardly understand, where she did not have friends, sleeping next to a marked man who would not stop drawing attention to himself. Back then, he took her on long walks with the kids so they could feel free for an hour or so, and he assumed they all loved those walks because he had. Because *he'd* always loved moving at night.

"I love driving at night," he once said.

"Me, too," I told him. "I love driving."

"Most of the time," he said, "I find an excuse just to have a night journey. At night when everything is dark, but still there are some lights, people coming, coming, going."

"Me, too," I said. "Walking at night, driving at night. Swimming at night. Have you ever been swimming at night?"

"I have never been swimming at all! Because I have never seen water." He'd laughed to himself then, like he meant something profound but wasn't quite sure what, and then we were quiet.

In Pakistan, the night was the only time they could walk, because he was known. He was famous with none of the benefits of being famous. He was accused of being a spy for the CIA, a spy for Israel, of working for the Jews. Others went mute in their exiles, Aziz grew louder. In the magazine he published, he blasted the pro-Iranian clerics, he pulled the curtain back on leaders in the Shia community. He criticized his own party. He treated his targets as if they were party to one big sinister gimmick and it was his job to yank out the false rostrum on which they were elevated. His articles were published in violent jihadi publications and in nonviolent but anticommunist publications; then he launched his own. *Our Today.* His writing was impassioned, but it was also officious, condescending. Religious leaders were threatened by him. They also just found him obnoxious.

Once, while driving past the Ayatollah's mosque in Kabul, he allowed how happy he was to have galled men like that. "I've had a good game with him throughout my life," he'd said, looking at the Ayatollah's massive seminary. "Though I have been very small, I really annoyed him. When you annoy someone big, really it feels good. You know Bertolt Brecht? There's a poem translated in Farsi, and he says 'I don't know what the use of me in this world is, but I know that without me my oppressors may sleep well.' I read that in Pakistan. Some people have really hated me strongly. But you know, I feel that as a sense of satisfaction for me."

Because of the school, he's learned vulnerability. Now he thinks, no, he does not deserve credit for how he treated his family during the war years. He was a good father, he never doubted that, but in a qualified way. Within the confines of the life he had to have, a mission he was obligated to serve. If that meant his family had to live with the constant threat of violence, well, he'd done the best he could, given the circumstances.

But he'd never given them reason to laugh. So when Abuzar went to the United States to study at "The Thufts" and came back smiling Aziz had been surprised. Surprised and happy, but happy in the way you are when someone you love succeeds, but not because of you, and maybe, you think, in spite of you.

Why is he thinking of these things now? The suicide bombers in the Desert and the threat to the school frighten him. More than that, they anger him. *It's supposed to be easier.* He thinks of the friends who have asked him for political advice. These men with a dozen cars and fancy living rooms, burlap sacks full of money from this new job he's started to hear about, "consulting," which as far as he can tell means not really doing anything. Meanwhile he is vulnerable, his family is vulnerable, and his school is full of children who are also vulnerable.

He had tried to make his kids free, but now he has had to put them in a house with two gates, two concentric circles of concrete. It was a nice home, as nice as any home he'd ever lived in, but it was a prison. A bunker at least, because he was beginning to understand that he was about to take a step forward again, and this time, he didn't have the excuse of not knowing what he was doing. With this next step, he knew with certainty that he was placing his wife and children directly in harm's way.

★   ★   ★

The phone rings. It's His Excellency, Second Vice President Karim Khalili. Aziz talks for a few moments and hangs up. Less than a minute later Ashraf Ghani calls. This new living room has become a nerve center where Aziz is putting together a political alliance with a cell phone that is falling apart. Ghani has come to depend on Aziz. It's Aziz who might convince Hazara intellectuals to support Ghani; it is Aziz who has Khalili's trust and might secure his endorsement for Ghani. When Ghani makes the fraught political decision to allow a brutal Uzbek warlord, General Dostum, to be one of his running mates, again Aziz mediates. It is Aziz, with his status as an intellectual like Ghani, but a past as a warrior like Dostum, who will help this odd couple get along.

Aziz alternates between amusement and anger that he has no resources and no protection but has found himself responsible for planning his country's future. The fragile alliance between all these people, of different ethnicities and vastly different backgrounds, rests on his ability to carry messages between them. He adjusts and calibrates so that a message from the bookish Columbia PhD with the CV full of scholarly publications won't offend the boorish general with the reputation for mutilating enemy soldiers and raping their women. He sits on the floor, covers his forehead with his hand, and concentrates now, as he passes Khalili's latest concerns on to the presidential hopeful.

The door handle wiggles, the door cracks open as if eased by a draft, and Farzhad's head pokes through, with a smile wider than his eyes. When Farzhad smiles he looks like a tiny clown; he runs into the room and begins tumbling on the throw pillows across the floor from his father.

"What are you doing, boy?" Aziz says. Farzhad mumbles while he rolls, pausing upside down, with his hands on his feet. Than he sits up and presses his hands against his hair, which Aziz now sees is wet.

"Ah," Aziz says. "He's making a cock peak." Then he frowns; he knows what he's just said is not quite right—he means "mohawk," but he's mixed it up with "peacock" and in the process, invented a new hairstyle. Farzhad tumbles again and lands in a resting position, cross-legged. He makes two fists, plops his chin down on top of them, and examines us. Aziz is amused. His kids are precocious, and he doesn't know where it comes from. They're tiny adults running around his house. Farzhad has begun using words from a translated Turkish TV show. He says *khatarnak* a dozen times a day. "Very generous." "Thank you, Dad, that is very generous of you," Farzhad says. "Astonished" is another. "Dad, I am astonished by you!"

"You are five! What does 'astonished' even mean for you?"

The school does its best to wash away the events of the previous month, and Aziz has a few events up his sleeve to help the process along.

Once a year, the school hires a couple of old German buses to take all the twelfth-grade girls for a picnic. For many of the girls, it's the first time in their lives they get to go out and just be girls, to goof around away from prying eyes without worrying about decorum. It is, for many of them, the only time they ever will. Even though many of them are outgoing, they're still restricted—by tradition, by family, by religion. As often as not, just by their own idea of propriety. They all have Facebook profiles; none of them use their own photographs.

But today, the girls will be away from the pressures of their community. A few male teachers will come; Mr. Bruce Lee and Aziz as chaperones—and their host will be there, a retired Hazara general, but one who's lived in London and is as liberal-minded as the friends he made there.

Other than that, it's all girls. It's their day to be outside, and to do whatever they want without worrying about anyone taking offense.

Many of the girls arrive for the outing in cars driven by their brothers, who look curiously at all the girls gathered at the school's front door. The atmosphere is festive, the girls full of energy. They have prepared mountains of food, rice dishes and chicken and long flat plates of pudding secured beneath plastic wrap. They've brought camp stoves and thermoses full of tea, and they all mill about and gossip, until they pile into the rickety old busses and venture across the city.

The ride is bumpy, through parts of the city Aziz remembers from the war but hasn't seen in years. The busses pass close to Afshar. The girls shriek, and they laugh, and shift constantly across the aisle to photograph themselves in different pairings.

The General's house is off an alley that looks as poor as any other part of the city. Silent children make careful passes through an expanse of garbage and stand suddenly erect when they see the busses, as if deciding whether a few dozen boisterous young women presents a threat to their enterprise.

Hidden behind big, plain, sand-colored walls, the General has a garden with grass such a deep green the girls don't believe it's real, and a variety of flowers so wide they're disoriented. They've never seen a place with so many different kinds of life. They stand politely while Aziz introduces the General to them, and them to the General, but they look past him to the green, and when the introductions are finally done, the girls begin to yell and sing and take off to explore all the far corners of the garden like it might at any moment disappear. They chase each other around the field and through the rooms of a house the General built on the property; they find any excuse to run. They can't behave this way at home; they can't behave this way any place, really, at least not any place they might be seen by anyone other than each other. Sometimes at school, girls will run down the halls clutching each other's elbows, and then stop short to see how far they can slide on the dust. But otherwise they're home, separated from one another, and obliged to show reserve and decorum. It's why Aziz dreams of a big open space on top of the school where the girls would be up so high no one would be able to see them being girls.

The General says he picked every plant himself and rests his hand on a mulberry bush he brought from Iran. He planted each one with his own hands because that's what a good soldier should do. The property is in an area people go mostly when the weather's nice, close enough to the city that you don't lose too much of a weekend getting to it, far enough that wealthy folks can justify having second houses there. The neighborhood surrounds a reservoir, and also houses a military base first occupied by Soviet forces, and later by international fighters allied with the Taliban. So this area, the closest thing Kabul has to a weekend getaway, was among the first places hit when U.S. airstrikes began in October 2001.

The girls split into two groups; half of them file into a big open room inside the house and form a circle, and then the girls begin to dance unreservedly. The other group stays out on the grass and a kind of dodgeball game evolves, with girls running in circles, pelting each other with a soccer ball, and shrieking. They take pictures constantly. They take pictures of everything: of themselves, of each other, of flowers, of Aziz, of the General. It doesn't matter whether the subject is looking at the camera, or is even aware a picture is being taken. The girls sidle up to Aziz, and a friend will take a picture of her posed with Aziz's blurred face in midconversation with someone out of frame. He's amused by this, by the girls simply taking what they want, like they're entitled to it. This is the first time he's ever seen the girls behave this way. He's taken them other places for their class picnic— to a recently rebuilt public garden, for example. There, the girls got to sit on the grass and be outside together, but they had no privacy, so they just sat and spoke quietly to one another, subdued by the stares of picnicking families.

The General's garden is different. It's a fortress, but a fortress full of flowers. It is both expansive and, at the same time, private. So the girls have space to roam, but they don't have to worry about people watching, two things they'll likely never get at the same time again. To be outside, and to be unseen.

The man who built this place is the type of man Aziz doesn't fully understand. They fought on opposing sides, the General with the Communists and Aziz with the holy warriors. Aziz has no complaint with him now, but he doesn't understand how the General got all his money. This huge house with its lush garden is his second house in the city—a weekend house. The General says he has a home in London, too, and kids who went to expensive schools.

"I bought this property right after 9/11," he says, by way of explanation. Everything was cheap then; afterward, real estate took off. He ran the country's Ministry of Counternarcotics for a while, so he has access to government officials and perhaps power to exchange for favors. But this information still doesn't solve the equation for

Aziz. All this, on a civil servant's salary? The General must have other income from somewhere. Probably consulting. Anyway, part of what sticks with him is the irony: a general who stuck by the Communist president, then cashed in and went to London. A traitor in two ways, then: a comrade who got rich and a loyalist to the Eastern Bloc who settled in the West.

But Aziz gets along with him because the General does not behave like other rich men here. He is genuine about his interests and wants to share what he has. He likes flowers, loves his garden, and knows the genus of everything in it. The title "general" is with him for life, and he still has sources from his days in the military, but he is no longer a military man, either by occupation or by demeanor.

The girls are loud for nearly five hours straight. They sit down to eat twice, they pull clumps of grapes from the General's vines and throw them at each other. The General wanders around, pleased that people are enjoying his garden, unbothered that they are colonizing his property. He finds a corner to discuss with Aziz his apocalyptic projections about next year. He's intent on addressing the Outsiders' departure, which is precisely the kind of thing Aziz is trying to keep off the girls' minds right now, but Aziz indulges, because he's a guest.

Another guest arrives, a trusted member of the General's inner circle so the girls don't feel intimidated. He's a former adviser to the minister of defense, a perfect counterpart to the General: staid where the General is expressive, severe where the General is comical. They lean on their elbows, and together they dissect a recent insurgent attack on a military outpost in a northern province.

"Twenty-four hundred troops were sitting there, why?" the adviser says, popping grapes in his mouth while the General nods. "Why were there so many there? It's not conventional fighting. There were maybe a hundred Talibs, but they were in mountains above. Those twenty-four hundred troops, they were in a killing zone."

"The military is politicized. Even though the men might be well trained, the leadership is not professional. They don't have accountability."

A series of squeals echo off the walls; the girls are inside trying to convince their teachers to dance.

The General turns to me. "This is your problem as Americans." He doesn't say it as an accusation; his tone is pleading. "All the troops are leaving, and you say you are going to leave eight thousand, or maybe ten thousand, just sitting at one or two bases. Doing what? I promise you, every day the Taliban will send a rocket. All the time they will be firing mortars. Every day you will get hit. What is the point?"

He knows no military argument, by its shear logic or passion, will overwhelm the decision to leave, because the decision doesn't have much to do with military strategy. He is deploying a tactical argument against a political decision. A few thousand troops staying behind, all concentrated on one base—that's not a general's idea of how to win a war. It's a politician's idea of how to not admit losing one. He seems resigned to the idea that the war will eventually be lost, that progress will be hemmed in, and that the calculations in the foreign capitals have already been completed. He knows no one with any say in the matter is listening to him. But he keeps trying to drive his point home anyway.

It has already been a special day when the girls start packing up; the plan was to go to the lake before the end of the day and they're running out of time. They reluctantly round themselves up, assemble for group photos, thank the General, load the bus, and head out toward the lake.

The lakeshore is barren: there's hardly any grass that's not guarded behind the walls of private restaurants. The army and police have checkpoints all around the perimeter. They've ramped up security since a Taliban attack last summer: gunmen in burkas walked into one of the lakeside hotels with rocket-propelled grenades and killed twenty civilians. But the lake is still a place people go, because really, there's no place else *to* go.

The water has begun to recede. No one is sure whether it's a natural summer ebb or something more permanent, but it's still striking, a twinkling blue basin like a precious stone that's fallen into the dirt. The girls run down toward the water's edge, right up to the line where dirt turns to mud—and then a little farther in, where mud turns to the kind of hard sucking sand that grabs hold of your feet so firmly it can trip you. A boy on a jet ski comes whizzing by, does stunts with a leg dangling in the water, and then turns around to make a closer pass. He makes no effort to obscure the fact that he's staring at the girls: he is plainly showing off for them. They, in turn, appear interested but unsure of how exactly they're supposed to react to the show. So they just stand there, quiet for a moment, looking intrigued but confused, as the boy goes back and forth, each time closer to the shore, in increasingly extravagant poses, looking more and more like some kind of ridiculous waterborne ballerina, until finally, unsatisfied with the girls' reaction, he gives up and motors off toward the middle of the lake.

There's a shriek from behind, and they all spin around to look: one of the girls has separated herself from the group, stopped a small boy leading a hungry-looking horse, and is sitting on top of it, doubled over in laughter. The horse stomps and shifts its weight, the girl shrieks again, and the boy tries to help her down as she inches to the side, then tumbles gracelessly into the dirt. Aziz turns around to watch another girl flop belly-first over the horse's back, and then wrap her arms around its neck and her feet over the saddle, easing herself upright. The horse stomps and whinnies, and she screams. Now all the girls are gathered around the horse, and the next one settles into the saddle, leans over, and whispers to the boy: "Do these things just stand still?" He makes a clucking sound and the horse takes off. It starts galloping down the beach with the girl bobbing on top of it and the little boy trying to keep up. The horse is faster but the boy won't let go of the lead, so the animal runs clumsily in one direction with its head facing the other, and the girl is laughing so loudly people are starting to stare. Mr. Bruce Lee, having realized too late what's happening, is running down the beach, his shirt coming untucked and flapping as he huffs and waddles angrily after them. It's all one big awkward menagerie, the heavyset man chasing a skinny horse sagging under a girl laughing hysterically, while the smudge-faced boy hangs on for dear life and clumps of mud fly up in every direction.

And then it's over. They've been at the lake for just ten minutes and it's time to leave. Although the girls are hot and dusty and thirsty and are beginning to smell of sweat, there's no suggestion of swimming.

They protest, they want to stay, but Aziz insists. They protest more; he herds them back toward the bus. He is patient but firm. When Aziz gets on board, he finds one of the girls sitting in his seat, an act of open defiance. He scolds her but doesn't raise his voice. The bus rumbles to life, and the driver begins to pull back onto the road, but the girls are in a chorus of defiance now, and one of the girls leaning backward against the dash reaches out, hesitates, considers what she's about to do for a moment, and then punches the gearshift into neutral so that car engine roars and the torque cuts out and the bus stops accelerating. Aziz yells, "Girl, what are you *doing*? Behave!" The driver, too surprised by the girl's act of defiance to be angry about it, nudges the stick back into gear.

The bus clears the lake and pulls back onto the main road, just as a military convoy goes by in the other direction. The trucks have slat armor, which is designed to deflect the shaped charges from rocket-propelled grenades, but which has the appearance of giant cages covering the cabs. "It's like our women," Aziz says. "We make them cover their faces, and then we say, 'Now go walk!'"

The bus stops for bottled water, but the seals are broken. Someone has begun to pad their margins, refilling recycled bottles and selling them as new. The girls don't care, and the bus is quiet again while they drink, the teachers enjoy a moment of calm. Then a girl shoots up and leans across a seat to look out the window. A Toyota 4Runner has pulled out from behind the bus and is accelerating alongside it; it's in the wrong lane and swerving to dodge oncoming traffic. Several of the girls gasp and cover their mouths. The SUV swerves in front of the bus, shimmying wildly on its suspension, then it brakes hard so the space between the vehicles closes. As the bus and the SUV are driving along at the same pace, a figure climbs up out of the SUV's sunroof, hands outstretched like he's about to perform some kind of action movie stunt. The wind catches his shirt and it flattens against him, rippling furiously as he steadies himself, and another arm reaches up from the sunroof to hand him what looks like a small electronic device. A gun? A remote of some sort? The girls go dead quiet, and the young man begins to turn toward the bus.

Just as his body stops with the device pointing at them, the girls break out into cheers: they recognize him. He's a Marefat student, filming the bus with a video camera—a car full of Marefat boys who spotted the girls at the lake and caught up.

The boy continues with his performance. He makes some poses, he performs some stunts in the wind, then he slackens his body and tries to look like he's not trying that hard. Finally he raises his hands and slips back down in the car, and it zooms off ahead and out of sight.

The next day is the International Day of Peace, and the school has a celebration planned. They maintain the extra security put in place to protect against the suicide bombers: a few extra boys wondering around on the roof. One of the U.S. military's radar-equipped aerostats hangs a few miles to the east—a hundred-foot long blimp with the most sophisticated surveillance technology available. Marefat uses teenagers.

Aziz walks between the rows of students forming in the schoolyard like a designer surveying his models before a show. "I'm wondering how this happened," he says, passing boys in the back who tower above him. "These boys aren't growing, they're just *jumping* up. I don't know how! Maybe climate."

There is nervous energy in the students' chatter. They're excited and invested in how the celebration goes. As Afghans, as Hazaras, as Shias, they have a whole collection of days they're told to memorialize, sad things from the past they have to remember. But at Marefat students care about obscure holidays because they're put in charge. It is the students who have planned this day, students who have recruited other students to sing the songs, recite the poetry, plan the spectacles. Teachers participate, but only when students invite them. They ask a literature teacher to give a speech; Aziz to write lyrics for a song. I was asked to talk about how International Peace Day is celebrated in America, but I can't remember ever celebrating it, or even knowing that there was such a thing. So when it's time for me to talk, I share a theory about peace I learned from the man who first introduced me to the school. He went to Pakistan during the war years, and then made it to the United States. He was smart and high-achieving, and he became an American, then went to a top-tier college, and an Ivy League school for a graduate degree.

When I first met him, at a café in Kabul six years before—before I knew anything about the tribes here, even what they were called—I complimented him on being unprejudiced. I just assumed, I guess, that he was, perhaps because he was educated. "Well," he said, "I come predisposed."

He was a kind and humble man, the sort of person who gives of himself constantly and requires someone at his side to make sure he doesn't run himself right into the ground. He'd hardened in his exile though; although he was away from all the violence happening in his country, he read about it every day. He learned of all the ways his people were suffering, the massacres in Hazara cities and neighborhoods. And then he went to rallies in America about the war crimes happening back home and felt impotent because he couldn't change anything. No one listened, no one seemed to care. His view of fighting in his homeland became binary. His people were constantly victimized; all others were constantly victimizing them.

It took me years to understand what that meant. He had a sadness about his people, because of the suffering he had been unable to do anything about, and that sadness had calcified. He was predisposed in that he carried resentment for ethnic groups that had victimized his own, and he had a hard time forgiving people even for belonging to one of those groups. At the university in Kabul, where we both worked, people whispered about his favoritism—that he hired only Hazaras. He didn't deny it. His people had been enslaved, oppressed, massacred, emasculated. It would be immoral *not* to give them a leg up.

I thought him a brilliant man, actually, but I became uncomfortable with how he thought about other tribes. I compared him to other people I met in this country, people who *hadn't* escaped the fighting. I had friends who actually saw and suffered physically from the violence done to their people by others, but who could still get along with them. I decided it must be easier to hate a person you can't see, because you can reduce that person to something uncomplicated. An enemy you never meet can simply be evil if you never have to walk by him in the market. He doesn't have a face, except the one you imagine for him. That, I figured, must be how highly evolved people at safe removes from the violent things they fled can have such visceral reactions, and such simplistic thoughts, about people from whom they've never themselves suffered.

I tell the 2,700 kids gathered there to find a time to leave this school if they can. You'll hate less, I say, if you have to hate people you've been around. I tell the students that honestly, I've never celebrated this day in my country but that in my country, there are many people from countries like yours, countries that have seen conflict. And if you stay at Marefat forever, in this haven that has been built for you, you will look at other people not as people but as oppressors, savages, simpletons, killers.

Two nights before, Aziz had reminded dinner guests that Hazaras and Pashtuns share fourteen hundred miles of borders in this country. He reminded them that Grandfather Mazari had said for this reason, "We should ally ourselves with the Pashtuns. Let *geography* determine with whom we make peace." This is what I'm thinking about as I speak to the students. I tell them how we have a saying, that you don't make peace with your friends, you make peace with your enemies. So leave if you can, go out of the Desert as far as you can afford to, and then come back. Then I decide I'm done.

Aziz looks across and gives me his version of a wink—he pushes his bottom lip up so that his chin wrinkles, and at the same time, he squints his eyes and cocks his head. He is either trying to tell me "You were very good," or "It's okay that you were not very good."

As the program continues, he puts his hand across my back and pulls me close to him, like we're celebrating something special I've just done. He leans over, and I nod toward him so that I can receive his congratulations. He whispers, "You're blocking the poster."

He pushes me a foot to the side so that all the letters of the peace day sign are visible to the crowd. "There you go."

A student walks up to the stage, dressed as a fairy, with wings and a wand. A tiny boy marches up with a white dove in a cage and sets it next to her. She gives a short speech, then bends down to release the bird. She struggles to unfasten the door and once it's open, the bird puffs its feathers, jumps up and down, can't get out, but refuses to be caught. A boy serving as event photographer puts his camera down and gets up on the stage to help. The dove finally leaps free from the cage, startling the girl and knocking her on her heels, sending a wave of laughter across the crowd as the bird flies out of the courtyard. With the bird flying away, the music starts, and Aziz grabs my hand. "Don't forget that I wrote all these lyrics." He gives me another nod-wink. A group of girls gathered on the steps of the schoolyard begin to sing, while waving flags, some of them tapping their feet.

> *You all are looking for a word that is the color of friendship and love, and*
>   *being one.*
> *You kids all together are in search of a word.*

Below, in the courtyard, Mr. Bruce Lee is unaffected by the poetry. He charges through the rows of students, grabbing them by the shoulders and shifting them to make the lines straighter.

> *It is in the image of water, it is in the image of sister, mother, rainbow.*

The students are organized by height, but Ta Manna has managed to skirt the order so she can stand next to her friends, and she looks on, not singing, carefully projecting a lack of amusement. Mr. Bruce Lee sees her, makes eye contact—he's on to her antics, knows she's out of place—but stays on the boys' side.

> *You kids all together, are in search of a word.*
> *It is alien to the color red, the color of blood.*
> *It is alien to black, which is the color of hate.*

The smallest students are lined up along the stairs to the podium and all around the balcony, swinging tiny Afghan flags in loose approximation of the rhythm.

> *You kids all together are in search of a word that is from the species of*
> *God.*
> *It is filled with love, peace, calmness, and gentleness.*

Aziz is in his rapture, head tilted, listening to his own words wash over the students, while all around him, as the song winds down, the students ready small contraptions they've prepared for the day: two balloons, tied to either end of a slip of paper, on which they've written hopeful slogans. PEACE IS THE SOURCE OF HOPE. PEACE IS A BEAUTIFUL EXPERIENCE. They hold the little inventions in front of them, and wait for the right moment.

> *One white morning, we find the word.*
> *We find the word in a box, a box the color of a bubble.*
> *Three tears on God's face: peace, reconciliation, and friendship.*

The song ends, and at the same instant, the students all let go. It's a striking thing to behold, the sky above Marefat filling with color. It's like a hot-air balloon festival, but one over the most crowded part of an overcrowded, polluted city. The contraptions go up with their messages, as if they were pleas to a higher power, and when they get high enough, the air pressure will break the balloons, and the messages will come fluttering down. Students get to decide for themselves whether the messages are meant for God or just for people in another part of the city. Two years ago a Tajik politician was assassinated just before International Peace Day, and right at the moment the students released the balloons, a thought occurred to Aziz. *The Tajiks are going to think we're taunting them! It looks like we're celebrating Rabbanni's death!*

Today he laughs at the misunderstanding. He doesn't care where the messages land. Maybe people will think God is talking to them. And anyway, this day it all becomes moot: the wind shifts, swirls around, and then dies, so the balloons stop their journey across the city and just hang above the Desert, as if they've decided nowhere else is interested in their messages.

And then as if the sky were replying, a message comes from London. Christa D'Souza, the British *Vogue* writer who'd visited the school before—and whose mother, Frances D'Souza, is now a baroness and speaker of the House of Lords—has held a fund-raiser for the school and raised almost £150,000. They'll send it posthaste, in three shipments.

Aziz calls the engineer immediately. "How soon can the men start filling the ditch in? Tomorrow? Can we have the roof by winter?"

The General summons Aziz to his other home. Aziz is tired and would prefer to be back at the school. He is spending more time away from Marefat than he ever has before, because there is more work every day for Ashraf Ghani and the campaign. But Aziz obliges. The picnic had been such a wonderful day for the girls, and he's grateful to the General.

Asef is unavailable, so Aziz takes a series of buses from the Desert to the General's house in Area Three. He has begun to sweat by the time he arrives.

The General had said only that he wanted to discuss recent events, but once they sit down, he quickly divulges the reason for the meeting: he's worried again, and he only allows a few moments for Aziz to have tea and try the cream fudges from Poland before he begins.

"You know how much defection there is in the military? The government is losing control."

Aziz takes his time responding. "The Taliban has control of many villages, I know. But the cities are still mostly fine."

"Well," the General says. "I cannot be that optimistic. I cannot predict the future is going to be fine. In the future, it's going to be very dangerous."

"I've seen many commanders are already fighting——"

"You civilian people," the General interrupts. "You are looking through different goggles. Different specs. Outside Kabul, it's different."

"Okay, but I've seen soldiers from other provinces," Aziz says, "and they say, 'We're not in a position to predict a collapse.'"

"Well, my belief is different." They smile at each other across the room. "I still believe we can't have a proper army. We have a factional army. The lower level is very good, okay, but at the top there's too much corruption. Those people don't have confidence in the future of Afghanistan, so they're not going to fight for it."

The General is echoing the concerns Aziz has had since he sat watching General Allen eight months ago, and listened to foreigners praise the Afghan leaders about to take over. It's too close to face now, too real, and Aziz doesn't want to talk about it anymore. He doesn't even want to think about it right now. There's no longer any way to keep this kind of fatalistic talk from infecting him. He can no longer put it aside as a concern for tomorrow.

"And remember," the General is saying, his finger raised, "Afghanistan has more weapons than before. When NATO leaves, the nature of the war is going to change. Maybe ten or twenty thousand NATO soldiers will be here, but they will not be involved in the fighting," he says. "They will just train. And the Taliban will not fight a conventional war. Now, they're fighting three kinds of war: they use IEDs, they use suicide bombers with their vests, and they use ambushes. But when NATO leaves, the Taliban will be on the ground, in villages, they will go up and face Afghan army forces." Aziz refuses to engage; the General doesn't slow down.

"The problem is, NATO made this war too spread out. They have bases everywhere. But when they leave, how is our government going to send logistical support to all these bases? We have fifty helicopters now. But six months after they leave, those helicopters will be broken. You'll have no close-air support. We should not be too optimistic that this government will survive." He puts down his cup. "And we must bring neutral people to the head of the national army."

Is it the General's intention to illustrate how dire the situation is, then remind Aziz that he's qualified to fix it? He knows more about the work Aziz has been doing with Ashraf Ghani than Aziz thought. Aziz is still silent, too weary to entertain what is looking more and more like an audition.

"These areas will collapse," the General says. "Especially the south."

Aziz finally tries limply for a Socratic lesson. "Then why haven't the Taliban hit the helicopters yet?" It doesn't work, the General already has an answer prepared.

"Because they've hidden their weapons. They're waiting for the foreigners to leave."

24

THE STUDENT

Najiba falls back into her domestic routine, and even though she is no longer studying, she encourages her children to. One day when her son has wasted a whole afternoon terrorizing his sisters, she loses patience. "No more of this nonsense! Do your homework, *now*."

"You didn't do *your* homework," the boy says. "You failed. Why don't *you* study instead."

It is the kind of wound only a son can inflict on a mother, and it festers in her. What's a sacrifice if no one recognizes it? All she wanted was for her children to acknowledge what she'd done for them, but of course they don't. She began to resent them, and today, in front of her son, it boils over. She hisses: "Because of *you* I was forced to leave school! If *you* had been responsible, if *you* had even just eaten a proper lunch and even just drank water and gone to bed at the right time, I wouldn't have had to quit! It's because *you've* been so careless that I failed, because I had to take care of *you!*"

After, she has dreams of her son coming to her and saying, "Mother, go to school! Continue with your studies, do your homework, and we will eat our lunch on time and drink enough water and sleep when we are supposed to."

At least leaving school has given her the chance to see how she changed. Conversations with neighborhood women are her only diversions again, and the things they talk about now seem trivial. They traffic solely in gossip. From the papers, Najiba knows things. She knows about the security agreement with the foreigners. She knows the president may not sign it. She knows what that means: that all the foreign troops will probably leave. While the others gossip, she thinks of the soldier with the long sun-colored ponytail getting down from the truck, their lives soon to be cleaved from one another. Her mind wanders while the neighborhood women talk. She wonders how she will get used to a city in which there's no chance of seeing that woman, or another like her, directing men, directing trucks.

She understands that President Karzai's reason for not signing this deal is that he somehow favors the Taliban. It seems he's formed a friendship with them. "Our disappointed brothers" is what he calls them in the papers. She wonders, when did the Taliban become his brothers? Does he say this because he's afraid of them?

They're getting stronger—she sees it with her own eyes. There are more attacks in the capital, more crumpled cars in the pages of the newspapers. More blackened skeletons of once colorful buses.

Or is it just that she learns of more attacks because now she reads the papers? This is the price of knowledge. Sometimes knowing more just means having more things to be afraid of.

And the prices keep going up, that much she's certain of.

She can't tell precisely why, but she goes to speeches. She's heard people talk about the economy, how the value of the currency is changing. The worse things get, the more interested she becomes. Kitchen gossip does not sustain her. She feels the absence from school as an acute pain, sharpening each day, it's nearly physical. She can feel it in her mind, too, like some restive part of it that was occupied by her lessons has been set loose and is burrowing in on her. She has anxiety attacks.

She notices something else: for most people in the city, winter is the hardest time, worse when the price of coal goes up and the value of currency goes down. For her and her children, it was summer that tested them. They're from the highlands, people of the mountains and hills. They can handle cold. And in the winter her older kids can help take care of the younger kids, because there are three months when they don't have to go to school.

Three months, maybe, when she can.

Maybe it's okay if her children make sacrifices for her.

She comes up with a new spin on it: she wants to study not in spite of being a mother but *because* of it. She wants her kids to be raised by smart parents. Smart parents are what's needed for them to avoid her biggest fear: that her children will be a drain on society. She wants to make sure they're not helpless, like she was. She wants them to contribute in some meaningful way. She wants them to push their country forward. For that, their mother must be able to teach them things. If it means there will be times when they might not eat well because she's studying, or when they're sick because she's not around to care for them, she will have to be okay with that, and so will they. She convinces her husband it's right for the children to sacrifice for her own education. In the end, after all, it's mostly for them.

Najiba decides she will return to school. If just for one season. But that's okay. If she has to move slower than everyone else, fine, she's no longer in any rush. Sometimes she wishes she had started sooner, but that's past, and now she'll move at the pace she can. Maybe she'll just study every winter, when the kids are off. And who knows what will happen next year. Benazir will be studying for the university entrance exams and won't be able to help around the house. Maybe Najiba won't be able to study at all until the next child is old enough to help.

For now, she will grab hold of the months she has at school; she'll wrap herself in them and pull as much as she can before she has to leave again.

25

TWO MONTHS LEFT

The winter announces itself with snow up high first. Against the white western peaks, the surveillance blimps begin to disappear.

Nights drop further and further below freezing. When the sun goes behind the mountains, the cold comes out and creeps through the classrooms, as if it were afraid to be seen in the light. The school hangs military-grade blankets over the classroom doorways to keep out the cold, but still the students shiver. "The wind is sneaky," Aziz says. "It finds a way in."

Next the rain, two days of heavy cold drops that make you wonder why you prayed for it to come when it wouldn't. None of the streets are paved, and the rain turns the dirt into a sticky, viscous mess that grabs at your feet and doesn't let go, then clings to your shoes when you finally pull free. As if even the mud wants to leave this place. In front of the school Shaiq goes into the street with a pick axe and hacks out a foot-wide runnel to guide the rain. A little stream dutifully forms down the path he's made for it, but still there are places where it dams up and swells so there's only space for one person to walk. Everywhere else is mud, all the way up to your knees. Once the rains come, the school looks less like something built on dry land and more like something risen from a bog.

After the rain, a dull, constant cold settles in. Kids follow behind cars and dance in the warm exhaust, and people burn everything. Wood, oil, plastic, any kind of refuse, coal from the old mine in Samangan that just collapsed. Twenty-seven people were in it, the news said, all of them dead. Their ghosts haunt the city now; when coal is burned a thick, emergent smoke settles over the city and everywhere you go it feels like the building next door is on fire. Some people just burn trash, and since the city is bowled in by mountains, the smoke doesn't go away. It settles over the city like a fog, it gets into your nostrils and your throat, it makes you dizzy, but it's how you stay warm.

Aziz has a new intercom system in the new house. It wasn't his idea, he doesn't see the point. When it buzzes at night the kids on the other end wrestle each other for the chance to say, "Who is it?!"

Aziz has little patience. "Let me in!"

"Okay, Uncle!" Or if it is his brothers' wives, "Yes, Teacher," they say.

Aziz, for his part, has an energy about him I haven't seen in years. He's more forceful, excited by the building on the auditorium that finally restarted. His work for the Pashtun has accelerated; he's been brought into the inner circle and is treated like the most important adviser. Official campaigning begins in just two months, just as the majority of the Outsiders are scheduled to be gone, but he won't think about that now. The elections are in four. He's electrified by the work. It's exciting and worrying. He's changing. He has believed for over a year now that the way to protect the school when the foreigners leave is to somehow win political power. Time is nearly out, but he thinks he's finally figured out how.

More than half a year has passed since Aziz first connected with Ghani to end the hunger strike. Since then, their relationship has deepened, and as Ghani's plans for a campaign have come into focus, Aziz's hopes for him have risen. When Ghani speaks, he sounds like a statesman from one of the books Aziz sometimes slips from the Marefat library: a man who cares about things like trade relations with neighbors and creative ways to train teachers. He thinks bigger and broader than solely protecting his own people. He was so transparently impressed when Aziz brought him to Marefat, blown back like he'd been hit with a gale when the students cheered for him, that Aziz was sure he wasn't acting. Ghani was genuinely moved, just as impressed by all the Hazaras as they had been with this important Pashtun man coming all the way out to the Desert to visit them.

The fact is, though, Aziz is not in the best of health. He has the vigor of a manic man, either a man consumed with a purpose he believes in wholeheartedly or else a man who has been pulled up from the things that ground him and is dangling, febrile, above them, a power line twisting in the wind and casting off sparks. He is sleeping no more than four hours a night, usually less. He feels weak. By six or seven in the evening, he feels his body is not working right, and when he holds his hands out in front of him, they shake. The fever dreams from Afshar have started again. He wakes up in the night with a storm of neurons firing, ideas and sensations whirling through his brain like they used to when he could feel—actually *feel*—that woman's blood and urine on his hands. It happens right around the time of night it was when he stood by that window looking back at Afshar, hearing gunshots echo softly off the hills, while his mind attached its own images.

His mind does loops, but now they concern the work he has left to do before the elections, so when he wakes full of frenzied energy, a to-do list for the morning is assembling and rearranging itself in his head. He is wide awake, then disoriented when the clock says it's not even midnight.

His insomnia doesn't strike him as unhealthy because now that he's coming up with so many good ideas in those hours, how could it be bad? He doesn't connect the waking, worried hours with the headache like a snakebite on the back of his eyeball that draws the heels of his hands against his eye sockets to block out the light. He doesn't connect it with the two-day toothache. The doctor gives him antibiotics—no matter what's wrong, it's always antibiotics—and then Aziz decides he's better.

It's in the quiet hours that he has his revelations. It's on one of these nights when he wakes up, his brain oscillating with energy, that he devises his plan to protect Hazaras after the Outsiders leave.

The night it came to him was after a meeting with Ghani's team. An adviser for General Dostum, Ghani's Uzbek vice presidential candidate, bragged about the number of votes he would deliver. "From the Uzbeks," the adviser said, "we have a million and a half votes guaranteed. We are a bank of votes for you."

Ghani had raised his eyebrows, and Aziz felt his own power slipping away. If the Uzbeks delivered a million and a half votes, they would have more influence in a Ghani presidency than Hazaras. Hazaras would be cast aside. He was sure Hazaras would then do what people here always did when they felt excluded from power: they'd try and take it back by force. They'd rally around the most militaristic leader they had.

So that night, when he opened his eyes just past midnight, what seized him was a question: Where did the Uzbek get those numbers?

Aziz got out of bed and began doing math. First, he found the voting numbers from past elections, broken down by each province. Then he found the ethnic breakdown of each province, and he put the two numbers together on a spreadsheet: voting turnout in one column, Uzbek population in the second. In the third he put the product of the first two, which was his prediction for Uzbek voters in that province. Then he added it all up.

In the morning, once a decent hour arrived, he called a friend in polling to check his numbers.

"I'm saying the Uzbeks have thirty-five percent of the votes in Balkh Province," Aziz said.

"That's definitely too high," his friend said. But that was good, Aziz wanted the numbers to be high, so that he could be sure his results were not just a function of his own bias. He rounded each number up, and when he added all the provinces together, he found that, even being generous, in the whole country Uzbeks had just four hundred thousand votes. Perhaps six hundred thousand if he really stretched his numbers, but that still wasn't half what the Uzbek adviser had claimed.

Had he been deliberately lying to Ashraf Ghani?

Had he not bothered to look at the numbers?

The adviser had said that the Uzbek population was growing; more of them were becoming old enough to vote than were dying.

Aziz believed that was true—the Uzbek voting bloc *was* growing. But not as fast as Hazaras. You only needed to look at how crowded the Desert became in the last twelve years to see how massive the Hazara population boom had been. Even though Hazaras were starting to leave again, the trend hadn't reversed yet. So perhaps there was an opportunity here. If the thing keeping him awake was the idea of Hazaras being cast aside because they didn't have a role in getting the next president elected, the inverse of that fear was: if they were *decisive* in getting Ashraf Ghani elected, Hazaras would be indispensable to the next president. Ghani would have to listen to them. That would mean protection.

Aziz did his own math again with Hazara votes. Only this time, he rounded down. If common knowledge held Hazaras at half a province's population, he put them at thirty percent. He rounded down every time, and when he added it together, he had to check his math twice: 1.5 million probable Hazara voters.

Well, that was something. If they voted as a bloc, they might even be able to handpick the next president. He knew Hazara voter registration was higher than other groups. So Hazaras might never be kings, but they had a chance to be kingmakers.

Here, then, was a radical plan, but one that had to work. There were 1.5 million registered Hazara voters. Aziz wanted every single one to vote for Ashraf Ghani.

It would be a hard sell. It meant convincing his long-oppressed people to support their historical oppressors. There were rumors now that Ghani was actually the Iron Amir's nephew, and there were Hazaras for whom that association was too compelling to ignore. For them, Aziz was trying to bring a new Iron Amir to power, inviting another war against Hazaras. And asking Hazaras to help.

For others, the fact that the candidate was Kochi would be hard to forgive. Surely if he became president, he would side with his own people, against Hazaras, in the ongoing conflict. Helping the Kochi was condemning one's own brothers and sisters and cousins to more

death and destruction. So to some Hazaras, Ashraf Ghani looked like
the Iron Amir, the worst oppressor in their long dark history. To others, it was enough that he was a Kochi, their current tormentor. Aziz
wanted them all to vote for him.

It was a wildly ambitious task, but even just in trying, perhaps
there was some deliverance. Hazaras rallying to support a Pashtun
would not just show their power as a voting bloc, but also their will-
ingness to cooperate. A capacity to forgive, to rewrite the pattern of
"our people versus their people" that had defined politics in this country, defined war in this country—that had defined *this country*.

And even if it *was* wildly ambitious, it was also a perfect test. Ever
since he was a teenaged holy warrior with the nickname "Teacher,"
this is what he was trying to do. *This* is why he wanted to teach: so
that his people would look at what was standing in front of them
and then question it. This man is a Pashtun, he's a Kochi, he's known
to have a temper like the kings from their stories. Maybe he *is* the
Iron Amir's nephew. But what else is he? What kind of ideas does he
have? What does he think about coeducation? Does he have a plan
to protect girls when the Outsiders leave? Can he reduce tensions
with Pakistan? With Iran and Saudi Arabia?

Aziz was confident he could get people to think about these
things. For the first time, to vote their minds and not their tribe. But
he had to act fast. Morale was sinking in the Desert and events were
conspiring to again demonstrate how high the stakes were.

President Karzai was in the middle of a dangerous game with the
Americans.

The countries were negotiating an agreement that would allow
some American troops to stay. Even after Aziz had finally accepted
that the foreign troops were leaving, he expected at least some small
contingent to stay behind. The troops that stayed wouldn't be able to
do much, certainly they wouldn't keep everyone safe, he knew that.
But if they *all* left, very soon there would be no place in this country
for the school.

The Americans were saying they needed time to prepare if they
were going to leave some troops behind, and if President Karzai didn't

sign the agreement, they were going to plan for the zero option. Karzai was stalling. He was flinging insults at the Americans, making new demands of them, and the Americans were getting impatient. U.S. officials began making public statements to show their frustration with this whole country, and at Marefat, it was a new reason for worry.

To students and teachers at Marefat, Karzai's motives were clear: He was having a legacy crisis. He didn't want to be the lackey who let the foreigners stay forever. He was worried about being assigned the role of puppet in history books. Still, surely he at least knew what disaster would befall them if all the troops left?

Morale at the school sank further as the Grand Meeting approached, a summit of elders President Karzai had convened from all over the country to advise him about whether to sign the agreement with the Americans. No law required this Grand Meeting, and out at Marefat the consensus was that Karzai's purpose in convening it was cover. The elders would vote no, and President Karzai would have an excuse to delay signing the agreement even longer.

Probably, the students said to one another, spies from other countries would come to the Grand Meeting. They'd hand out bags of cash in return for "no" votes. The Americans would abandon them, the rest of the Westerners would, too, and then Pakistan and Iran and the Arabs would come pick at the country's carcass.

Here it was, then, the beginning of the end. Once the meeting happened, the Americans would leave, and they'd leave nothing behind.

But then a remarkable thing happened. The elders at the Grand Meeting voted yes, the president *should* sign the deal with the United States. They voted almost unanimously, and without condition, for the president to do what the Americans wanted. When it came right down to it, everyone seemed to agree that whatever they thought of the foreigners, the country would be overrun if they all left.

Karzai looked stunned. At the meeting's closing ceremony, he got up on the podium, took a moment to compose himself, and then, in a voice that halted and guttered like he was short of breath, admonished the participants. They'd done wrong, he said, and he would not accept their recommendation. Not until the Americans made more concessions. The elder who presided over the meeting got up on the stage in front of President Karzai, and in front of everyone, right there on TV, the two men bickered like schoolboys.

At Marefat, the whole thing was torture. From despair to a moment of hope, and then back to despair. If a big meeting of tribal elders telling the president to sign wouldn't make him sign, nothing would. The students watched closely for an American response to the meeting, hoping they would say something reassuring, to show they knew President Karzai didn't speak for everyone.

There was no hope there either. "Without a prompt signature," the U.S. National Security Advisor said, the United States "will have no choice but to initiate planning for a . . . future in which there would be no U.S. or NATO troop presence in Afghanistan."

The zero option was happening.

Aziz saw more worry on the students' faces than ever before. No one paid more attention to the news than they did. That's what he'd wanted after all, for Marefat to breed curiosity. The students had to know what was going on around them if they were going to participate in it. That's what he thought the country would need: you could talk about democracy, but it was little more than marketing if people weren't ready for it. It needed cultivating; it needed involved and alert young people to staff it. Marefat students were alert. But now they were looking around, seeing that they'd never been so powerless.

When he substituted for a sick teacher, a girl came to him and said, "If the Americans leave, we know there is no chance for us to continue our education." It wasn't even a question. She'd gone silent after saying it, and the whole class had gone silent along with her. Aziz couldn't think of anything to say, and that never happened. Even worse than the fact that they wouldn't be able to continue their education was the fact that they already knew it. He'd wanted a generation of people with built-in resistance to the big men wielding religion like weapons, the ones who claimed to be descended from the Prophet; to any man who would demand reverence simply because he was standing on a podium. But now Aziz wanted to be the man standing on a podium so he could tell the students they needn't worry and have them just believe it.

He can't. They question him. If he wanted the students not to worry, he'd have to show them proof of why they shouldn't.

After the fireworks at the Grand Meeting, President Karzai went quiet for a week. Then the office of the president made a startling announcement. America, it said, in a bold attempt to pressure us into signing, has cut fuel and other military support to our government.

The city went into a frenzy. No one knew what a fuel shortage would mean. How much fuel was Afghanistan getting from America? Do we even have another way of getting it? Would there just be no fuel? And if things were so bad that America was cutting off the fuel supply, wasn't that more proof the Americans were all leaving? People began offloading U.S. dollars, the value of the afghani shot up so quickly that moneychangers folded up their cases and closed for business, shops shut down, army and police filed out onto the streets in riot gear, and the city stood on alert. Aziz had a familiar feeling. It was one he hadn't felt for thirty-five years, but it was unmistakable: strident words from the government, men in uniform standing armed and expressionless, a jittery kind of excitement passed between the people just by eye contact.

To Aziz, it felt like a coup.

It took a series of public denials and the rest of the day before the Desert settled back into an uneasy equilibrium, but the trust in the president that had been fraying for months had finally snapped. Hazaras were presented with conclusive evidence that their president was going to sink the whole ship with them in it, just to make a point. He was telling the foreigners "None of us want you here," and in every classroom Marefat students wanted to jump up and yell "No, wait, he's wrong! We do want you here! We *need* you here!"

The trouble didn't stop; it accelerated. The next day a fight broke out in the middle of Parliament. The old bearded men standing up and pushing against each other, leaders again yelling like children having a tantrum. They were arguing over whether a person's ethnicity should be listed in the nationality field of the country's new identification cards. On TV, two Pashtun commentators and a Pashtun moderator on a Pashtun television channel discussed the debate in prime time, and with no one in a position to dissent, the three fed off each other until a general said, "These bastard Hazaras, Tajiks, Uzbeks—if they want to be in my country and don't want to use our name, they're all just sons of prostitutes and they should leave."

The outburst ricocheted around the Desert. *Even after all this time, they still think we don't belong here. As soon as they can, they'll get rid of us all.* In classrooms at Marefat, the effect was chilling. A general had argued for ethnic cleansing. No one had challenged him.

That the television station was known to be biased, that the general who had made these threats was a known provocateur—these were qualifiers that all receded in importance. The overwhelming sense that washed over the Desert and seeped into classrooms at Marefat, despite Aziz's best efforts to bulwark some optimism, was this: a lot of people don't want us here, and the rest don't care.

The on-air call to arms proved to be a story with legs: it kept circling around in the media, other TV channels picked up the comments, then newspapers, more TV channels. A central roundabout in the city was pasted over with signs criticizing the general's comments, and it gathered momentum until it became not just a revelation of one man's anger but, in a tribal society where a man of status is perceived to speak on behalf of his people, a position statement. The general was a Pashtun. More specifically, he was a Kochi, and his clan was Ahmadzai, which placed Aziz in a very specific predicament. Ashraf Ghani didn't always use his clan name, but he was born "Ashraf Ghani Ahmadzai." So the general on TV was from the very same ethnic group, the same sub-sect, and even had the same clan name, as the candidate Aziz was helping.

He spent the next week fielding calls and emails from friends, all of them variations on the theme of "How could you possibly support such a fascist as Ashraf Ghani, who will surely bury Hazaras the first chance he gets?"

Aziz, they said, was not just digging his own grave, he was going to bring the rest of the Hazaras down with him. It simply didn't matter that Ashraf Ghani had not himself said those words. His tribesman had, a member of the same clan, and, by the way, hadn't his brother said something like that, just a few years before? Also on TV? *To you?* How could you not see! You're a pawn, you're being played, used by Ashraf Ghani in a scheme to repress Hazaras even more and undo all the progress we've made.

Aziz is exhausted. "He's really under very bad pressure," he says, driving home after meeting with Ghani about the fallout. He corrects himself. "Not he. *We.*"

It's raining, and mixed in with the smell of damp asphalt is the smell of gas leaking from the car. Aziz doesn't complain: the driver and the tiny red Toyota have been provisioned to him by the Umron Group. Umron is a Hazara success story, a business owned and run by Hazaras that's become hugely profitable since the Outsiders came, and which is helping the campaign because the second vice presidential candidate on Ghani's ticket is a Hazara, from the same region as Umron's founder. So the company has given Aziz his own office in Area Three, a driver, and a car that they've sworn they'll upgrade soon.

His father calls. They talk briefly, Aziz sighs, says he will be home soon, and hangs up. "My father says we don't have electricity tonight in the Desert."

When city power is out at night, and you drive out into the Desert, it feels like going back in time. Some of the stalls have single bulbs connected to generators, but the deeper you get, the more sporadic they become, until they disappear entirely.

It used to be that just about every storefront and most homes were hooked up to generators, because an enterprising person with cash on hand could buy one and wire in twenty of his neighbors. But when the Desert finally got city power, everyone left the little co-ops. City electricity is cheaper, and as long as it's working, it's more powerful, too. People began using space heaters, fridges, washing machines, many for the first time ever.

But it meant that with the winter's first heavy rains, when the power goes out and the car headlights are all behind you and the stars and moon are forgotten, hidden above a ceiling of smoke and rain clouds, it becomes so astoundingly dark out in the Desert that the school begins to feel like a place both man and nature have forsaken.

"All the time when it is raining," Aziz says, "I don't know why, but there is cut power. Stop power. Power stoppage?"

In the house the kids are unbothered by the dark. Even though the power goes out all the time, it's still exciting, a game to them. With the Desert's power out the windows become like boards of black paint, so they can pretend there's nothing out there and the whole universe becomes child-sized. They run around and try to catch each other with their hands, pale and ice cold now that all the space heaters are dead. Even Roya has a new spirit to her in the dark. At three and a half years old she's found her voice, and when she talks to her father, she talks and talks and doesn't stop. She bounces around now like the other kids, smiles all the time, and is starting to resemble her brother Farzhad in both appearance and demeanor. She drags a battery-powered lantern along the carpet and places it in front of her father, then sits down inside the globe of light and begins to babble contentedly, unbothered that no one is listening. She has grown, too. She's just tall enough now that if she stands on her tiptoes, and reaches her hands all the way up above her head, she can get her fingers around door handles. When Aziz has guests over for serious meetings, she lets herself in. She's not afraid, even though the handle is high enough that her feet are nearly off the ground, and she doesn't open the door so much as rides it. The men will be talking, there will be a rattle, the handle will shimmy, and then the door will move with Roya affixed to it, holding on for dear life, as if the door's purpose is not to keep people out of the room but to convey giggling children into it.

Farzhad plops down inside the light next to her and puts his arm over her shoulder. Five years old and he already knows to be protective. He wants to show off; he's been working on his English. Following his father yesterday, he said, out of the blue, "My name is a dog." Aziz frowned.

A little farther, he passed a sedan parked next to the ditch. "My name is a car."

"Ah-hah!" Aziz identified the problem. "Not 'my name' is a car," he says. "*This* is a car."

Farzhad laughed. "My name is a school."

Aziz goes to bed coughing. He clears his throat and tries to drive the dust down with water, then coughs anyway until he falls asleep. The house seems never to rest, the doors screech, the heavy wooden panels still aren't broken into their fitted steel frames, so small movements make them whine in protest. Every draft gives the house its own motion.

Finally, at around eleven, it's quiet for a time.

At midnight, there's a strange noise. It's different from the groans of a house adjusting to wind and cold; it sounds animate. It recedes, then rises again. Aziz's ears adjust; the sound resolves. People talking. Two, maybe three. These are unfamiliar voices, they belong to no one Aziz knows. Their voices are distant and tinny, but grave-sounding, like people whispering over an illicit plan they're about to set in motion.

Then, laughter. An orange glow rises from the floor, so faint at first it looks imagined. It becomes sharper, vivid. It takes a moment to make sense of it—all the space heaters are turning on, at the same time.

Power has come back. The voices are from a downstairs television, which someone was watching when the power went off. It's come alive in the middle of the night with the returning electricity. All clear. Adults get up, turn off lights, heaters, and appliances that were left on, and everyone goes back to bed.

Then it's morning. The light is pale and gray like an unclean sheet hanging over the school, and the rain has again turned the dirt lanes to mud so thick it's hard to believe they were ever solid. It's a marsh, a place from which a tide has gone out. It's on this morning that Aziz decides to put his endgame into motion.

He has tried everything he can think of to prepare the school for what comes next. He's led them forward into protests, he's taught them to understand what they were entitled to and to demand it. He's begged them to do the opposite. He told the students to stand down. Do not be the unruly Hazara who arouses the wrath of another Iron Amir, because there will be no one here to protect you. He's advanced; he's withdrawn.

And now he feels he's stumbled upon a third way.

This man he's helping, Ashraf Ghani: yes, he's a Pashtun, a Kochi

even, a member of a tribe that has a violent history fighting and usually defeating Hazaras. But he's a man who believes in education.
He's spent most of his life either studying or teaching. He is, after all,
an academic. A professor. A *student*.

If Aziz can get people at Marefat to think *that* way, then this
whole campaign has a chance. Instead of supporting a leader based
on race, or whether his kin killed yours, maybe people will support
him because he sees the world like they do. Maybe Aziz can help
them see that this man has more in common with them than cause
for conflict.

If Marefat students and teachers could see it that way, it wouldn't
so much matter whether your uncle was killed by a Kochi or your
mother was beaten by a Pashtun Talib or your great-grandfather was
enslaved under the Iron Amir. What would matter was who had ideas
more like yours.

Today, Aziz begins to plan meetings.

The school year, meanwhile, ends in a whisper. What would otherwise be a lively celebration today is almost trivial. There's too much
anticipation for what lies ahead. Still, the students gather for their last
lineup of the year, while the men working on the auditorium hurry
to finish the roof before the winter brings its full might. They work
at a comical speed, turning the concrete, paving it out, running across
the plywood with jumpy wheelbarrows always an inch away from
some Chaplin-esque slip. It's an urgency that seems bizarre given how
long the ditch sat empty. The plan is to finish the roof first so the
men can work through the winter on what goes below, weather no
longer an excuse to stay home. But the roof is taking shape over what
looks like not nearly enough structure to support it. Under the roof
slab, the hundreds of red metal rods look like a mesh of exposed cap-
illaries you aren't ever supposed to see, and the fact that you can
suggests something injured and vulnerable. The workmen's urgency
feels less like creating, more like a desperate attempt to resuscitate.

The students file past the workers. It's now the middle of December and winter is no longer just a suggestion. Even though the
students are still wearing their uniforms, they are also wearing coats,

so everyone is a different color on top. The rows don't have their usual order; they seem scattered and broken down. The cold has the kids giddy to keep warm; boys laugh and pinch one another, and girls yank at the headscarves of whoever's lined up in front. The game catches on and each time the fabric slips off, the victim grabs at the top of her head with both hands, so it looks like a wave of girls making some terrible discovery, one after another, in exact reverse order of age.

With Aziz gone out of the Desert at a campaign meeting, his brother Hafiz takes over emcee duties. He makes a plea for the students to come for extra winter classes, and then the top students in each class are announced. After he dismisses them, the lines of students collapse into hives with teachers at the center handing out grades, and that's it.

The school year is over.

26

THE DRIVER

The snow starts at a little after 7:00 a.m., thick and wet so windshield wipers snap and the world goes blurry. Everyone skidding, everyone driving slowly: the new speed bumps have no signs and are big enough to detach a car from its traction, send it lumbering into a fruit stall. The vans slide sideways and diagonally down the road, foals stumbling only vaguely toward any destination. Motorcyclists drive with their feet out and hovering over the ground. Everyone is cautious. Men come out onto the street with wiper blades for sale protruding like fractured limbs from beneath blankets. Asef shakes his head at them politely as his van moves past like a big sleepy animal. The municipal workers in their incandescent orange look like flashlights cutting through the snow. They scoop the hardening sewage from the open drains before it can freeze and overflow. Aftermarket bumpers on offer hang from awnings for after the small tragedies that will happen today.

Everything is slow. Asef, too. He can't make much money now. The number of riders and the amount they can pay has fallen for months. With school out, he doesn't have the daily fare from the students. He misses the Marefat kids not just because of the money though, but because they give him something else. *Freshness* is how he thinks of it. To him, they're energy. Now he doesn't see them, and that's what's hardest about winter.

If he gets up early enough, he can catch some of the people looking for rides to early shifts. In theory there's money there, because people don't like walking through this weather. When it snows, though, he has to use four-wheel drive, which strains the engine and costs an extra half gallon of fuel every day. That's three dollars extra, just to move, almost not worth it. Often he stays home.

He tries to embrace the changes happening around him. It helps him feel some control. He adds fur to the upholstery in his van for the cold; he hangs a dinosaur from the mirror. A cartoonish T. rex that lasts only two days before succumbing to a higher kind of carnivore, his daughter, who rips it down and proclaims it her new best friend.

He follows politics on TV, eavesdrops on his passengers whenever he has them, and speaks to other drivers. He watches *Beyond the News* every night at 10:00 p.m., but tries not to worry because he knows men in power make a spectacle of their disagreements. That's how they keep themselves relevant, and let the people know they care.

It was only when President Karzai announced the fuel cut that Asef felt it all start to overwhelm him. That day, he drove around a city sent tumbling into chaos by just a suggestion that the Outsiders would stop giving his country fuel. He didn't even know the Outsiders *were* giving his country fuel. He'd been proud because he thought he'd built himself up on his own; now he was being told he hadn't. The conversations between President Karzai and the Outsiders keep getting worse.

Also, Aziz has a new driver. Aziz is now working for the Pashtun all the time. Most people know about it. The Pashtun is running for president, and they've given Aziz his own car and a driver, so he doesn't need Asef anymore. A nice car, too, an SUV, with everything working. Aziz said it was better for Asef, because Asef is for the school, really, not for Aziz's personal use. But there's no school now.

27

―――――

THE MECHANIC

There's even more to do now, even with all the students gone. There are new building projects. The school year ended, but Marefat's ambitions don't cease. There's work on the auditorium, the roof needs a new weather coating, the rooms need paint, copies need to be made for the students now studying for university entrance exams.

Most of all, a million chairs need to be fixed. His one resentment for students: they break so many chairs in the course of the year it's like they're doing it on purpose.

His to-do list is as big as ever and money is tight. Everything is expensive. Prices shot up when the president called the Grand Meeting. Shot up and stayed high. It costs twice as much to get even simple things like flour and oil. How could no one have accounted for that? It was a simple mechanism. If you assemble all the important people in one place, you create a target, if you create a target, you need to secure that target, to secure a target, you need to control traffic, to control traffic, you needed to shut down borders. When you shut down borders, fewer supplies get in, when fewer supplies get in, things cost more, and now he can't afford enough okra for his kids.

He had to move. When the Desert got electricity he was excited, but then rent went up because his apartment building had city power to offer. He moved his family farther out toward the provinces, so getting to Marefat costs more money and he has to leave earlier. His days get longer, even though in winter, for everyone else, they get shorter.

He used to save a hundred dollars every year, but everything is more expensive. Even after the Grand Meeting was over, prices kept rising. When the president made the surprise announcement about Americans cutting the fuel supply, the price of gas doubled and the price of flour became preposterously high, especially for something you can't very well live without. A sack of flour used to be ten dollars, now it's four times that.

These days his children want so many things. They have expensive taste—how did that happen? They're old enough now to know what they like, but not old enough to understand how expensive it is for their father to bring it for them.

More than anything, it's hard because it's a winter without Aziz.

It's always lonely when the students are gone, but there's a finality to the end of this year. It takes two weeks into the winter to understand that this big old complex Aziz conjured into being feels empty without its creator. The school without its people is cold and cavernous. Aziz is now off playing his dangerous game with the politicians. Nasir believes this is important; he sees immediately that what Aziz is doing, partnering with an ethnic rival, is ahead of his time. Nasir is proud of that. Still, he's sad. Aziz has been pulled from the school, and Nasir has to get used to Marefat without him. This is what it will be like when he's gone.

28

ONE MONTH LEFT

Aziz holds the first meeting at the office the wealthy businessmen gave him.

It's not in the Desert, and everyone has to travel an hour to get there. He chooses a room on the first floor even though it's smaller and less elegant than the conference room upstairs, because he wants the meeting to be intimate. It's a room with no furniture besides a small bench, and a TV with bad reception that shows faded players on a football pitch somewhere far away.

Aziz watches while he waits. He doesn't know or care who's playing but he likes that it's motion. He's unsure how many people will come, which is another reason he's chosen this room. He knows from the G-72 that if you put people in too big a room, they spread out to fill the space. Like particles of gas, he's read this somewhere, and he doesn't want his people too diffuse. He wants them squeezed in together, a unit, because one way to pull people together for a cause is to actually pull them together. If enough people come today, if his students show up to at least hear him out, each will *feel* the person next to him. Their bodies will touch and they will sense some reassurance that none will be alone if they decide to do what Aziz is about to ask them to do.

Not everyone waited for him to ask. Najiba came right away.

Just as soon as she heard the rumors he'd dispatched through Marefat that he was helping the Pashtun, she got in a taxi by herself and rode out of the Desert to his office in Area Three, just to let him know she wanted to help. She'd read about all the candidates and she approved of his decision; it didn't matter what other people said about the Pashtun. She convinced her family too, they were all ready to help. Whatever he needed, she told him she was ready to go to work. To go back to the highlands if need be, to the place she'd fled and the people she'd fled from, to win their support for the Pashtun. Although it would help, she said, if Aziz could compensate her for her time.

Aziz shifts on his knees as people begin arriving in waves. Two, five, seven at a time, they arrive by the taxi-load. Marefat administrators, teachers, recent alumni. They file past the guards, and the room becomes its own organism, fogging up the windows, flesh shifting and settling to fill the space between the walls. The girls take the bench without discussion, bodies align on the windowsill, and the rest sit on the floor, even Aziz. People keep coming in until there's no room even to open the door. Animated chatter rises and falls, and the room becomes charged with the feeling of something exciting or dangerous or new or perhaps all three.

Aziz puts the phone down by his side, slides it back and forth along the carpet, a silent gesture that does gavel duty. He looks up. The room falls silent. Aziz begins.

"This is the first official announcement of my campaigning," he says.

He corrects himself. "*Our* campaigning."

He takes his time because he always takes his time when he alone is talking. And because this is not an easy sell. Everyone in this room knows the history between Pashtuns and Hazaras in graphic, excruciating detail. The Taliban, the Army of Islam, the parade of kings throughout time who have oppressed Hazaras, the Iron Amir— they've all been Pashtun. He's going to ask them to put another one in power.

He begins his case. Hazaras have come a long way, Marefat has come a long way, but now it's time to be realistic. We must accept that the Outsiders are leaving. No Hazara has ever led this country, and probably no Hazara ever will. But if we all help this Pashtun with his campaign—if all of us, all million and a half Hazaras, cast their ballot for this man—well, we may never be kings, but right now we have the chance to be kingmakers.

Mr. Bruce Lee gets up and leaves the room. He finds a couch outside and sits there, gets up, sits back down. What Aziz is talking about will bring more attention to the school. A school with still no protection to speak of, other than him. What happens if the Ayatollah attacks again? If he sends another mob to Marefat? Would police still come when there are no foreigners to punish them for neglecting Hazaras? There was a school meeting a few days ago in which the attendees discussed security, because already things were moving so fast. Aziz was becoming an activist again. He was appearing on the news and in TV debates about the elections, drawing attention to himself and to the school. The school needed to do something to protect the students. The head of the English language program was the most vocal about that. He stood up and talked in his resigned, palms-up way, about how badly they needed guards, walls, anything, something. Aziz wouldn't have it. It's a school, it can't be a prison, and he guided the rest of the room away from it, too.

Back inside, Aziz brings his case to a close and opens the floor for questions.

"We shouldn't take Mohaqiq as a weak figure," one of the alums says. "He has a lot of support among Hazaras. He's strong, and he could defend us."

"Yeah," another says. "Why shouldn't we use all this support for Mohaqiq and Abdullah? We can finally transfer power away from Pashtuns."

Aziz anticipated this. These two are the biggest challengers. Abdullah will be a frontrunner and he's not Pashtun. Or at least, he's only half Pashtun, and he identifies more as Tajik. The chance to yank power away from Pashtuns for the first time is too delicious to ignore. Add to that the fact that one of his vice presidential candidates is the Hazara commander Mohaqiq. Though Mohaqiq is the same man who tried to stoke the hunger strike into an ethnic wildfire, and who once put a bounty on Aziz's head, still, he is a strongman for the Hazaras, and Hazaras have few strongmen to speak of. For Hazaras who feel theirs is a history of cowering in the face of bullies, he represents brawn. Together, those two candidates have obvious appeal to Hazaras. A president who does not identify as Pashtun, and a vice president who has fought and killed on behalf of Hazaras.

Rather than attacking the candidates though, Aziz takes a thinking man's approach. Because, really, convincing these people at this meeting isn't enough. They have to arrive at the same conclusion he has, but on their own terms. If he changes their minds, he gets their vote. If they feel they've changed their own minds, they each become teachers. They can change others.

"Dr. Abdullah would not change the system," Aziz says, "He would just change the people *in* the system. And even Zalmai Rassool," he adds, using another candidate as an example, "will not change the system, *or* the people in it. But you see, what Ashraf Ghani wants to do, he will change the system, but he will *keep* some of the same people in it. That's the way progress can happen, but without big disruptions."

Someone asks about the Kochi issue. Aziz has a response prepared. "What is Abdullah going to do for you? Say 'Okay, Kochis and Hazaras, let's sit down'? If anyone can solve this issue, it's a Kochi! It's Ashraf Ghani! But don't take his word for it though—take your own. He will not be some sultan sitting up there, making these commands by himself. He will be there because of the people who put him there. That's you. So what do you want? Do you want to solve the Kochi issue? Then you make this government. Get everyone to vote for him."

Another question from the back: "I know he's made you promises, Teacher Aziz, but what is the guarantee that he doesn't forget all of them?"

Aziz smiles, and gives his sideways nod. "We have a proverb, have you heard it? If a law comes that all the drunks should be arrested, there will be no one left in the city. Who can claim he's perfect? This is a universal disease no one is immune from."

★ ★ ★

That night, Aziz wakes up to one of his private frenzies. *What if I just succeeded?* If people signed on to his idea and his plan took off, would he actually be able to manage them?

This new benefactor, the Umron Group, has given him the office space, the driver, and the car. They won't give him much more, though, and he has far too few resources to actually execute the complex operation he's trying to launch. So has he just made an empty promise? If people agree to work with him, he won't be able to support them. He can't afford to pay for cell phone minutes: how will he coordinate people who need to be all over the Desert? All over the city even, maybe the country. How will they talk to each other?

His mind spins; he needs a solution. He runs through the stacks of stories in a corner of his mind like a hard drive scanning for a file, some common thread—someone, from some point in the grand course of human history who faced this problem, and overcame it. There has to be someone who ran a complex operation relying on people spread out over space but with no telecommunication. The prophets and apostles of different religions; discoverers, explorers, conquerors—and then it all resolved. A needle in his mind dropped into its groove and the answer revealed itself: Genghis Khan.

In the stories Aziz read, Genghis Khan mastered a cascading kind of leadership. He devolved power. Each ten soldiers reported to a commander, who himself belonged to another group of ten, reporting to another commander, all the way up to one of Genghis Khan's own sons. It was exceedingly simple and most militaries since did some version of the same thing, but it was in this way that Genghis Khan unified the Mongolian steppe and moved on to conquer the known world. All with an army composed of semiautonomous units moving about the land. Ten soldiers, and one hundred, and one thousand.

Aziz would call his take on it "ten plus one." Each of his volunteers would recruit ten others, and would be rewarded with authority over them; each member of that ten would recruit her own ten, and so on. It was a kind of phone tree. A strategy inspired by his people's most controversial figure—a strategy mastered by one of history's most violent men for the purpose of violence, but which Aziz would redirect to the mission of political armistice. So a usurpation of history, too. A rewriting.

Aziz was identifying problems and divining solutions rapidly now, everything moving at a frantic pace. The next night another problem, another solution. He'd been thinking about the other candidates who were going to open campaign offices and mount giant billboards all over the city. He can't do that. He has no money for it; Ghani doesn't seem to have nearly the resources the other candidates do. Aziz thought the Americans would help, because it'd be worth it for them to have a friendly president in office. But he miscalculated. The Americans aren't providing any support at all. Or if they are, Aziz isn't seeing it.

In the middle of the night, he conjures up a way to get by without big campaign offices. Maybe, in fact, he can do better. Maybe the best place is not prime real estate on a busy street that everyone sees when they're passing by in a rush to go somewhere else. Instead, he'll send Marefat students out to find space in the poorest places. Down the farthest lanes in the dingiest corners of the Desert. Why have an expensive office in a place everyone passes when you can have a cheap one where everyone's trip ends? Even if just one or two people a day come in, at least they'll have time and privacy so they can actually talk about the elections. Less campaign offices, then, and more like small classrooms. Less to sound rallying cries than to set up space for debate.

At the next Marefat political meeting, this time with some students, he floats the idea and within minutes three of them are talking over each other about plans for their own offices. They're invigorated by the idea: their own little courtrooms, where they will do their part to elevate the debate. They want to help move past the era in which they chose leaders based on who looked the most like them. This much, at least, had been surprisingly easy: the students were taking to the idea of nudging history along.

Another day, another campaign meeting, another crowded room. Again the girls get the seats, again the men sit mostly on the floor. A few chairs are wheeled in. None have all their castors in place; most have yellow foam tufting out from where big chunks of upholstery are missing. The chairs look like they've survived some kind of predator. It's a long meeting; Aziz hands out a few thousand fliers he hopes will reach all corners of the Desert through the ten-plus-one network, because he's trying to get at least a thousand young Hazaras to attend a speech on Friday. The students take the stacks and have just begun passing flyers around the room when a student airs a complaint about his first week of campaigning.

"We asked people to open these offices and they asked for money. They're not used to this, Teacher Aziz. They're used to people coming right before elections and just giving them something for their votes. We're just offering words and everyone else offers cash."

A young women interrupts, a graduate who joined Marefat at seventeen and went through all twelve grades in five years.

"Teacher Aziz, we're hearing . . . things, out there. This is dangerous. We don't want to see you risk yourself." Her tone is imploring, like a concerned mother, but one confident in her authority. "You should be alive, you're no good to us if you die. You should be here, for the next generation after mine."

"Yes," Aziz says, "but what if that generation never comes? Because if Abdullah wins, if someone else wins, there might not be a chance."

"And what's the guarantee that when Ashraf Ghani wins, he won't poison you? Or not him, but those around him? There are so many cases of people being wiped out. What's your guarantee?"

Someone makes one of Aziz's plays against him, deploying an old proverb to make the case: "You don't have a grain of wheat in your house, but you're waging war on the whole kingdom."

"How can we forgive ourselves if we sit aside? And tomorrow something happens to the country? And we are just witnesses?"

Afterward, as the people file out and Aziz goes down to the SUV, his mood is still buoyant. There is energy here, even if it's not wholly positive. The teachers and alumni he's recruited are pushing back, but they're taking it seriously, and for now that's enough. The fact that they came, sat on their knees until their legs fell asleep, and argued with him about the danger he's inviting—these are good signs. People are at least entertaining this.

It's rush hour, and the old Soviet road system fills with a few hundred thousand more cars than it was designed for, all muscling for space. Progress is slow. The car inches along next to an old city bus, and then the two vehicles sit next to each other for a time, unmoving. An old man standing in the back of the bus turns and looks down at Aziz. The man is standing in exactly the place Aziz stood, on exactly the same bus route Aziz took when he went to see the frightened Hazara general two months ago. The old man stares. His expression is not one of malice but of distance, as if Aziz were interesting and unfamiliar, a visitor from another place. Aziz has become one of the men in suits, who ride in the back of SUVs. Aziz senses the man's gaze, but doesn't look up to meet it.

In these moments moving between places he reflects. The vehicle stops, his mind moves faster. He's *not* one of those men in suits riding in the back of SUVs. He doesn't fit here. His suit doesn't fit. It's too big, and too shiny, there's a rip he hasn't fixed from when he got swiped by a motorcycle taxi. He doesn't *want* to be here. Not so long ago he spent his days moving through the school. Teaching, substituting for other teachers, pushing students, ministering to skittish parents. That's where he belongs.

But if being pulled from the school has allowed him to see how much he wishes he were back there, it's also allowed him to see if his plan has worked. Whether he's succeeded in doing something here that the United States couldn't do, that the United Kingdom couldn't do, that none of the foreigners could ever do. For better or worse, the school of his, once just a dozen refugee kids crammed into a friend's basement, has institutionalized free thought. Who could have predicted that the future would be determined not by whether his people could conquer their enemies, but by whether he could convince his people to join them? It's the ultimate test, because even the most persuasive orator, the most skilled campaigner, couldn't make people bring a man to power if they've been told their whole lives he's their enemy. It only becomes possible if those people have been primed to take statements apart and see their different angles. If the people are confident enough that they can make a decision their fathers say would be fatal. Aziz will soon see whether he severed the guylines that hold their thinking in place, whether he has truly freed them from the constrictions of history, religion, tradition. He will see whether he has prepared his people to really decide for themselves.

There was a time, seven years back, when I still thought the foreign troops in Afghanistan would be there forever. The Taliban had only just begun to reemerge when I began making the long drive through the Desert every week. I was teaching an English class; I thought that knowing English was the sole prerequisite to teaching it (the students made sure I knew that I was mistaken. "Sir," one of the boy's said, "you've learned more from us than we have from you").

Already my class had endeared themselves to me, and they knew it. There was one student, though, who over the course of the class emerged as the most pious, and I struggled to reach him. He was severe in his faith, a child who never smiled. The day class veered into a discussion of religion and government, I worried we were offending him. His silence unnerved the other students. Finally, the boy stood and said, "In the name of Allah, no, sir, religion should have *no* role in politics or government. It does not matter if our leaders are religious. Religion should have nothing to do with how we're ruled. Religion is between man and God. Government is between man and man. Government is no place for God."

Aziz had not convinced all of his students that religion could lead them astray, or that it was a destructive force in the country, as he had believed at the very beginning of Marefat. He did succeed in making them come up with their own arguments, whether they believed Islam to be indispensable or destructive or something in between. Whatever they thought, they had to argue it, and they were not allowed to parrot anyone else's ideas. It was always heartening that the students didn't have the opinions I expected them to, and that they always had good reasons. The school was a place of logic in the midst of a chaotic time, when natural laws seemed to no longer apply.

In this, the final year of occupation, during another debate at the school, a gaunt young man with inquiring eyes leaned forward and said, "Sir, why do we need religious freedom when Islam is the best religion?"

He didn't mean it as an offense. He said it softly, his tone was earnest. A girl responded before I could. "It's best for you and me," she said. "That doesn't mean it's best for everyone." The boy listened. He seemed to be considering her answer.

The next class, that same boy argued forcefully against arranged marriage. He said neither families nor religious elders ought to determine who marries whom. He defended love. And a girl who had emerged over the weeks as a forceful advocate for women's rights took the other view. Arranged marriages are more sensible she said, because "love is the opposite of logic." She reminded the class of what happened to Romeo and Juliet.

Another day, Ta Manna argued for stricter Islamic law. I was dumbfounded. It contradicted everything I knew about her to that point: that Islamic extremists killed her cousin and best friend, that tradition stifled her, and that she found her most religious relatives to be simpleminded. But she explained: "Islam would be good for women if people followed it more. Islam says we can't keep dust in the house. It says we can't cut our nails in the house, and we follow those rules. But it says women should be equal, and we don't follow that. We should just all follow Islam more strictly."

It had been apparent to me from the very beginning that these kids had been successfully conditioned to question. The students had the tools to make up their own minds—to *change* their minds—which right now has to happen.

Ta Manna changed her mind. When she first heard Aziz was trying to help a Pashtun become president, she thought it was proof Aziz was a fool, as she'd begun to suspect. She believed this Pashtun candidate was surely no different than all the Pashtuns who at best didn't care when Hazaras died, and often helped to kill them. As time passed, more information about candidates became available. She read, she processed, she argued with her father about all the choices, and then she changed her mind. Aziz might be a fool, but he had chosen the smartest candidate. She warmed to the idea of Ashraf Ghani, who would be the smartest leader the country had ever had.

She decided he was a man who really did believe in education, whether you were boy or girl, Hazara, Pashtun, Tajik, or something else, and that he would help even her Hazara school. She decided she would support him, even though she blamed his people for most of the bad things in her life.

For Aziz, that was the point. Right now, he sees that his own role is secondary. The success of his school won't be decided by anything he does preparing for elections or preparing his people for what happens after the Outsiders leave. It will be decided by what he did in the classroom. The revolution he started in the Desert.

If he succeeds, it will be because he built a school to change people's minds, and it worked.

The next day, after another round of meetings in the city, Aziz finally has some time at the school planned. Just a few moments before he has to turn around and leave again. Just enough time, if he's quick, to check on a searchable database he had the Marefat tech director design for the ten-plus-one network. An entry for each volunteer, and the ten she presides over, and the ten to which she belongs. So he can see how everyone is connected to everyone else.

As we drive toward the school, we try to activate a new smartphone he'd asked me to bring him so that he can stay connected to his friends abroad, too. I read off the security questions, and though his mind is elsewhere, he answers.

"What was the name of your first childhood friend?"

"Jeff Stern," he says. I can't help it, I feel a proud smile on my face.

"Okay. Let's see. Next is 'What's your dream job?'"

He doesn't need time to think. "Teacher."

29

THE STORYTELLER

In the beginning, there was a rainy day and lightning came. A jagged yellow bolt that flew from the sky and struck a tree. The tree caught fire, and at first it was frightening, but then the people discovered they could use fire to keep warm and cook food

She's not sure where this happened, or when exactly—she'll know for certain later, she's only in fifth grade—but it was maybe two hundred years ago.

That's one way it might have happened.

The other way is that there was a caveman—this also is two hundred years ago, maybe three hundred, just a guess, you understand—and he saw two stones hit against each other, making a spark. Then he took two stones himself and made a spark on purpose, and he impressed the other men and women in the cave with his on-command spark making, probably they grunted in admiration or something, and together, they learned how to turn the spark into an ember and an ember into a fire and that into heat and good salty chewy lamb kebabs.

But it's actually not that easy to make a spark with two stones, and the lightning story makes more sense to her anyway. So, that's an important thing that she knows from history.

The other important things she knows from history are all about the people she belongs to. How everyone in this country has always been cruel to them. Until Hazaras learned to fight, and then to edu-cate themselves. It was a proud history. First sad, then violent and tragic, but, in the end, it was proud.

She knew about "the forty girls" from as far back as she can re-member knowing anything about anyone. The evil king, the Iron Amir, was killing her people. Why did he want to kill her people? She can't ever remember. He sent his soldiers to a Hazara place, rap-ing and shooting and killing—shooting? Did they have guns back then? Maybe it wasn't shooting, but more like stabbing—and forty girls ran away from the men until they reached a cliff, and then they held hands, and together they jumped.

They were going to be raped. That's why they jumped off the cliff. She doesn't know how she knows they were going to be raped, but she knows. Everybody knows. When her mother told her the story, the part about being raped was always there, assumed, con-veyed, in the knowing way mothers communicate to daughters without always saying the thing directly.

She was so proud of those girls jumping off the cliff that her eyes welled up and her throat tightened when she thought about them. They did the right thing. Her mother would also cry when this part of the story came, sad for the girls but happy for their people and always proud.

She puts this story on a shelf in her mind next to the one about the Lion Boy. A brave Hazara. To her, the Lion Boy avenges the forty girls. That's the way she sees it: he settles the ledger and repays the suffering and puts everything back into the proper balance. The way her mother spoke about him, this Lion Boy, it was like he could have been one of their lost prophets. When another king—actually the Iron Amir's son—came to hand out certificates at a graduation cer-emony, the Lion Boy told the king, "I have a gift for you, too!" and then courageously shot the king in the face. She was proud of the Lion Boy for what he did, she felt she could reach out through his-tory and hold his hand, like he was her brother but just by accident they were flung off to be born in different times.

Her mother had her own stories, too. Like how she was called "Hazara pig" by her history teacher in school. How the class shrieked in delight. How when she was in the tenth grade, the teacher said, "Okay, class, remind me: who is first position here?" And when her mother raised her hand, the teacher turned to another student, and said, "Aren't you ashamed that you've let this Hazara be first in your class?"

It was her mother who told her that their people had an embarrassing history at first. Right up until the civil war. "You still weren't even born yet," her mother says, as if on purpose she'd waited until Hazaras had something to be proud of, before bringing a girl into the world. The way her mother explains, it was like Hawa could only start life once Hazaras proved they could end others.

From her mother's stories she knows her people have changed. She knows to be thankful that the street in front of her house is paved. When she was younger, it was just dirt, with big wide holes. You couldn't drive a car down it.

She knows to be thankful that Hazaras are in universities, and that they are professors and engineers now. Those are all new things.

It's why she likes President Karzai so much. Ever since he was president, girls could go to school. Before him, they couldn't. Before him was the Taliban.

Now is a sad time though, with school over, because she and her friends all live in different parts of the Desert. Soon the streets will fill up with so much snow and mud they won't be able to get across to see each other. People will climb up onto their roofs and shovel snow off onto the streets, so first God will block her way with snow, and then people will.

She remembers that from last year, being packed in.

Not that snow is always bad. Her mother once took her to a part of the city outside of the Desert. "This was my house" she'd said, "where I grew up," and she pulled Hawa close.

The street was on a hill, and her mother would sit on a sheet of metal and slide all the way down. Hawa has never done that. She can't think of where in the city there's any space to do it now, but thinking of her mother sliding down a hill on the snow, screaming the whole way down, Hawa laughs out loud.

At home, she can only ride her bike in circles around the yard for so long before she gets bored and lonely and wants to come back to

Marefat. Since she and Sima miss each other in the winter, she makes up projects all the time that she can only do back at Marefat. Then she and Sima go to school, even though school is over. It's freezing cold, except for the offices with the stoves that leak smoke into the rooms they're supposed to warm, but Marefat is where she loves to be. Marefat is where she can see Sima, so her mother shrugs and lets her go.

It hadn't started out as a happy day. It was raining that morning, a cold spring rain like winter didn't want to leave peacefully. It made her sad. Going to school was marching off to prison. She knew from her older friends that it was a place where adults yelled at you and sometimes even beat you. Being a kid was an offense you could get hit for. She walked out into the rain that morning and felt she was marching off to a place where people would tell her all the ways she was wrong, and then she would be punished.

Marefat, when she arrived, was so big it saddened her even more. A big mud-colored prison. The way the students all lined up in the morning was frightening. Everyone in their perfect rows, and a heavyset man moving through them like a big wobbly barrel. She could see anger in his motion. Sometimes he would grab a boy by the shoulders and yank him into place.

But in class, her first teacher, on that first day, was kind. Ms. Maliha: even her name was without hard angles. *Maliha,* it felt like a breath. She didn't seem to Hawa like the kind of person who could hit children or torture them with sticks, like what usually happened at school.

It turned out Hawa was right. Ms. Maliha never once hit the students. In this class, where the students learned about their own language, the teacher was always kind.

So it was, then, on the first day of class, Hawa decided her language was a place of refuge. The way it was used as a vessel to pass stories to kids and grandkids, that's where comfort for her was.

It was first grade when she decided she wanted to write a book. Writing stories made her think of Ms. Maliha. Just as soon as she learned to read sentences, she wanted to make them. She began looking at magazines, reading stories with photographs that seemed to hold the words up, somehow make them more important. She wanted to be on the other side, creating that. Once she learned how to read an entire story, she wanted to put one together, too.

First, though, many things changed. Her street was paved, new buildings were built in the Desert, new buildings were built at the school, the school grew.

She grew, too, but not as fast.

Boys. That was also something else that changed. Each year, she saw fewer and fewer of them. In first grade she had classes together with boys, but then in second grade, boys and girls were taken apart from one another. They used to have all their extracurricular activities together; now they don't have many at all. That was okay with her. Better, actually. Sima says, "They're lazy, and also, during break time when they run in the halls, they make so much noise and kick up all the dust." The boys have learned about American wrestling now, and two of them got in a fight in the halls.

"I'll be John Cena! You be someone else."

"I'm John Cena. *You* be someone else!" Then they wrestled about it, so it seemed both of them were John Cena. Anyway, what's so good about Marefat is how disciplined everyone is. Her mother says, "It's good you're there, everything is serious, everything is in order." Boys just bring trouble.

The thing about boys that frightens her most, though, and which she doesn't understand, is the same thing she sees in all these stories that have carved themselves into her mind. All this violence, all the time. Sima told her the story of the father and son from hundreds of years ago who were torn apart by fate and then reconnected, just like Sima and she would be, but with a different ending, because girls knew how to reconcile. The story goes like this:

There was a boy named Rostam. In the story, he was a legendary hero. Hundreds of years ago, this happened, when the young hero Rostam was asleep under the shadow of a tree—

See! Sima laughed at that part. Boys were lazy even back then.

When he woke from his nap, his horse was gone. He searched and searched but found no sign of the horse, until finally, he found a set of its footprints. He followed them through the woods and all the way to the king's palace in a place called Samangan.

Samangan—she had heard that word in the news this year. It's a real place, it turns out. It's where her people get the coal they burn. The place they dig the coal from the ground, the big hole, it collapsed this year, a lot of people died.

The people of Samangan informed their king that someone named Rostam has come, and so the king did the polite thing and invited Rostam to his house.

In the king's palace Rostam met the beautiful princess, her name is Tahmina—

Almost like Ta Manna. Hawa thinks she knows someone in Marefat with that name.

So the two got married soon. Not married, exactly, but they . . . had a relationship. Princess Tahmina wanted a son by the handsome soldier, and she told him she knew where his horse was. She would bring it to him if he agreed to have . . . a relationship with her.

The man and the woman each did their part of the relationship. But before Rostam left, he said to her, "Tahmina, I have to leave here. But before leaving, I want to give you this bead, made out of a precious stone. If you give birth to a baby boy, tie it on his arm. And if you give birth to a baby girl, put it on her forehead. That way I will know my child if I see it."

Sure enough, Tahmina gave birth to a baby boy. He grew to be well built and sturdy, just like his father, and he was named Sohrab.

One day, Sohrab asked his mother what his father's name

was. He begged and begged, and then he threatened her. He said, "You must tell me, Mother. If you refuse, I will leave here and never come home." So finally Tahmina agreed. She told the boy his father's name and tied the bead onto his arm.

Now, Sima says, the boy Sohrab thought just the way all young boys think. He thought he was like John Cena, and he wanted to fight, so this is what he decided:

"If my father and I join forces, we'll be the most powerful army in the world. We'll conquer all the other kingdoms."

So Sohrab set out to find his father. First, he had to go to war against neighbors, and he did, and his troops conquered two kingdoms. Then they went to war with a third kingdom, where his father was said to live. The tradition of war at that time was to have a match between the strongest man from each army, before war.

When Sohrab asked to fight the strongest man in the kingdom, the king brought Rostam. Father versus son, but neither of them knew it!

The match began. Sohrab beat his father in wrestling, but he didn't kill him, because the tradition was that the champions would not kill each other on the first day.

On the second day, this time Rostam won, and he mortally wounded his own son.

"It doesn't make sense," Hawa said. How did he still not know it was his son?

"Because they're boys, they fought even before they talked."

Anyway, Sohrab, when he was in the agony of death, told Rostam, "If my father learns that you killed his son, he will find you. Even if you try to hide deep in the earth like a drop of water, or if you become a cloud in the sky, still he will find you and take revenge."

Rostam asked the young warrior: "Who is your father?"

And Sohrab replied, "My father's name is Rostam."

Rostam was shocked. "How can you prove you are the son of Rostam?" Sohrab pulled up his sleeve to show the bead on his arm.

Rostam was filled with remorse for his deed. He yelled for a messenger to run as fast as he could to the king and ask for *noosh daru*, life's water. It was a cure-all, a precious substance that could save the young fighter.

When the messenger reached the king, the king took sympathy, but his scheming advisers had other ideas. They told their king, "If the boy survives, and these two heroes get together, they will form a powerful alliance. More powerful than you, and you will lose your kingdom."

So the king came up with a plan. They sent the life's water to Rostam so that Rostam wouldn't be angry with the king. But first the king made sure the messenger arrived too late to save the boy.

And that's what happened. The king's messenger arrived with the life's water, but by then, it was already too late. Sohrab died. His own father killed him. The king didn't save him.

Sima thinks the story says that war is evil; it makes fathers kill their sons. She thinks it says how boys can be foolish and violent, for no good reason.

Hawa thinks it is saying the lesson she learned in English class: "A friend in need is a friend indeed." Politicians always think of their own gain, not people's loss. Even if those people are from their own tribe.

The story is also important because it says even life's water is no good if it doesn't arrive on time. The most special medicine in the world is worthless to a dead man. If you don't have it at the moment you need it, a precious piece of gold is no different from a dirty old rock.

By fifth grade, Hawa was confident she could read and write enough for a magazine, maybe even a book, but she was missing two things.

She needed a subject and she needed a partner, because she wasn't sure she could do it alone. And then, like a bolt from the blue, she got one.

It was the morning the teacher came in and said "Okay, girls, today we're going to rearrange the seating." Hawa got moved back two rows and the dark-skinned girl who smiled all the time got moved up two rows, and the two girls sat down right next to each other.

The dark-skinned girl was pretty. All the other girls liked her; she always had a smile on her face that dimpled her cheeks. She was looking down all the time, putting her chin to her neck, because it was the only way to hide her smile. This was Sima. Since Sima couldn't stop smiling, it made it hard for you not to smile too. Something was always funny; you didn't even need to know exactly what it was.

It turned out that beneath her smile, she was a serious girl. Or at least, she was a girl who thought seriously about the things that had happened to their people. She kept a journal and she wrote in it every week. Hawa found it hard to picture that—Sima, alone with a diary, smiling (she smiled so much you couldn't even picture her not smiling—it'd be like trying to picture a girl with a beard or a dog with wings). But Sima swore she wrote about everything. She wrote a long entry about when Teacher Aziz came into their class, with a writer from America and an engineer from one of the snowy countries in Europe, and a student asked the American, "In your country, is it possible for a woman to become president?" And then Aziz interrupted to say, "Why do you ask him about his country? *Here in Afghanistan* it's possible! Even if *I* can't become president, because I only passed fifth grade, you girls can. In fact, I'm sure one of you will."

Sima had been so surprised that she went home and wrote all night all about how Aziz said she could be president and the American hadn't disagreed and neither had the Swedish or Norwegian guy.

She wrote about their quarrel. After she and Hawa had been friends for two years, they got into a fight. They reconciled after a while; Sima wrote about that, too. And later, she said, she went back often to read her own words about reconciling with her best friend.

It was pleasing to her. Resolving a fight with a friend felt better even than making friends in the first place. Maybe because it showed that together, you could pass a test, and that both of you are pretty grown-up about things.

Hawa learned all these important parts of Sima and realized that now, she had a writing partner.

She just needed a subject.

The final piece for her book fell in place just after midterms, in language class. The same subject in which she'd first decided Marefat was going to be okay, when Ms. Maliha was teaching it, six years before.

The teacher had moved so quickly through their language lessons that they finished all their work and there was still two months left in school. With nothing else to do, the teacher said, "Well, you know what? Tomorrow, we'll start just talking about the history of this country, all the legends and stories."

It was then, during that class discussion, that it struck her: she didn't need to come up with a brand-new story all her own to write a book. She could just retell the stories that had been there all along. There were no new stories anyway, not really. Just the same stories, told different ways.

She and Sima split up the tasks, who would write what: the story of how fire was discovered, the story of Rostam and Sohrab, the story of the Lion Boy, the forty girls who'd killed themselves. And the next thing she knew, she and Sima were in Teacher Aziz's office, holding each other by the sleeves of their tunics and tugging signals of courage to each other, while they asked the most important man in the world for help.

The book was a success. Aziz agreed to write an introduction, give the text a light edit while he was at it, and then Nasir oversaw the book's production on one of the school's Xerox machines. The initial run was thirty copies, but the important thing was that there was a book out in the world that she had written. People could hold in their hands something she'd made.

The other students started making fun of her, but she knew they were jealous. "Why didn't you tell us you were writing a book?" Suddenly everyone wanted to have written a book. She heard them calling her "author" sarcastically, behind her back. But that was okay. She was proud, and she'd done something no one else had thought of doing.

As the school year wound down, things were looking up. But then her father began getting angrier and angrier at the news. Her mother was as sturdy as ever; she put on a smile, but her father couldn't. He's weaker than her mother, and Hawa sees in him the things he thinks he hides.

Sima says it's the same with her own dad. Sima says he yells at the TV, like the TV was misbehaving. Like you could change what it said if you were firm with it.

Sima says the reason people fight is because they only think about their own tribe. They have a narrow perspective. But Sima doesn't always know, because even though Sima watches the news, her brother likes cartoons, and he usually gets his way. He watches the same cartoons over and over and over while things blow up in her city, and Sima can't find out about them because they're blocked by animals dancing around on the TV screen.

So who knows how the rest of the winter is going to go. So far, it's been as cruelly cold as ever before, but the snow came late to the city. She's happy about that, even though she knows it may mean trouble soon. Already, out in the Desert, the wells are running dry.

For now, she's also happy because she can still walk the streets. She can still see Sima, and when she wears the hood with white sparkly fur over her headscarf, she's warm enough, though her feet still get cold. And people are civilized now. Now, people have fire!

But there are more explosions on the news, it's true. Once a week, at least, she watches her father while he watches the men on TV. Men jog around on the screen in their boxy green uniforms and the trucks drive too fast through the frame. Too fast for the screen to keep up, and the groups of women in burkas huddle together like shifting mountain ranges made of fabric, wailing into your living room like there was something you should be doing to help.

She's watched the news with her father for as long as she can remember, and this year it's too much. She knows what people say, that the Taliban are angry about the agreement with the Americans, and about the elections, so they're making more threats. To show people that if the president makes the agreement or if people vote, they'll keep increasing their attacks.

She knows Sima is worrying, too, beneath her smiles. Sima went on a trip to the central highlands, she said, and with her own eyes she saw a truck all burnt up because of fighting, and she admitted to Hawa that these days she has nightmares all the time. Sometimes she can't sleep because she thinks of girls like her, whose fathers are killed by bombers, or whose fathers *are* bombers.

Do those girls keep going to school?

There are other things that bother her, too. Like even though there are no kings to be cruel to people now, people are still cruel to each other. Her mother told her about a Pashtun man on the news saying the same things they've always said, about how Hazaras are "guests" in this country. She's been taught that hospitality is something sacred, and she wants to grow up to be good at it. She wants to welcome people into her living room. How can you do that when someone comes along and tells you that, all along, it hasn't been your living room at all? That you've been trespassing in somebody else's?

"The Hazaras should leave," the man said. "The name of the country means 'Land of Pashtuns.'" So it's strange, then, about how there are these elections coming up. Because she has a secret. She decides not to tell her family. It's this: she likes a Pashtun candidate.

Maybe her mother wouldn't be so happy. But Sima said the Pashtun candidate is going to build five hundred thousand houses for poor people. Sima said her father met him once, too. In class she heard rumors about how Teacher Aziz was helping him. Once she heard that, she wished she could be eighteen, or could find a way to pretend she was, because then she could vote for him.

She thinks: so what if it's against the law? She knows from Teacher Aziz that you shouldn't let anything have power over you just because. They better have a good reason. What's the good reason why a girl in fifth grade can't vote?

It would be something good she could do. All year, the news is all about the Outsiders leaving. Like everyone thinks it's the End of Days. It's boring, really. If they leave, fine; nothing will happen. There won't be war, the Taliban won't take over the whole country, everyone is just going crazy for no reason. She knows this because when she was working on her book, she had the chance to have extra conversations with Teacher Aziz. He told her, and he knows more than her father, and more than Sima's father, more than anyone. He put his head to the side and smiled, like she was the most special thing in the world, and he said, "By next year, you're going to have a new auditorium. Every morning we'll gather under a roof, instead of outside. And I'm thinking on the top there will be an area for you mischievous girls to run around and play. What do you think about that?" He was asking her for advice. He was not worried at all.

She tries to make her family understand this. That there is nothing to worry about. Because there are so many people who are literate and so many people understand so many more things than anyone did before, and because the street in front of her house that used to be dirty and full of holes is now smooth and clean and she didn't use to have a book but now she does and it can't be unwritten so how could people start fighting again? You can only take steps forward, you can't take steps back, that doesn't work. That's what she thinks.

EPILOGUE

The Taliban dispatched thirty-nine suicide bombers in the two months leading up to the elections.

The capital was ravaged. Twenty-one people were killed at a restaurant frequented by foreigners. Nine were killed at an upscale hotel. Among them was Sardar Ahmad, who helped me transcribe interviews for this book. He was having dinner with his wife and three children when gunmen entered the dining room. Only his young son survived.

Foreign organizations hastened their departures. The National Democratic Institute pulled its election observers, so did the Organization for Security and Co-Operation in Europe.

During the Taliban's brutal two-month offensive, an apparent paradox occurred: the first calendar month with zero U.S. combat casualties. The reason foreign soldiers were no longer dying was that foreign soldiers were no longer fighting. Foreign civilians were bearing the brunt, as were—as always—Afghans.

To myself and others in Kabul at the time, it was a foregone conclusion that very few people were going to vote. It would simply be too dangerous, and with so few poll observers, the elections were bound to be fraudulent anyway. It would not matter who was elected, because whoever it was would have no mandate. The winner, it was increasingly clear, was going to be the Insurgency.

Plus, on Election Day, it rained.

Then, a remarkable thing happened. People showed up to vote in huge numbers. By noon on Election Day, turnout had nearly equalled the entire day of the previous presidential elections. So many people turned out that election centers ran out of ballots, and by the time polls closed, seven million people had voted, almost twice as many as the previous election. Despite the ruthless Taliban offensive—or perhaps, to spite it—people voted. Even more remarkable was that over a third of the voters were women, and among the photographs beamed around the world from that triumphant day, there was one that stayed in my mind for a long time after. Twenty or thirty women, lined up outside a polling center, holding above their heads a long plastic sheet to shield themselves from the rain.

The image stayed with me, I think, because it was a reflection of the one that inspired this book.

At around 2:30 p.m. on April 29, 1975, a Dutchman named Hubert van Es was in the darkroom of United Press International's Saigon bureau, getting ready for the regular 5:00 p.m. transmission to Tokyo.

By that point, the American mission in Vietnam was over. The final evacuation had begun, most Americans were gone or on their way out, and the plan had been to use an airbase in the city to airlift the last few thousand. The North Vietnamese were moving quickly though, they'd shelled the base and the runway was blocked by the wreckage of downed planes. The city would fall at any moment. South Vietnamese soldiers were trying to escape, stripping off their uniforms and leaving their weapons in the streets on their way down to the Saigon River, where they hoped to get boats to the coast.

Van Es stayed behind after the press evacuation began, and already had what he thought were iconic images of the fall. A photo of South Vietnamese people burning documents that might associate them with the United States; a U.S. Marine with a Vietnamese mother and her boy.

He was exposing the photos when his bureau chief started yelling, "Van Es, get out here, there's a chopper on that roof!"

He picked up his camera and a 300 millimeter lens and went out to the balcony; from there he had a decent vantage point of the Pittman Apartment building at 22 Gia Long Street, where a helicopter was perched, its rotors still spinning, on top of the elevator shaft housing. The building had no landing pad. He recognized the helicopter as a Huey operated by Air America, the CIA-run airline, which made sense to him: CIA officials lived in that building. The people he saw were almost all South Vietnamese though—a mass of them, crowded onto the roof and climbing a ladder leaned up against the elevator housing. Van Es guessed at least thirty, and knew a Huey could carry only a dozen people at most, maybe less. It lifted off, and more than twenty people were still waiting to escape the falling city. Van Es looked up at the sky and said a prayer for more helicopters, but none came, so he went back into the darkroom to process the photograph that would become one of the most famous from Vietnam, and an emblem of the moments our foreign wars end.

The photograph became famous, I think, in part because it is an open question in visual form: What will happen to those people, up on that roof? What happens when we leave?

A line of South Vietnamese on a roof in Saigon; a line of women at a polling center in Afghanistan—perhaps the two have little in common beyond the superficial. In comparing them I oversimplify, maybe I make the same mistake I blame generals for: the tendency to reason analogically, to see every situation as simply an iteration of another situation that happened before.

Still, in both places we fought, and killed, and died. In both places we brought money, tried to defeat an enemy, and tried to build beachheads to protect the values we believed to be universal. There were less altruistic motivations, of course, but Marefat is proof that good things can happen when we clear the space for them to happen. So when we launch our foreign wars do we inevitably raise in people the desire for things they cannot have forever? Will there always be some sort of helicopter lifting off, a line of people who are desperate to get on board, but can't?

In the line I looked at forty years later, I saw a benediction. I felt maybe we had figured it out. The image from that day was not of desperate people trying to escape a country, but hopeful people exercising their new power over one. It was people peacefully transferring power for the first time in their country's history. We said we wanted to bring democracy to Afghanistan, and the thing we wanted to happen was happening, just as we left.

On that day, I lost cynicism. Afghanistan was going to be fine. The Hazaras would be okay, Marefat would keep growing.

Ashraf Ghani came in second place, with 37 percent of the Hazara vote. If it's remarkable that so many Hazaras voted for a man from perhaps their most bitter ethnic rival, it was still a failure of Aziz's plan. Most Hazaras voted for someone else, and Ashraf Ghani did not win.

Both Aziz's plan and Ashraf Ghani were given a reprieve because the winner, Dr. Abdullah Abdullah, failed to secure the fifty-plus percent required by the constitution to become president. Two months later a runoff was held between the top two vote-getters.

Again, turnout was strong despite the ruthless Taliban offensive, the shrinking foreign military presence, and, critically, severely reduced election monitoring: allegations of fraud were so widespread that the contenders couldn't even agree how the ballots should be counted.

Months of deadlock followed. Optimism faded. U.S. Secretary of State John Kerry flew to Afghanistan to help broker a power-sharing agreement, in which Ashraf Ghani would be president, and Abdullah would fill a newly created role as the country's chief executive. It was an uneasy political alliance, and every decision required painstaking negotiations. Important government posts remained unfilled for months.

For Marefat, the outlook grew bleaker. Aziz's choice for president became president in time to lead the country with our armies gone, but not because of Hazaras—Ghani won in spite of them. Aziz believed Hazaras had the chance to seize influence, and that they missed it.

Security deteriorated. As foreign armies stopped fighting, the Taliban launched large-scale attacks. Afghan forces tried to step into the breach, but they were simply not as good. The International Committee for the Red Cross collected twice as many bodies from battlefields as the year before.

It wasn't just soldiers dying. More fighting took place in more populated areas, with less precise munitions. Mortars fell on towns and cities. Civilian casualties rose dramatically.

More improvised explosive devices hit more people.

More people were hurt and killed by unexploded ordnance. Kids tried to pick up landmines and cluster bombs to sell for scrap metal. Or, sometimes, because the explosives looked like toys.

There were other ways in which children and women suffered more due to the withdrawal. More casualties meant more widows, and more women compelled to take children out of school to earn money, or force daughters into marriages to settle debts. Women without husbands were more likely to be abused by members of their extended family.

The police began abusing more people, too. They killed more people than ever before. Perhaps unsurprisingly, incidents of insurgents dispensing their own justice jumped by a factor of four. Often the offense was supporting the U.S.-installed government; often the penalty was death.

So the number of people fleeing their homes increased, too. There are now close to one million internally displaced people in Afghanistan. The economy sputtered. With foreign armies leaving and foreign NGOs following them out, money left, too. Foreign investment kept falling, remittances kept rising—less money coming in to the country, more going out. The value of the currency shrunk lower than it had ever been; GDP grew less than 4 percent (in 2012, it had grown 14 percent).

The deadliest wave of suicide bombings yet hit Kabul in December 2014. Faith in the new government withered. Then the spring fighting season began, and it was the most violent in fourteen years. Taliban fighters actually captured and held district administration centers in the north of the country, which they hadn't done since the war began.

And it was no longer just them. Reports of ISIS or ISIS-affiliated groups in Afghanistan have multiplied, and the interior minister reported that foreign militants infiltrated six northern provinces.

Hazaras started going missing. In February, thirty-one Hazara men were taken in Zabul province. Gunmen stopped three different busses, separated Hazaras from other ethnicities, and took the Hazaras away in cars. This happened on the country's one major highway, near two different government checkpoints. The families found it inconceivable that no one saw what was happening. As frightening to Hazaras as the violence rising against them, was the government's unwillingness—or perhaps just inability—to do anything about it. They were on their own.

Around the country, beheaded bodies of Hazaras began turning up. Beheading was a new Taliban tactic; Hazaras believed the Taliban was mutilating their bodies because that's what ISIS did, and ISIS was getting all the attention.

In July 2015, Talibs attacked Hazaras manning a security checkpoint west of Kabul. Other local police were stationed nearby but did not help, and the Hazaras ran out of ammunition before the government sent reinforcements. They were overrun, thirty were killed, and their bodies were mutilated. Many were decapitated, and there were reports that they were "chopped to pieces" and set on fire.

Marefat feels the changes acutely. The violence happening all around is harder than ever to ignore. More jobless people roam the streets. Government staffers are not being paid on time, fewer NGOs are providing jobs or aid, and fewer donations are coming in. The number of Marefat students applying for aid from the school's "charity box" has increased dramatically. There's not much left in it, and when its empty, kids will start dropping out.

Despite it all, so far, Marefat endures. Classes have not stopped. Girls have not stopped going to school; girls have not stopped arguing with boys. Aziz was named a finalist for an international teacher of the year award, and afterwards decided it was finally time to pursue his own education. He took a high school equivalency exam, and passed. In addition to his work at Marefat, he is now studying law.

By the summer of 2015, enough progress had been made on the auditorium to hold a holiday celebration there. Aziz began using it to show movies, too, as a diversion. A recent favorite is *The Hunger Games*.

Although it's now in use, the auditorium is, as of this writing, still unfinished.

AUTHOR'S NOTE

The preceding is a work of nonfiction. The material came from research of various kinds, including exhaustive interviews with people generous and brave enough to let this foreigner into their lives. For that I will always be grateful. Many gave me permission to use their real names. In a small number of cases I have changed or withheld names, for example, in the cases of several minors in this book.

Many of the people in this book have lived eventful, trauma-filled lives, and do not perfectly recall dates and places, particularly from when they were children—as few would, of any age or extraction. Where their stories included provable facts, I have checked them against the historical record. When appropriate, I have presented people with disparities in order to resolve them. In many cases, however, the person's own memory was the only record available. I have tried to remain faithful both to what actually happened, and to what they experienced.

There are terms in this book for which I've used English translations, in order to orient the reader to the experience people in the book are having. For many of the words, there is no precise English translation—it is a constant irritant to those who write in Farsi that English is, in their estimation, not comparable as a vector of poetry. Because language is both an extension and incubator of culture, word choice is sensitive. My purpose was to be consistent and illuminating.

Much of Afghanistan's past is debated. Many excellent histories are inconsistent. Things as seemingly innocuous as the origin of the word "Hazara"—just a breath away from the word for "thousand"—are the subject of debate, as is much of the history of this people. For that reason, I drew the sentiments about Hazaras in the background chapter, "The First Thousand," from the people who expressed them.

The opinions of Babur, the first Mughal emperor, came from *Babur-Nama in English (Memoirs of Babur)* translated from the original Turki text of Zahiru'd-din Muhammad by Annette Susannah Beveridge.

The opinions of the Iron Amir came from his autobiography, *The Life of Amir Abdur Rahman, Amir of Afghanistan*. They also came from a history written by his palace historian, Fayiz Muhammad Katib Hazarah's *The History of Afghanistan Volume I*, translated by R. D. McChesney, and *Volume 3*, translated by McChesney and M. M. Khorrami.

(Hazarah was, as his name suggests, Hazara. It's a great paradox of the country's history that a Hazara served as palace historian for a leader overseeing a brutal war against them.)

The words of the visiting British physician, Dr. Lillias Hamilton, came from her memoirs, *A Vizier's Daughter: A Tale of Hazara War*.

Further historical information came from Sayed Askar Mousavi's *The Hazaras of Afghanistan: An Historical, Cultural, Economic and Political Study*. Patrick Camiller's translation of Alessandro Monsutti's *War and Migration: Social Networks and Economic Strategies of the Hazaras of Afghanistan* was also vital to this work.

For the history of Genghis Khan as it relates to one particular Hazara origin story, I drew from Patrick Porter's *Military Orientalism: Eastern War Through Western Eyes*, and *The Mongol Art of Wars: Chinggis Khan and the Mongol Military System* by Timothy May.

Abbas Changezi shared his exhaustive research on recent Hazara history with me. I also owe a debt of gratitude for the work and knowledge of Aziz Royesh, Saeid Madadi, Besmellah Alizada, and the aspiring scholar and champion pedicab driver, Nasim Fekrat.

For more information, or to donate to education for at-risk communities in Afghanistan, please visit the Bamyan Foundation at www.bamyanfoundation.org.

ACKNOWLEDGMENTS

Thank you to my amazing editor, Nichole Argyres. Rarely, I think, are such brilliant people so patient. I'm blessed to have her influence on this book. And to Laura Chasen. Rarely are artists so skilled at managing such complex, long-term projects, or at managing the writer's fragile ego. You have a gift. There are so many skills in these two people.

Writing this book has been a difficult and often painful journey, but the people who came forward with advice, encouragement, and love have made the whole thing worth it. I've been given the chance to feel, again and again, how people often want to help, and perhaps as surprising, how they are often able to, in ways unexpected by them and me.

Someone once said that when you take a difficult journey, you take your loved ones with you. So to my mom and dad, I owe a debt of gratitude. They didn't choose to have their child take ill-advised adventures, but they've chosen to do all they can to lighten the load. Their support and forbearance are more than should be asked of anyone, and are more than anyone is entitled to.

To Margot, who gave me sun, food, company, and lodging, and who read thousands upon thousands of pages, and was there, dispatching with minor crises no matter what the hour was or how many time zones separated us. To Jenna, who is the funniest, smartest person I know, and who gives me patience and perspective—these things are more important than you know. Thank you, Decima, for all your love and care.

To Gene and Jeff No. 2, both of whom provided food, advice, patience, well-timed whisky, and most important, friendship. And lodging. To Justin, who has always, always been there for the important things, for as long as I can remember. To Davis, who is a steadying hand and a source of wisdom when I needed it most, and of humor. And of lodging.

To Kathy, without whose wisdom and perfectly aimed encouragement there would simply be no book, and who is pretty good at drinking beer. To Ted Achilles and Farima, who provided endless assistance and support, and to all the girls of SOLA, another amazing Afghan institution, who let me laugh with them.

To my friend Dave Larabell, who bought me many lunches over many years without me producing anything for him, still took my calls, and dispatched with many bad ideas. To call him an agent is an understatement. To Gary Morris, who picked up where Dave left off, despite having no idea what he was in for.

Ken Rogerson, your wisdom and direction, to me and my family, kept me from quitting this line of work a long time ago—you continue to go above and beyond the call of duty. Bob Bliwise, thank you for taking a chance on me all those years ago, and for providing the right book, the right article, the right painting, the precise inspiration I needed, always at precisely the right time.

Thank you to Saeid Madadi for your skillful, delicate translating, and your encyclopedic knowledge, and your patience in sharing it. Thank you to the kind and wise Besmellah Alizada. Thank you, Esmatullah, for your insight and wisdom, and for continuing to help me with this book in the face of tragedy. Timor Karimy, for his ceaseless and patient imparting of knowledge. Qais and Steve, who pushed me when I needed it most to make this thing happen. Nasim Fekrat, you might not have the paper quite yet, but I consider you a professor already.

To James Khanu, Aimal Naheb, Lovely Oberoi, all the people in all the places who've kept me safe and happy and shared their lives with this visitor.

Thank you to The Pulitzer Center on Crisis Reporting, for taking a chance on an ambitious young journalist, and to RISC, for the lifesaving work you do.

Thank you to Hugh Allen, who is something like a perfect coach, putting people in positions to succeed, and then withdrawing to watch them do it on their own. Thank you, Joe Torsella, whose faith in me is motivating; who always takes my calls and takes the time, and never lets me know from what important matters I'm keeping him.

To Hafiz Royesh, who arranged so much for this book despite having to take over the school in his brother's absence, and who gave me a place to do them in his office, in the spaces closest to the stove.

It is perhaps atypical to thank a source and a character in a work of nonfiction, but I trust the reader has by this point no illusions of objectivity when it comes to my regard for Aziz Royesh. So to my friend, mentor, and teacher, who continues to be a cherished member of *my* family, to make me laugh, make me frustrated, make me learn, who built a school and opened it and himself up to me, and who answered the million and one little queries that followed. Thank you for letting me be your friend.

And to the students and teachers and parents and janitors at Marefat, who always open their homes to you, ask nothing in return, and make you want to give everything.

Or at least something.